DISCARD

SAVOR

SAVOR

..

A Chef's Hunger for More

..

FATIMA ALI *with* **TARAJIA MORRELL**

FOREWORD BY *Farezeh Durrani*

BALLANTINE BOOKS

NEW YORK

Published in the United States by Ballantine Books,
an imprint of Random House, a division of
Penguin Random House LLC, New York.

BALLANTINE is a registered trademark and the colophon
is a trademark of Penguin Random House LLC.

Grateful acknowledgment is made to *Bon Appétit* for permission to use
excerpts from "I'm a Chef with Terminal Cancer. This Is What
I'm Doing with the Time I Have Left" by Fatima Ali (October 9, 2018),
© 2018 Condé Nast and from " 'Top Chef' Contestant Fatima Ali on
How Cancer Changed the Way She Cooks" by Fatima Ali (May 1, 2018)
© 2018 Condé Nast. Reprinted by permission.

Library of Congress Cataloging-in-Publication Data
Names: Ali, Fatima, –2019, author.
Title: Savor: a chef's hunger for more / Fatima Ali with Tarajia Morrell;
foreword by Farezeh Durrani.
Description: First edition. | New York: Ballantine Books, an imprint of
Random House, a division of Penguin Random House LLC, [2022]
Identifiers: LCCN 2022000429 (print) | LCCN 2022000430 (ebook) |
ISBN 9780593355190 (hardback) | ISBN 9780593355206 (ebook)
Subjects: LCSH: Ali, Fatima, –2019. | Women cooks—United States—
Biography. | Cooks—United States—Biography. |
Bones—Cancer—Patients—Biography.
Classification: LCC TX649.A425 A3 2022 (print) |
LCC TX649.A425 (ebook) | DDC 641.5092/2 [B]—dc23/eng/20220225
LC record available at https://lccn.loc.gov/2022000429
LC ebook record available at https://lccn.loc.gov/2022000430

Printed in Canada on acid-free paper

randomhousebooks.com

2 4 6 8 9 7 5 3 1

FIRST EDITION

Book design by Barbara M. Bachman

BUT, BEHOLD, AS FOR THOSE WHO ATTAIN TO FAITH and do righteous deeds—verily, We do not fail to requite any who persevere in doing good: theirs shall be gardens of perpetual bliss—through which running waters flow— wherein they will be adorned with bracelets of gold and will wear green garments of silk and brocade, and wherein upon couches they will recline: how excellent a recompense, and how goodly a place to rest!

—THE QURAN, SURAH 18:30–31

CONTENTS

PART II

PART III

ABOUT THIS BOOK

By

TARAJIA MORRELL

It was mid-october 2018 when I got the call.

"Are you familiar with Fatima Ali?" my literary agent began after niceties.

"I am," I told her. "I just read her second essay in *Bon Appétit* yesterday."

"Well, she wants to write a book about the time she has left," she explained. "She needs a collaborator."

"Yes," I answered without a pause. "Yes—I want to be considered. Please put me forward for it."

I hadn't watched fatima on *Top Chef;* I didn't know her personally and I'd never tasted her food, but I'd read her essays in *Bon Appétit* and, just like many, I admired her. In her first essay, from May 2018, I'd recognized a hard-working, charismatic young woman on the cusp of coming into her own—of becoming—when cancer callously interrupted her. As she fought the vicious disease, I inwardly applauded Fatima's stalwart grit. After reading her second essay for the magazine the day before my agent called, in which Fatima revealed that she was terminal, I was in awe of her pledge to live the rest of her abbreviated life to the fullest in the face of a literal death sentence: her vow to accomplish her bucket list against all odds in the year that she was given to live. If I could, I wanted to help this ambitious, spirited young woman to go out fighting.

I submitted some writing samples and embarked on a long-planned trip. While I was gone, Fatima was a guest on Ellen DeGeneres's TV show. I watched on my laptop: a pale Fatima, on crutches but poised, conceding her diagnosis but not letting it curtail her plans. She was determined to make her last year count, to travel the world, to eat at her dream restaurants, to go on safari. Her humor and cheekiness were contagious as she gracefully, wittily volleyed back to Ellen, the professional prankster. Fatima impressed me anew.

Our appreciation must have been mutual, because our agents facilitated a conversation. Over Skype, she and her brother, Mohammad, reiterated the proposition: to write a bucket list book based on her dream travel and meals. I encouraged her to journal, to write down anything—words, fragments, memories, recipes, smells, lists—whatever felt too important to forget, and I offered a few memoir suggestions for her to read while they sorted out the specifics. Mohammad and I mostly glossed over the details of where and when the project might begin, other than that they hoped to start on it as soon as possible, and we said our goodbyes.

In late November, I learned that Fatima had chosen me as her collaborator. The plan was for me to record the reflections of an intrepid young woman living as best she could for what would be the last year of her life. I'd write down what she saw, heard, tasted, and felt so that she could simply *be* in the moment, for the moments she had left. She mentioned wanting to go to

Noma in Copenhagen, Chef Rene Redzepi's nature-driven temple of New Nordic gastronomy, and Osteria Francescana, Chef Massimo Bottura's storied jewel in Modena, Italy, which I longed to visit as well. *What,* I asked myself, *will I see with this stranger? What might I learn from this impermanent life force?*

I returned home to New York and awaited my marching orders, but a week passed, then two, and none came. Several days before Christmas, Mohammad called from Los Angeles and explained: Fatima's condition had deteriorated rapidly and she was in constant, harrowing agony. She was about to undergo a procedure that would help her better manage the pain, and he wanted to give her a few days to recuperate before we began our work together. We decided I should join them right after the holidays. The parameters were rapidly changing.

I flew to Los Angeles on January 3, 2019, concerned and nervous, feeling ill-equipped for whatever lay ahead. I'd never written a book before. I'd never written a book with a dying woman. Already this hardly resembled the poignant but delectable voyaging that I'd signed up for. How could we make Fatima's book come to life from a hospital room in Santa Monica?

Upon my arrival, I was met by a hollow-eyed family with faces worn down by preemptive grief, still playing at being strong for the woman in room 435 of UCLA Medical Center's Cancer Ward. My initial conversation there with Mohammad left me with a series of questions: What was I doing there? How could I best serve this woman I'd never met, her family, and my assignment, the framework of which shifted hourly?

The promised year from her terminal diagnosis had been cruelly pruned to four pain-filled months. Mohammad admitted that unless something changed drastically, Fatima didn't have long. I'll confess that I considered excusing myself. *What can we achieve together,* I wondered, *under these tortured circum-*

stances? And with so little time left, why does she want to spend it with a stranger?

"You'll see lots of people here with us," Mohammad explained, as if reading my thoughts. "Fati's friends, my mom's friends, our family. I don't want you to worry. I've explained to them why you're here and they understand that what you're doing is for Fati."

"I don't want to intrude," I told him. "At any time, someone can just ask me to step out or away."

"Yes, that's right, but for now this is what Fati wants to focus on. She wants to work with you. And the rest we just check in with her and follow how she's doing. She fades off sometimes, but she's there. She's still really there."

So I stayed. I decided to give this young woman whom I'd never met before all I could for the week I'd committed to spending with her, whether a book came out of it or not. What would it cost me to keep this initial commitment to a dying woman? How often in life is simply showing up of such value to a stranger? If life and control were being torn from *me,* how much would I appreciate those who kept their word?

I followed Mohammad into Fatima's hospital room. She was propped up in bed, wearing glasses, head shaven with thick black hair starting to grow in. Her twenty-nine-year-old face was symmetrical and void of makeup or wrinkles; her dark eyes were haloed in black lashes. She was all the lovelier for her lack of ornamentation, but I sensed a sallowness had snuck into cheeks that were meant to be a richer hue of toffee. I reached for her hand in greeting, and she didn't draw back, but serenely said, "Not a lot of touching," and my worried withdrawn hands quickly found each other, as if in prayer. Though I knew she was unwell, my first impression was that she exuded a sort of regality: as if it was not her infirmity, but her distinction that made us orbit around her quiet, reclining frame. We three were together for the first time then, in the same positions we'd inhabit in every session over our one week together: Fatima in her bed, me on her right side by her ankles, Mohammad by her left hip. And then, so near the end, we began.

I asked questions. She spoke slowly. I listened. I recorded. Sometimes her faithful brother pressed her further for a hard answer, trying to stave off the inevitable sleepless nights and cravings for more clarity that stay with us when we lose those we love.

After that first day, I left Fatima's room feeling exhilarated by her storytelling but dazed by the circumstances: speedy and drowsy at once. My legs were heavy, as though I'd been trudging through sand, and I was thirsty for fresh air. I wanted to run out into the cool January evening. I wanted it to rain, though I knew it wouldn't because it was Los Angeles. I wanted to scream open-mouthed into a deluge as my skin was pitted by cold sharp drops.

Instead, I encountered Fatima's mother, Farezeh, for the first time near the elevator bank, and she embraced me. She asked if we could find time to speak and I told her that I wanted that too, that "there would be time." I flinched inwardly as I said this, knowing that there would be nothing but time, that when Fatima was gone, it would be Farezeh who was left, endlessly. Farezeh would outlive her daughter and together she and I would sit and fill in the gaps, the history from which Fatima had sprung. Farezeh, with hands like my own mother's, would be left, surviving, without cessation, forever trying to solve the broken riddle of why.

It was on our third day together that I caught the thread and understood why I'd been summoned. There was, of course, more to this woman than tales of culinary school and exhausting services on the line in bustling New York City restaurant kitchens; more even than far-flung internships and a star turn on *Top Chef.* Fatima wanted to leave a different sort of story in her wake: a deeper one. Less palatable, perhaps, but more human . . . more urgent.

So, I became a pastor of sorts, a receptacle of secrets, ones that I was meant to sort through and figure out how to impart despite the complications of her truth. Someone they all shared and whose words carried the weight of a separate entity, beyond the family's grief or flock. I was overwhelmed, yet committed: to listen, to wait, to gently prod, to encourage, to lead them into loving corners in which they already lived.

This book was born out of that strange liminal week together. Woven into the narrative are essays that Fatima wrote at various points in her adult life, including those she published in the Lahore *Sunday Times,* in a university food journal, three from *Bon Appétit* magazine about her battle with cancer, and pieces she was working on when she died on January 25, 2019. Over that week together—and in the three years since—I've thought of Fatima and how to do this project for her as I fall asleep at night, struggling with the responsibility of imparting her experiences, her smells, her thoughts, her secrets, and transmitting them in her absence. I've spent countless hours asking questions of her grief-stricken family (and friends and colleagues) about a woman they wish were here to answer for herself. *She hired you,* I told myself. *She chose you*—perhaps because she sensed our similar command of language, our mutual fascination with the truth, with the undercurrent.

In our week together in a hospital room in Los Angeles, Fatima invited me into her memory, her experience of a perplexing life, unjustifiably brief but replete with love and adventure, hardship, culinary inspiration, and ambition in spades. In a few short days, we established a rhythm that felt comfortable and even somehow sustainable. *Perhaps we can go on like this for weeks, months: recounting her history, keeping each other's secrets. Perhaps if I postpone my flight,* I thought, *we can keep at it, keep working together*—as if our shared goal of making a book could keep her alive. As if we could trick the cancer into waiting for us to finish. The fallacy was irresistibly sticky and sweet.

"Tell her your secrets," Mohammad said one day in the dusky waiting room after we'd wept together. *My* secrets! "Your secrets are safe with her."

Indeed, I let snippets of my own story seep into our conversation. When she'd asked, I'd shared of myself, my circuitous professional and personal path to her bedside, thinking it unfair to hold back when she was being so open. And her brother was right: my secrets were safe with her. I'd signed on to help Fatima write a book about living life to its fullest over her final year, flavor rich. But that notion had fallen away like sand and I found myself making promises, taking oaths.

On our last day of physical proximity, she was past pain. There was a wildness in her eyes, that of a child, a seer. She was punchy and alert; she'd begun to have visions and she could see around edges and into dark corners.

"You're going to throw yourself into this like you throw yourself into everything you do," Fatima informed me before I departed for New York. Fourteen days before she passed, my marching orders had finally come. She knew enough of me to recognize my tenacity.

"You have my word," I promised, unsure at the time of how exactly I might manifest it, though my allegiance to her had bloomed with our rapport.

This is Fatima's story, but essential to its very existence is her mother, Farezeh, who gave her life, whose own story shaped her. We stand on our parents' shoulders, inheriting their choices. Whether we embrace or rebel against their perspective, it's a jumping-off point to become who we are. Fatima and I cut to the quick of it in our week. We never left food behind; food was where we began, and from talk of feeling melons for their ripeness and the essential trifecta of ginger, coriander, and green chilis, we delved into the universal gorgeous and gnarled complexity of family and of life—the space between the meals. I listened to her in a time beyond hunger, when all that mattered was love: the love of her family, who shared her with me when time together was its most precious; the love in the room full of friends who waited for us to finish our truth-telling sessions before they gathered around her wilting frame. Their love was something visible, tactile, a haze in the room, a vapor that would billow if I swung my arms, and it changed me.

What Fatima gave me in our week together—the faith, the intimacy, the open-heartedness—was one of the great gifts. She taught me how to expand my heart again, unafraid of who might score it. She reminded me that it's the feeling that matters, not whether the feeling is good or bad . . . that it's all both.

FOREWORD

By

FAREZEH DURRANI

AT BEST, TWELVE MONTHS: THAT'S WHAT THE DOC-tors gave Fatima in October 2018. They had told her that her cancer was back, and that it was bad. There were some experimental treatments she could explore and perhaps that was something we could consider, but there was not much that they could do.

We flew back from New York to our home in San Marino, California. Fatima was on crutches by then, and we were all in pieces.

Two days later, I woke up feeling uneasy. I slept with the door to my bedroom open at night so that I could hear Fatima if she called out for me and be right there if she needed me. I made my way to the kitchen to make my cup of tea and peeked into Fatima's room.

There she was, huddled up under the covers. She looked so small, too small for the enormity of pain she was learning to live with. An image of her as a baby flashed in my mind, as it often did during her illness. It was my way of holding on to time. If I thought of her as a baby, then I had twenty-nine years left with her.

I noticed that the trash can that would normally be in our laundry room was by her bed.

My heart sank. She wouldn't have said anything, but I knew Fatima had suffered all night. She had probably not slept a wink, had been in pain and did not want to worry me. I went back to the kitchen.

She must have sensed me. As the water came to a boil, Fatima hobbled out on her crutches.

"Mom," Fatima said, "I want to write a book."

Only Fatima could have hatched an ambitious plan on a night when she was constantly vomiting.

"I think that's a great idea, Tatu," I said encouragingly.

She paused.

"No, Mom. I need your permission."

Permission?

"You don't need my permission, Fatima. Write whatever you want to write about. Go ahead."

She shook her head. "Well, for this one I do."

"Why?"

"Because I don't want to write just any book. I don't want to write about my cancer. I want to write an honest book about my life—my story."

She continued, "And I will be gone, Mom, and you'll have to bear the brunt of it."

I blinked at her. Did she really think I had anything left to lose after her?

I reached out and, as always, put her hand in my own and repeated what had become a chant that we both so desperately wanted to believe: "It's okay, my Tatu. It's okay."

We held each other, rocking back and forth. She felt my tears on her shoulders. I felt hers in my bones.

She made her way back into her room on her crutches. A year earlier, she would have been running, dancing, skipping, pacing in kitchens.

I turned to my now cold cup of tea and rolled Fatima's request around in my mind: an honest book.

Perhaps what drew Fatima to food was how it never lied. Ingredients could never betray a misstep in the making of a dish. If the heat was high when it was meant to be low, it would show. Food was sincere, and that's what this chef expected out of everyone else in her life.

And in that spirit, this book contains many truths.

Painful and inconvenient truths. Truths that are often brushed under the carpet. Truths that we would do anything to believe were lies. How many of us deny our truths, our realities, our honesty, because we fear judgment? How many of us have tried so hard to protect our sons and daughters that we lose sight of what really matters?

I spent so much of my time with Fatima wanting to protect her from becoming a topic of judgment by others. I have lived my own life in fear of this. But not my Fatima. Fear didn't have a chance with her. Never did. She came from me, but Fatima wasn't afraid to break invisible boundaries, and always followed her heart.

Even as she took her leave, she was not afraid to share her journey if it meant that it could change the world—like we all want to. Fatima wouldn't even let death get in the way of her trying, and so, at the end of her life, she looked back, putting memories on the page and recording heart-to-hearts with her brother.

She wanted to inspire conversations, difficult as they may be, to shift the way people think, the way we accept, confront, and deal with death, not just life. And more than anything, she wanted even just one little girl who might have been going through the same experiences to feel less alone.

She knew, from the very beginning, what has taken me decades to fully understand and accept: *What people think does not matter.* In the end, my fears of judgment were dwarfed by the terrifying truth that I was going to lose my child. Nothing else mattered or has mattered since.

Putting Fatima's story into the world has proven a difficult assignment. My grief accompanies me everywhere, never more than an inch beneath my skin and always hovering around me. Reliving those moments has only fueled it more. Times when I have wanted to run away from it all and hide in a hole have been spent painstakingly recalling her abbreviated life, as well as my own uncertain journey.

I want to knock on her door, sit by her, and talk to her. Find the combination of words that we pray exists to undo all that I regret in our relationship. I would only need a moment, and it would carry me through the life that I must now live without her. And I will never get that. I thought there would be time. We always think there will be time, and when time runs out, we are told that time itself will be the healer, that the pain will subside, that she is in a better place. But I only miss her more; the pain only seems to grow with time; the seed of her loss has bloomed into an orchard that I roam every day in search of her. I wish that people understood that no words can comfort, that there is no comfort to be had or given, and that is okay.

———

CONTRIBUTING TO THIS BOOK has stripped me bare, and I feel exposed. It has not been easy, and I cannot say that I am unscathed.

But for the first time, I have no fear—as I remember and connect so deeply now with her words: "Only God has the right to judge me."

This is Fatima's parting gift to me. She gave me the tools to chip away at the insecurities and anxieties that have plagued me throughout my life. My daughter gives me that courage, both by example and by instruction.

And so, to my darling Tatu, for persevering with your book, even in the deepest, darkest moments and despite the mental and physical pain you endured, thank you for guiding me, and giving me clarity that I wish I could have grasped sooner. You gave this book its power. I hope in turn, that power helps people turn the page and share their truth.

—*Farezeh Durrani*

FOR HE IS GOD, SAVE WHOM THERE IS NO DEITY.
Unto Him all praise is due, at the beginning and at the end;
and with Him rests all judgment; and unto Him shall
you all be brought back.

—THE QURAN, SURAH 28:70

SAVOR

PART I

chapter 1

ITWAAR BAZAAR

———

Fatima

———

I GREW UP IN PAKISTAN, PLAYING CRICKET, BASKETBALL, oonch neech, and pithu gol garam with my brother, Mohammad.

When it was rainy season or too hot to be outside, we canvassed our grandparents' basement for hints of a world that predated our small brown hands and hungry minds. I idolized my grandmother, my mother's mother, who I called Nano, a tenacious, fair-skinned beauty whose shalwar kameez always carried with it the powdery rose elegance of Chanel No. 5. From when I was six and we lived with her, I often joined her on her weekly excursions to the Itwaar Bazaar, the Sunday market that unfolded like a circus on a plowed plot of dirt in a skeletal, undeveloped neighborhood in Karachi. At my grandmother's behest, we set out early, in order not to miss the best produce. While we guzzled water and used the toilet, Nano counted her cash and had Qadir, our family's cook who had been with us since my mom's youth, check the boot of the car to be sure it was empty and ready to be filled. Nano ruled the house, our small staff—a member of which delivered us to the market in our

Honda Accord, bedazzled with its Italian Momo rainbow steering wheel cover—and our days, particularly in those in-between years when my mom was building her business. Nano was a second mother to me, and it was more than obvious that her prowess in the kitchen was connected to her confidence in the world.

Before we made our way through the rows of stalls—vegetables on one side, fruit on the other—the mazdoors would line up, chests puffed out, shoulders back to imply strength and stamina. In Urdu, a mazdoor is a young boy—probably home-less, possibly orphaned, certainly too poor to attend school—who works as a porter and makes money carrying groceries for wealthier patrons at the market. Past the mazdoors, the farmers sold their produce: lauqat, jaman, lychee, cheekoo, small sweet green sultana grapes; yams, gourds, arvi, and ruby red carrots. The pungent fragrance—a saccharine crushed guava underfoot, wilting greens, the rank damp shirts of farmers who awoke be-fore dawn to haul their loads to town, potatoes with a film of dusty dried soil still clinging to them—made for an intoxicating perfume at once bodily and of the earth. I was supposed to dread these market runs, as all children and most adults did, but secretly I loved them. I followed my grandmother, sometimes pressed right up against her damp silk-draped frame—her sweet signature scent still discernible amid the odiferous hubbub—as she perused the bright stalls, surveying what she planned to purchase, sweat forming rivulets between her shoulder blades and at her temples, which, like all the other matrons, she dabbed with the corner of her dupatta. *Who has the greenest beans? The snappiest okra? The onions have to be large but not too large, because those ones are the sweetest.*

Produce was selected not just for its ripeness in the moment, but for its future perfection. Nano taught me to feel melons near their stems, that they should be heavier than they appear; to press pears gently; to smell mangos for sweetness to determine their readiness. Then came her masterful bargaining: first mild interest, then an ambivalent *How much?* No matter what price the vendor told her, it was always too much. *Fifty rupees?!* she scoffed with feigned horror. *Your friend there just offered me the very same dates for forty rupees. I'll buy them from him.* Then she turned gravely on her heel with dismissive finality, but every time, the vendor rushed to her, leaving his stall to block her path, a wagging head and smiling eyes offering her a nicer price. *Wait, Baaji Malik, I'll match his price, but only for you, tell no one,* and she'd give a barely perceptible nod to confirm her approval. At the market, my glamorous Nano was notorious and revered, and from her I learned how to shop—to select, to haggle—in that drenched tent, that humid carnival of perishables.

After the produce, trailed by a mazdoor who carried our haul in jute and plastic bags that Nano brought from home, we made our way to the meat market, where we chose our chickens from the specialized stalls that sold only chickens, and from its owner my grandmother once again tried to get the best possible deal. Nano signaled to the butcher which of the birds she wanted from the piled-up cages and he pulled each bird from its cage, rested its feathered neck on a wooden block held between his feet, and slit the chicken's throat. The blood—thick, crimson and clotted as fresh cream—gushed out into a waiting bucket, and then he tossed the bird, still pulsing, into a large industrial blue bin, lined with feathers and crusted gore of chickens that had come before, where it gave its final thrusts. Hidden behind the tall blue walls of the large drum, the bird became a shadow phantom that rumbled the bin from within. Once it was still, the butcher pulled the chicken's skin off in one fell swoop, like a mother undressing a sleeping child before bed, and gave us the still-warm poultry to take home and turn into a karahi with a rich tomato base and a fragrant finish of green chili peppers, cilantro, and ginger.

I loved the organized chaos of the market. I tried not to give much thought to where the mazdoors slept at night or what they ate for supper. I would figure out how to feed them someday, I told myself: *When I am big, I'll know how.* And I was not sentimental about the birds and beasts who died to become our suppers. It was simply the order of things: brutal but digestible. There I felt exhilarated and at ease.

Back from the market at Nano's house, Qadir met us at the car to help us unload and carry our plunder to the kitchen. Bags of rice were deposited into the pantry and stored on the cool terrazzo floor. The raw chickens, still warm with life, went into the old 1970s icebox or directly into the sink for Qadir to clean and make into that evening's supper. Fruit was piled in wicker baskets, where it ripened and tempted us over the days to come, its scent evolving from bitter to honey-sweet. The parlor and entrance of the grand Tanzeem house were intended as the house's center, but, as with any home, the kitchen was always its heart—the nexus of the most action, aroma, and appetite—and where I needed to be. Kitchens were where the love began. That much was already clear to my seven-year-old mind.

The Tanzeem house was a majestic three-story home on Khayaban-e-Tanzeem, the first street of the Defense neighborhood's tony prized Phase V, which was developed in 1970 not far from Zamzama Park. My grandfather built it as his dream project, dignified but not ostentatious: the perfect place to coddle his wife, my Nano, raise his offspring, and care for his own father.

"Your grandfather laid those stones with his own hands,

Fatima," Nano told me exactly every time we walked through the foyer together.

Nano never missed an opportunity to reference my deceased granddad: the koi pond he'd insisted upon beneath the skylight in the entrance; the long, graceful lines, devoid of gaudy motifs, that, at his direction, the architects realized throughout; the ten-foot oak front door surrounded by light-giving glass windows, all these were relics of my grandfather's good taste and prescient vision, she explained.

Nano was often my caregiver in those early years when my mother and brother and I returned from Texas to Pakistan and lived with her, first in Shamshir, the house my grandmother and Saby Khala—my mother's eldest sister—lived in together after my grandfather's death, and then in the stately Tanzeem house. I longed to know Nano's kitchen secrets: the graceful witchery of her ingredients; the mystical logic that fed us. The essential question was already nascent in me: What greater expertise could one possess than to feed those they loved?

"Let me stir it, Nano," I begged. She discouraged me half-heartedly, lest my small tender limbs be speckled by hot oil or lashed by vicious steam burns. But her concerns for my safety were no match for my conviction, so first Nano brought me a pot of hot water, into which I was allowed to drop cabbage leaves and carrots to make my first "soup." Upon tasting it and realizing it lacked any complexity (after all, it was only hot water, some salt, and wilted vegetables), Nano brought me a footstool from which I could see inside a pot of golden daal, the better vantage point from which to stir it.

"Hold my hand while you stand on that, Fatima," Nano instructed me.

"No, Nano. I can do it myself," I promised her, and true to

my word, my brown arms—darker than my pale mother's and grandmother's—were never burned in her kitchen.

From photographs, I knew my grandfather as a Pakistani version of Clark Gable—that's what everyone said. He was tall, like the rest of the Afghan side of my family. His hair was thick, combed precisely into a widow's peak and jet black apart from slicks of silver around the temples. His mustache, manicured and precise, added unmistakable masculinity to an almost feminine plump bottom lip. My great-aunts loved to tell us children stories about their adolescent years, when he picked them up from middle school at St. Joseph's Convent (thanks to British colonization, there are many Catholic schools in Pakistan) in a cherry-red 1940 Siata Sport Spider. When the shrill final bell echoed through the stained-glass chambers of the cathedral, the modest schoolgirls in traditional shalwar kameez and sashes symbolic of dupattas impatiently grouped near the convent's gates. My grandfather's Spider purred up to the curb, his little sisters clambered in, and no sooner had the doors shut—because apparently back then cars didn't even *have* seatbelts—than my grandfather slipped a sleek Rothman's Royals cigarette into his mouth, flicked his Zippo, and sped off in a puff of tobacco, horsepower, and silver screen fantasy, leaving the other girls at the gate to sigh and swoon unrequitedly.

He was the picture of sophistication: an educated and cultured gentleman who reigned over his well-appointed house of four children and an adoring attractive wife. It's said that there was a gracious sense of order, of quiet opulence in the house in the early years of my mother's youth . . . until there wasn't.

My grandfather died in 1980 at age fifty-one, when my mother was only fifteen. Every morning, rain or shine, while his brood slumbered contently in their warm beds, my grandfather diligently woke at five a.m. to walk the five-kilometer perimeter of the neighborhood. One ordinary morning, very early before the sun was up, he suffered a cerebral hemorrhage in his sleep and never woke up for his walk.

If I were to pick one incident that altered the trajectory of our family, and of myself, it would be this: the death of my dashing grandfather, a man whom I never even met, because, of course, my story is not only my own. It couldn't be. My story began long before I did with those who came before: the nawab great-grandparents, the enterprising grandfather and his beloved wife—my Nano—and most significantly, my mother. She, more than anyone else, made me who I am and painted the outlines of my life. As I often remind her, she and I are for a reason.

chapter 2

DAYS THAT SHONE
LIKE POLISHED STONE

———

Farezeh

———

My CHILDHOOD WAS SO UNLIKE FATIMA AND Mohammad's, and of course Karachi was different then: the 1960s and the 1970s were golden decades, when the city felt grand and full of civility, moving toward a bright future, and I was born into a family and existence that epitomized those promising times.

It was 1954, only seven years after Pakistan won its independence from British rule, when my parents, Malick and Asif, met. My father, Asif, who we called our Agha Jani—Light of Life—out of love and respect, was from an esteemed political Sindh family. His great-uncle was one of the original Pakistani senators after Partition, and his aunt was married to the first chief minister of Sindh when India and Pakistan split. My father's first cousin is a sitting minister for the Pakistan Peoples' Party (PPP), and Agha Jani was great friends with Prime Minister Zulfiqar Ali Bhutto, the Sindhi founder of the PPP, who served as president and secretary to the United Nations before becoming PM.

Though from a political dynasty and friends with the former

PM, Agha Jani was no politician. He'd studied mechanical engineering at the University of Michigan in the United States and was a star engineer at Pakistani Railways, where my maternal granddad was managing director. One day, my grandfather invited his star mechanic home for lunch and Agha Jani's fate was sealed the moment he met Mummy—my mother, Malick—then sixteen years old. Though my grandparents planned that Mummy would marry a nobleman (my grandmother was from a family of nawabs—descendants of viceroys of the Moghul kings), Agha Jani and Mummy's chemistry was inarguable. It was a marriage based on love at first sight.

By the time I came along, his third child, Agha Jani owned and operated Daihatsu Pakistan as its chairman, overseeing the Japanese motor company's production facility in our country. He also owned several Pakistani mines that he leased out to men who extracted the stone. It was perhaps where his passion really resided, carving out raw onyx and marble from the earth and polishing it until it shone.

My elegant, coy, and perfectionist mother was the object of Agha Jani's affection. She focused on her prizewinning gardens, learning flower arrangement techniques, perfecting her khaosuey recipe; she managed the staff and planned menus, ran the household meticulously, like a practiced ballerina giving off a pleasurable sense of effortlessness.

Mummy took great pride in caring for us, showing us her love through food and the comforts of home. Every day, she surprised us with a treat at dinner—a homemade pizza or lemon pie.

She was years ahead of her time when it came to cultivating her interests, learning to cook cuisine many Pakistani households had not even heard of, let alone sampled. She signed up for Chinese cooking classes, conjured up Italian dishes, even cheesecake—before a bakery in Pakistan had ever sold one. She brought the world to our table, and no one encouraged her more than Agha Jani.

Mummy's table always had plenty. She made sure that no matter who came to our house unannounced, they would leave with full bellies, delighted, and joyous having eaten an assortment of dishes she either had prepared, or was able to produce in an instant. She made her own cheese, which was fried off for a snack, or made its way into a warming slice of lasagna. Depending on the season, there were rotating jars of jams, and chutneys—apricot, strawberry, or apple jams, a mango chutney that in summer was dolloped on every bite of my plate. Falsa berries become a sherbet; almonds, too, to cool us off in the summer heat. Mummy's kitchen was in constant production, never chaos, instead an orchestra with its indisputable conductor. Every few days, a new culinary experiment, a recipe she had clipped away from a lifestyle magazine or from one of the many cookbooks she accumulated. Spicy prawns with spring onions, thinly sliced beef with green chili and soy, a chicken fricassee, and the infamous "supgetti keema" as our Qadir called it for decades to come—a Pakistani-style spaghetti Bolognese. Her elegant china and porcelain dishes enticed and enchanted our guests, for whom there was a perpetual all-you-can-eat policy.

It brought Mummy joy to make those around her happy, and it was infectious. In our extended family, she was everybody's favorite. And her marriage was no exception: Mummy was the perfect housewife. She and my father made an excellent team.

Though our family was urbane and educated, there was a different standard associated with us girls. Under Agha Jani's watchful eye, my two older sisters and I had very sheltered early lives. While the Western world was partaking in the swinging 1960s and rebellious 1970s, we were attending an all-girls con-

vent school; we were not allowed to go out on our own, to socialize with boys, or to dress in a Western or contemporary way.

My parents dreamt up the house they wanted and, brick by
brick, brought it to life when I was eight years old. We called it
the Tanzeem house, for the name of the street it was on in a
wealthy and up-and-coming neighborhood with large lots and
impressive homes. It was a six-bedroom wonderland, with two
dining areas lit by Iranian crystal chandeliers, a huge drawing
room for entertaining, two gardens, and a swimming pool, an
unusual extravagance in 1972, but one Agha Jani had earned.

The Tanzeem house also sported an airy four-bedroom staff
house, where our maids, drivers, and cook lived and set up their
home. Chief among them was Qadir, who went on to take care
of three generations of my family. Most of them were like family to us, and my father paid for the education of all the staff's
children, as his ideology was that our wealth was meant to be
shared.

When I think back on my early childhood, before Agha
Jani's death, there was a pervasive rosiness to our everyday life.
It was imbued with music and fragrance from my mother's
magnificent garden, where she grew and clipped chrysanthe-
mum, pansies, marigolds, daisies, chandni, din ka raja, and roses.
On the terrace that opened off the parlor and near the front
doors were potted jasmine plants that climbed the walls around
each doorframe. My father awoke early, while the rest of the
house slept, went for his morning walk, and then left for work
by seven a.m. My sister Tammy got me ready for school, where
I was deposited by and later collected by Mummy and the
driver.

Our meals and daily life were filled with aunts and uncles
and cousins who were like my siblings, all held together by the
glue that was my Agha Jani. He anchored us, and we knew that

safety, protection, and love resided where he did. He was the sun, under whose gaze his family rose and bloomed. I had no concept of friends. Life was about family, family, family . . . and with a family so large as our extended one, it was more than enough in terms of camaraderie.

Even so, amid our nuclear family, I often felt overlooked. My eldest sister, Saby, was my father's clear favorite, who, although a daughter, played the role of a firstborn son. Opinionated and courageous, Saby showed interest in his business, rode a motorbike (in fact, my father gave her a Sizette on her fifteenth birthday, before realizing it was an utterly inappropriate gift for a daughter of a good family and rescinded it), and managed to elude all the suitors that approached her or whom he suggested for her. My next older sister, Tammy, who was often included in what the grownups did, looked after me, five years her junior, until she married in 1979. My little brother, Mohammad Ali, was the baby—the long-hoped-for boy—and the instant darling. And me? I was simply the middle child, a mostly well-behaved little girl who didn't want to create waves, who hoped to please, but who mostly went unnoticed.

Dignity and manners were central to our family identity, as was hospitality. My parents entertained often with the finest food and liquor, and an invitation from the Durranis, an attractive, charismatic, well-to-do couple, was too appealing to ignore, something Karachi society vied for. I couldn't help but imagine that someday I'd lead a similar household—full of love and music. For a time, the beauty of our daily lives seemed completely normal. Then, as sudden as an earthquake that destroys a stately building, our lives were upended by Agha Jani's death.

chapter 3

A CONVINCING FEAST

———

Farezeh

———

I T HAPPENED WITHOUT WARNING. AGHA JANI, THE picture of health, a literal life force, went to sleep one September night in 1981 and did not wake up. We were told it was a brain aneurysm. His sudden death was such an ill-fitting end to a life so well lived that people thought there had been an error when his obituary was published in newspapers the next day, assuming it must have been Agha Jani's *father* who had died.

I was almost catatonic at his funeral, in disbelief of what was happening. I was fifteen years old and stared at the frenzied mourners who had congregated in his honor: an indelicate reminder that life is fleeting, that their time in this world is finite. The grief was as visceral as the sense of injustice—of the light of our lives being snuffed out so soon.

I watched Aba Jaan approach his son, who had been thriving not more than a day before, wrapped in a shroud, a cloak of death. I saw Aba Jaan's shoulders bow, and then shake. It was the first time I saw my grandfather cry.

Then he said, to the son who could no longer hear him,

"Asif, you have broken my back today." Aba Jaan died just six months after Agha Jani.

I'VE SAID THAT AGHA JANI was the main fixture, the sun around which we all orbited, the center of a very patriarchal and cloistered house. He was our protector, our governor, our linchpin, our provider, and the light of Mummy's sheltered life, so when he died, our world shifted on its axis. Mummy, still young at forty-one, was inconsolable and depressed. She receded into the cavern of her darkened bedroom, where she more or less remained, lost and grieving, for six years. Her gardens showed her grief, neglected in small ways. Perhaps she felt there was no point in perfection, without my father's gaze to praise it.

When Agha Jani died, so did my family's main source of income through Daihatsu, and the bills began to pile up. We had to leave the Tanzeem house and lease it out to cover our expenses. My eldest sister scrambled to try to save Agha Jani's onyx and marble business, just as an eldest son would have. Saby was clear about her disdain for commitment to a man. My next older sister, Tammy, had already married and was living in Austin, Texas. That left me and my baby brother, Mohammad Ali, to account for. I was fifteen and it became clear that I would be married off to a suitable husband who was educated and had good prospects with which to support me.

In those years following Agha Jani's death, with Mummy inert from the loss, I could get away with a bit more and began to sneak out on occasion. It was quite innocent, but I started to meet new people, including a boy I fancied. At this time— Pakistan in the early 1980s—it was unacceptable for a girl to have a boyfriend; girls who had boyfriends were called *taiz,* promiscuous. Of course, it was not only normal, but *encouraged* for boys to have girlfriends, typical of the pervasive gender bias and societal double standards at their most basic. So when Mummy found out that I had a crush on a boy, her fervor to marry me off hit a fever pitch, as she feared that a girl who had a boyfriend would open herself up to all kinds of slander and gossip. All this, to her, was another inevitable and unwelcome consequence of my having lost the protection of a father.

By this point I was eighteen, and as fate would have it, someone was interested in marrying me. I came from a well-respected family and I had inherited Mummy's pale complexion, an attribute that had historically been associated with beauty and privilege in Pakistan, and so my name was suggested as a suitable wife for an educated young man with aspirations and a bright future.

The Lahore-based Punjabi family of a twenty-eight-year-old man whom I'd never met approached my family through my phupho, Agha Jani's younger sister—a friend of one of their friends. Their son, Ashtar, had just gotten a degree in law from George Washington University in Washington, D.C. They were Shia, as were we. He had no money yet, but a bright future, so the two basic attributes—a good education and our common branch of Islam—were enough for Mummy to accept their proposal of marriage sight unseen and promise me as his bride. There was no discussion: Mummy simply told me that I would marry him. Ashtar's parents sent a photograph of him, as was the custom then—for photographs to be exchanged before a boy and girl physically met.

"Fari!" Mummy shouted when the mail arrived. "Fari, come quick!" she said. I rushed downstairs from my room to see what

she was on about, and Mummy greeted me at the bottom of the
stairs, holding Ashtar's photograph. "My goodness, Fari, this
boy looks exactly like Barry Manilow!"

I can't possibly tell you why *now,* but in 1983 at age eighteen,
I thought Barry Manilow was incredibly captivating. I swooned
at his voice and listened to his records every chance I got. Knowing this all too well, Mummy tried to soften the blow of my
arranged marriage to a stranger by likening my betrothed to the
American singer of "If I Should Love Again" and "Copaca-
bana." She meant well. And to be fair, it *was* a good photograph
of Ashtar. Ten years my senior, he appeared intellectual and curious. The angle of the shot made him appear tall and burly, just
like the Prince Charmings in the fairy tales on which I was
raised; this appeased me slightly, as I was also tall and curva-
ceous.

As I stood in the foyer, I tried to allow myself to be convinced that this stranger was my destiny. I was utterly naïve and
believed in the fairy-tale fantasy that my knight in shining
armor would sweep me off my feet. I'd seen the way my petite,
pretty Mummy looked at my six-two, jet-haired Agha Jani, and
it was the very same expression that these helpless women wore
when their princes kissed them, which reaffirmed the illusion.
When I saw my sister Tammy marry the man she loved (a marriage that wasn't arranged, but which my father endorsed), I saw
the very same look on her face. I tried to imagine my Agha Jani
pushing me to marry the stranger in the photograph, and simultaneously I wondered why Mummy wouldn't trust me to
choose a partner whom I loved, as she had for herself with Agha
Jani when she was only sixteen.

It was organized that Ashtar would come from Lahore to
Karachi for ten days to get to know me and my family. I sat in
the drawing room with Saby and Mummy, waiting to meet my

future. When Ashtar arrived my heart sank because I immediately realized that I was taller than he—a superficial observation, but around him, I just felt bigger, which made me feel even more ill at ease. We three greeted him, without any handshaking or touching, and then sat in the living room together awkwardly in near silence. First Mummy got up and left. Then a few minutes later Saby departed, leaving Ashtar and me to discuss topics as banal as the weather.

The following day, Ashtar wanted to buy some new shoes, so Mummy and I took him to Tariq Road, the bustling street that's lined with clothing stores. We went into Service Shoes and Ashtar picked out a simple pair of utilitarian black shoes. As he was trying them on, I realized with horror that my feet were far larger than his. *How could we possibly fit together?* I thought to myself, fixated on the impossible ideal that I'd been spoon-fed since childhood. I expected the perfect package, one that I believed in and had witnessed in other unions, from that of my own parents to those depicted in Walt Disney movies—one I wanted for myself.

"Mummy, I don't think I love him," I told her meekly as she watered some potted croton in the drawing room later that afternoon.

"Of course you don't love him, Fari," she responded. "You don't even *know* him. But you will *grow* to love him when you have a child."

Perhaps my mother had knowledge that I didn't, one that comes from a great love like she had shared with my father. Maybe she believed that chemistry would come. Maybe it would grow out of something I hadn't stumbled upon yet. But at that time, all I saw was the robbery of my romantic dream.

I wanted to object and remind Mummy that she had fallen in love with Agha Jani when she *saw* him. I wanted to remind her of what I knew to be true: that she had loved Agha Jani *before* they had a child, that having four children had reinforced their *pre-existing* love. *Listen to me! Protect me! Consider ME!* I wanted to scream at this dainty, formidable woman who had given birth to me but who seemed utterly unconcerned by my instincts or heart. But I was afraid to say anything more—afraid of disrespecting an elder, afraid of a fight. Mummy seemed so sure that I was too young and naïve to know what was good for me. She seemed certain that having a child would solve everything, a refrain that would become ever more familiar, if nonetheless false, in the years to come. Was there chemistry between us? Did I like him? Could I see my future with him? Those things were not important to Mummy, and neither was I asked. With Agha Jani gone, money was scarce and unmarried daughters were prime targets for trouble and gossip.

One afternoon, when he'd been in Karachi for three days—an endless procession of socializing, hosting, and pretending—he and I were sent on an errand with my cousin to fetch a forgotten item from her home. I soon realized that it was a ruse orchestrated by my family to give us a bit of privacy, unsupervised by an adult. I was standing toward the bottom of my cousin's stairway waiting for her to find the item when Ashtar came up behind me and flirtatiously grabbed me from behind. I was so startled that I screamed and tore away, shrieking, dashing toward where my cousin had disappeared. Ashtar was bewildered by my dramatic response to his unexpected touch. He was so confused by my overreaction that he mistook it for coquettishness and followed me. He must have thought that I was playing games, engaging, being silly and flirting right back, which frankly, I ought to have been.

"We aren't a good match," I told him, rather cruelly, when

I'd calmed down. "I think we will be unhappy together, but my family won't listen."

"I don't know what to say," Ashtar responded frankly and not unkindly.

When I made a final attempt to dissuade Ashtar from marrying me, he confessed that his family didn't care what he wanted any more than my family cared what I wanted. *You can marry either of the Durrani sisters,* his father had apparently told him. *But you're going to marry one of them.* Ashtar and I weren't adversaries; rather, we were both victims to traditions we had no part in making. He was under just as much pressure as I was, and so I knew then that it was pointless, that we would certainly be wed.

I thought of Agha Jani, and what all of this would have looked like if he'd still been by my side. Would the rules have changed? Honestly, probably not. My sister Saby, who evaded all suitors, would likely have found herself with a husband too. But I did know this: Agha Jani never would have pushed me to marry the first person or into the first family who asked. He would have sought out a suitor that actually suited me. He would not have forced any of his children into an ill-fitting marriage, because his instincts would have been the same as mine: Ashtar and I did not belong together.

There was no further discussion between me and Ashtar, no formal proposal between us. The families had decided our future before we'd even met, and the date was set for April 10, 1984. As is customary, wedding celebrations began a month ahead. Mummy arranged for daily ubtan massages, during which ladies rubbed ubtan paste all over me, warding off blemishes, fading scars, and lightening my already pale complexion. The ritual of the ubtan massage, followed by the olive and almond oil rubbed all over me, was meant to prepare me for my wedding, but it was an odd experience to be touched by strangers and to know that my body was being prepared for someone else. While the women's hands ought to have made me feel attractive, their daily pressure instead made me feel trapped.

Family arrived from near and far and extravagant festivities with music and extensive menus became a thrice-daily ritual in our home. The scent of Qadir's freshly cooked halwa (semolina pudding) roused me in the morning, and in my half-sleep, I sometimes lost my place in time and believed I was still a child, a little girl whose Agha Jani awaited her downstairs at his desk, home from the office because it was Eid. By the time I descended the stairs and round perfect puris tossed in a pool of desi ghee were being served to our guests, my reverie had been dismantled: I wouldn't find my father in his study playing Connie Francis's "Lipstick on Your Collar" on his gramophone. He wasn't there to protect me; I was a young woman about to marry someone I hardly knew.

At lunchtime platters of chicken biryani, chapli kebabs, and baigan ki burhani—Mummy's signature yogurt and eggplant dish with fresh garlic chips—adorned the dining room table, a daily exercise in proving we had plenty. Then at dinner Mummy showed off her Chinese specialities: chow mein, sweet-and-sour prawns, fried rice, and her famous beef with dried chilies. The house took on the liveliness and cheer of the holidays, and a large dining table was set in the family room with an array of hot and cold snacks that guests could nibble at throughout the day, ever at the ready to satiate a visiting family member or friend for whom my wedding was an excuse to drop by to socialize.

Weddings are pretexts for excess. At teatime the table became an elaborate pastel collage of fresh butter biscuits, pound cake, black forest cake, and all sorts of mithais (Pakistani sweet pastries), the treats that we begged for as children, rewards given by a doting father or leftovers pocketed after our mother had her society friends over. Here they were—gulab jamun, ras malai, rasgulla—available by the tin and by the platter, and yet my mouth remained dry.

The aromas that found their way into every corner of our house should have stoked my hunger with their references to happy memories and the jovial meals of my youth, sitting with my parents and my siblings and eating Mummy's sindhi biryani, but leading up to my wedding, they had the opposite effect: I barely ate.

The day before the wedding, my mehndi party took place. Surrounded by women who were also being decorated ahead of my wedding festivities, the mehndi artist drew the intricate patterns in henna on my forearms and hands, front and back, and my ankles and feet. I knew that these ceremonial celebrations were meant to build excitement about my imminent marriage, that I was meant to rejoice in the blessings that were being scrawled onto my skin and delight in the fact that my betrothed's name was probably hidden among the ornate motifs. But I didn't. Instead, it felt like it was happening to someone else.

For the shaadi ceremony, my bridal dress was a beautifully embellished and handcrafted red and green farshi gharara—an old-fashioned style of dress worn in Muslim courts of Oudh by royalty and the privileged classes, which I changed into at the salon after getting my hair and makeup done professionally. No expense was spared. Amid the flashing of lavish fabric, the whir of hair dryers, the *shhhh!* of hairspray, and the chatter of female voices, perhaps I should have felt like royalty—it was all about me, after all, wasn't it?—but gazing at my made-up reflection, I felt only disassociated. Later, my sister Tammy arrived with the family jewelry, now a part of my dowry to complement my very heavy wedding dress. I wore a gold kundan teeka on my forehead (as every Pakistani bride must) along with rows upon rows of necklaces that started at my collarbone and ended just below my waistline. I wore gold bangles on both wrists, rings of all stones and shapes on all ten fingers, and gold earrings with emeralds and rubies that were so heavy that strings of pearls were wrapped around my ears to support them to keep them from ripping through my earlobes. I felt trapped beneath the weight of gems and tethered by the silk. Amid the merrymaking around me, I had an urge to tear off my elaborate shackles. I saw myself running away from it all in just the thin slip that was closest to my skin, but even as I pictured it, I knew that I lacked the armor to survive without the approval of my family, the shelter of a marriage that had been prescribed for me. There was nothing but for me to remain motionless in my gown and jewels, shaking inwardly but outwardly serene for the nikkah, when the marriage contract was signed and we were on display for all to see.

Dressed as the perfect virtuous bride, I sat beside my elegant and traditionally clad groom in his gray raw silk sherwani, crisp silk kulla, and stiff starched white shalwar. This was the moment, where I sensed that my life had taken a turn, that there was really no going back. I had taken a handful of anti-anxiety pills to numb myself and I did what I was told: I married Ashtar Ali with a wan smile.

The food at the reception was extensive, extremely elaborate, and rich in its flavors and cooking style, intended to impress: thick, creamy Mughlai badami korma (curried chicken with almonds); gamy, fragrant kabuli pulao (lamb with rice pilaf); verdant palak gosht (spinach and mutton curry); rack of lamb; roasted chicken with an assortment of vegetables and an array of fresh tikka (spiced marinated grilled meats); kebabs and mutton chops on skewers made on the spot and served on platters to guests by hired servers and staff. Fresh sesame naans and rotis were baked and served from a tandoor. Pakistanis love their sauces, and a host of chutneys and achars and salads to add as condiments was perpetually refreshed and tidied on a sideboard. An entire table was devoted to desserts to tempt our guests: gajar ka halwa carrot pudding; the Afghan custard known as firni; fruit trifle; frozen kulfi dusted with pistachio; cold faluda in pretty little glasses arranged on a tray; and rose-scented fresh gulab jamuns in delicious syrup.

When the ceremonies and festivities were drawing to a close, my family walked me to the car for the rukhsati, when the bride leaves with the groom for his home. Because Ashtar was not a local, we'd booked the Karachi Sheraton Hotel after the wedding, where I locked myself in the bathroom and wept. When Ashtar knocked, I told him through the door that I didn't feel well, that I needed more time. But it was inevitable; my time was up. I was his bride, whether I was ready to be or not.

chapter 4

A FOREIGN HOME

———

Farezeh

———

I MOVED TO LAHORE TO LIVE WITH MY NEW HUSBAND and his parents. It was the expected thing to do. The Al-Abbas house—so named for the devoted Shia biblical figure Abbas, brother of Hussein—was on a quiet leafy street in an old part of Lahore called Garden Town. It was deceptively large, two stories with a set of steps that led into different sections of the home. In the large backyard, there were guava and citrus trees and a big old mango tree with a bee colony in its trunk that generously donated honey to us every year. Al-Abbas was sunny and airy enough, and although it was beautiful, it didn't feel like home.

I was very much in the spotlight, the center of attention, and was entrusted with supporting my new parents with the little details of everyday life. From picking fabric and designing clothes for my in-laws, to refurbishing our home's furniture, to playing hostess when guests came for tea, my judgment, my taste, and my approach were celebrated and sought out, and this attention and faith in me made me feel valued and appreciated.

But it was also as if my new parents were more in love with me than my husband was.

I was keen to live up to the expectations that went with being the prized wife of the eldest son. I wanted to rise to the status they had bestowed upon me, and do my new and old families proud.

The dynamic at home, however, was not always conducive. There was a simmering volatility—conflict that I was unsure how to manage because of how foreign it felt—that occasionally boiled over and escalated, and I missed my old home most in those instances, and in my quiet moments when I felt isolated. Ashtar, who was starting his own practice, was almost always busy with work and I was always left at home. I was beginning to recognize the contrast between the marriage of my parents and my own. I craved the partnership and symbiosis that seemed to be ever present in Agha Jani and Mummy's relationship. Until Agha Jani passed, I'd observed such a strong and mutual love that vibrated between them, and I wanted the same from my marriage.

Perhaps my mother-in-law sensed my loneliness, perhaps she took a liking to me, or perhaps she simply felt it her duty to help me become a good wife for her eldest son, but whatever her reasons, she took a special interest in me. "You are going to change my future generations"—it was one of the first things she told me when I moved in with them in Lahore. Clearly it was a compliment in her mind, putting the betterment of her lineage heavily atop my inexperienced shoulders.

In the mornings, I accompanied my mother-in-law to the Ichhra and Akbari Mandi markets and did the daily chores at home. She and I spent many stifling afternoons lying on her master bed, the air conditioner buzzing to offer some relief from the oppressive Lahore summer, and in the evenings, we attended family gatherings. A predictable rhythm was starting to build.

I'd never been in a rickshaw before my mother-in-law hailed one from the line of rickety three-wheeled dinkies whose sunken-cheeked drivers stood leaning and smoking on our corner in Garden Town.

"Akbari Mandi!" she said as she hoisted herself into the seat beside me, practically onto my lap. As our shoulders, rib cages, hips, and thighs pressed together, as if we were intergenerational Siamese twins, I felt a particular intimacy I'd never before sensed, a physical proximity I couldn't recall ever sharing with my own mom. "And quickly, before there's nothing left!" she added as we swerved into menacing traffic.

The first time I entered Akbari Mandi, a walled city of freshly ground spices, it overwhelmed my senses. Narrow lanes littered with overflowing shops poking out of any space one could find. Tall hessian sacks with mounds of freshly ground turmeric, Kashmiri red chili, garam masala blends, and whole spices of all sorts were brought out in little bags for us to smell and taste. My mother-in-law kept moving, waiting for her taste buds and nose to tell her where to spend her money; the crack of a cinnamon stick, the pinching of cardamon to unveil its fragrant jewels, the feeling of the dried chilies—are they leathery and malleable, or do they threaten to crack and break? The market changed colors and smells as you walked through it, the muted hues of white and brown where so many different types of rice and flour could be found, to the bright and provocative colors of different masalas. Each shopkeeper trying their best to attract you into their square foot of space, to seduce you into buying from them and only them.

As I trailed a few steps behind my mother-in-law, the protruding baskets of lentils and semolina flour snagged my memories. I felt a rush of nostalgia, recalling occasional childhood trips to Karachi's Empress market with my own mother, where my brother and I followed in awe as Mummy selected her seafood and vegetables for the week. Fresh pomfret lay as flat and gray as our father's daily newspaper, as if God had pressed it under his palm. Pink-fleshed fish lay in vibrant rows beside tiger prawns, crabs, and lobsters freshly caught from the Arabian Sea. These bright creatures smelled clean and salty, but there was always the pungent scent of rot and death beneath, the unseen debris from last week's offerings caught in invisible cracks.

My mother-in-law dropped a small bag of something into the giant baby blue plastic bag I carried and our eyes met, bringing me back to the present: Lahore in 1984, ready to head to the main market for our weekly visit to the butcher shop. They would be ready for us there—my mother-in-law was an old customer who commanded the attention of the top butcher. Freshly slaughtered and skinned goats hung from hooks, their pink flesh, white fat, and sinew swaying macabrely, their hairy little tails curling out of their now bare bottoms. Heads, feet, lungs, kidneys, livers, and all sorts of unidentifiable bits were stacked on one side of the red-and-white printed vinyl cover, and at the top of the plastic blanket, the butcher, Ashraf, sat in front of his gigantic misshapen wood chopping block. Within arm's reach were his "fly flickers"—wooden sticks with old gray wet-looking cloths bound to one end. With a flick of his wrist the cloth whipped over the flies, menacingly close to them, threatening them enough that they buzzed off momentarily before they kamikazed back to the exposed piles of flesh and bone. Ashraf's kameez was splattered with blood, no matter how dark in color it was. There was a metallic taste to the air, and a gaminess that came from the barnyard animal carcasses that awaited our hot stoves.

"Fari . . . *Fari!*" I heard her voice distantly, as if under water; I was lost in my thoughts. My mother-in-law was exacting in her instructions to the butcher. The goat must not be more than twelve kilos, in order to offer the most possible meat and the tenderest cuts. "You see how he's cutting the chops? You have to make sure it is a double chop, otherwise it's pointless," she explained in Urdu, pointing. "Those will be perfect for Bhunay howay champs. And the maghaz [brain] we will make into a masala. The keema we will NEVER pass through the mincing machine, no! It must be hand-chopped to have the right texture. Soon you'll know all this yourself."

Indeed, soon, through observation and repetition, I would know all her secrets to being a "good wife." As if that was all it took. As if knowing how to cook, how to take care of him, I would qualify. Every day, I became a better wife, or at least that's what I told myself through my fog of despondence. This was what had worked for her, and she gave me the same template.

I suppose that's what Ashtar wanted too, and the connection I sought didn't really figure in to what he had seen growing up. What was foreign to me was normal to him. What was an expectation for me was not natural to him. We were both trying to duplicate the marriages we had observed in our own parents, and those were clearly two very different marriages.

A full month into my marriage, resigned that nothing about my circumstances would change, I realized that the only aspect I could control was my own outlook. I had not chosen this man, this family, this house, or this new life, but it was mine, and perhaps I could make it more pleasant and less something only bearable if I could shift my perspective.

I woke up the next morning and said to myself, *Fari, you must at least try to make this marriage work*. At that moment, I decided to try to change my approach. I asked Ashtar not to go to work but to spend the day with me instead, and though he was surprised, to say the least, he was easily convinced. We didn't do anything monumental, just went to a nearby park and walked and spoke and swung on the swings. I listened to him and flirted with him. It was my way of committing to the relationship, of creating intimacy, becoming vulnerable and bonding, and it seemed to work. His parents noticed the changed energy between us and doubled their warmth toward me. I was from a sheltered home, lacked confidence, and above all hated conflict and confrontation, so I decided to go with the flow and keep the peace.

I knew Ashtar was busy building up his practice, which was good for all of us, so I didn't want to agitate about how much time I got with him or what impact that might be having on our relationship. Instead, we made the most of the time we did get. Some nights after work and after the entire city had gone off to sleep, Ashtar and I would zip away for a late-night drive and meal. While I enjoyed these times together, I still had to fight off the sense of being trapped, without any real life of my own. When I shared this nagging sensation with my husband, he made my feelings and desires even more diminished, as if it was wrong for me to even have any needs in the first place. Ever the talented lawyer, when I shared my perspective with him, he put me in the role of opposing counsel: he'd pick apart my words and slowly dismantle my case until he emerged victorious, and without any burden or responsibility.

Ashtar's practice began to thrive, and we found ourselves invited to every party as a result. It was at one of these cocktail parties that I met three women about my age: Yasmin, Eram, and Afshi. I felt an immediate kinship to these genuinely warm women with joyful, kind eyes. Eram had just given birth to her first child, Usman, and Yasmin had recently had her second, her son Ammar.

Eventually, with these newfound friends, I began to uncurl. It was so organic that I almost did not notice it. They accepted me for who I was, cheered me on, protected me, and showed me what it was like to be prioritized. Feelings I longed for in my marriage appeared instead in my friendships. These women were my sanctuary from our home, where I felt like I could not be anything less than perfect. I didn't need to play a part with them. I could just be myself. These brilliant, wickedly funny, endlessly generous women would remain my best friends for life—my soulmates.

Not long after this, I became pregnant. The pressure from my in-laws was immediate and incessant: They wanted a boy to further their name and they wanted him to be fair-skinned like me, as this was perceived as impressive and ennobling. At that point in Pakistan, there were no ultrasounds that showed the sex of the baby.

Mohammad arrived into our lives male and pale. I had produced the ultimate grandchild for my in-laws, according to their standards. It showed in the way they doted on him, and in turn how they doted on me.

I began to anticipate the blossoming of my relationship with Ashtar that my mother had promised would follow the birth of our first child. I kept waiting, and it did not happen. When he was gone, which was often, I missed him . . . or at least I missed what I imagined a relationship between the two of us *could* be like. The busier he got, the more I felt a sort of vacuum inside, in the part of me where affection should reside. He was gone for days on end traveling for work, and I missed his attention and the fragile spark of romance that I'd worked so hard to stoke.

The loneliness in our marriage took over. When Mohammad was about two, the charade became too much for me and I took my baby boy and left for Karachi in the hopes that Mummy and Saby would welcome me and accept my escape from unhappiness.

This was not to be.

When Mummy and Saby realized that I had no intention of returning to Lahore and to my husband, they were horrified. They simply couldn't comprehend why I would leave him.

"Fari, only a father can provide properly for a child," Mummy said flatly.

"Why can't I work?" I asked them. "I can earn money."

"You're not capable of it," Saby said definitively.

"I can write. Perhaps I could get a job at a magazine," I tried again. They just shook their heads: *No.* "I could work at a hotel, I could check people in or do guest relations," I offered, to their disdain.

"Working at a hotel is not a respectable job. You are young and naïve," they told me.

"You've worked at Agha Jani's factory since he died," I countered to my sister, who had made sure our father's marble and onyx business stayed afloat since his death.

"That's different, Fari. I didn't just go out and look for a job. It just wouldn't be appropriate!"

I couldn't fully grasp why it was so impossible for me to work, other than it had something to do with our class, with social perceptions, and of course with the fact that I was a woman. My family had been struggling financially since my father's death, but somehow our "class" was independent of our (lack of) wealth. One thing they made clear was that I had no grounds to leave my husband and marriage. Ashtar was a provider. We had a son. Everything else was irrelevant. I felt disposed of anew. As I flew back to Lahore, with Mohammad asleep in my arms, his steady, sweet breaths on my neck as familiar and essential to me as oxygen, I wondered: *How could a father who was rarely home be so instrumental?* It was impossible for me to reconcile, and yet, with no other options, I returned to Lahore and to my husband.

Not long after, Ashtar moved us out of his parents' home and into our own place, the F.C.C. house, where I finally had more autonomy. Every day I convened with my girlfriends and our young children at our house or at one of theirs to talk and laugh. When the men weren't working, they joined in too.

Our new life coincided with a steady expansion in our social circles as well. We now had multiple bubbles of young families to which we belonged and were constantly hatching one plan or the other to spend time together. Entertaining became a regular occurrence in our home and began to dominate my focus and role. It was far easier to surround ourselves with distractions than to pay attention to the widening cracks between us. Our relationship was becoming more about convenience than anything else: We took care of our self-assigned duties and not much more, speaking generically at the end of each day, avoiding any meaningful topics or issues that were moving from a steady simmer to a rapid boil underneath us.

In 1989, when I became pregnant for the second time, the expectation and pressure were the same as they'd been with Mohammad, but this time I did not deliver to my in-laws what they wanted. My water burst in the wee hours of August 8. We were told that the obstetrician was at home asleep, so I could not give birth yet. The nurses told me to cross my legs; they told me to hold my baby in.

There was no epidural—it was a natural childbirth and I was in a great deal of pain. Mummy was there throughout, but when I cried out from the pain, she shushed me, reminding me that there was another young mother in my room who was also suffering and who my moaning might disturb. It was not considered good breeding to express your pain, but with my contractions coming fast, there was only so much I could take.

By four a.m., I knew that my baby was in the birth canal and needed to come out, and so I channeled that pain and kicked the nurses off me and pushed with all my might. Out Fatima flew—my little baby girl, projected into the world. She could not wait to be born.

And in her struggle to come out of me, she inhaled amniotic fluid into her lungs and the next day was diagnosed with double pneumonia.

Fatima was immediately taken away to the intensive care unit. I felt the life drain out of me and pour itself into the baby I could not hold. Did Fatima know she held my life in her tiny body, which had tubes sticking into every part? Did she know then that my very survival was tethered to hers?

I watched her, in complete isolation, from behind a glass window outside the ICU. I would stand for hours, staring at her, willing her to be okay. The nurses would tell me to go sit down somewhere, but I wouldn't even hear them. I was crippled by my hopelessness, not knowing if my baby girl would live or not. I wanted to break down the door and comfort her, comfort myself. I began having conversations with her pain, urging it to find its new home in me and leave her body. I was ready to strike any deal with any power as long as it would soothe my baby. The doctors had no answers. Fatima's chances of survival fluctuated by the hour.

But baby Fatima fought. Like hell. She had no reverence for her weaknesses.

She was a warrior even then, resolute as a baby about what she wanted to do: live. Her sickness and the doom doctors had predicted for her were no match for her fight and her strength.

Could I have predicted it then that for Fatima the odds did not matter? That the might of her willpower would carry her through her difficult life? That she would always persevere, no matter what?

She was in the ICU for two months, and it took her a full year to recover. But recover she did. She negotiated with death—breaking with her destiny even when she was just weeks old—and bought herself time.

While my in-laws had said they wanted another pale male baby, they couldn't help but fall in love with Fatima. Even as a sick infant, she was sunny and strong-spirited, and my father-in-law in particular was besotted by her bright life force and resemblance to their side of the family when I was finally able to bring her home.

Ashtar, for his part, loved his children. He went along with their hide-and-seek games when he got home from the office early enough to see them before bed. He brought us treats from his work travels, always bringing something for each of us as his way of showing us that he had us in his thoughts.

"You're a great mother," he often remarked upon returning from his many trips. I know he admired me as a mother, if not in other ways.

chapter 5

THE VERY FIRST TASTE

———

Fatima

———

I N THE BEGINNING, IT WAS THE FOUR OF US. DAD WAS home most Sunday mornings in our three-bedroom townhouse in Lahore and would call out to us when it was time to watch *Yan Can Cook,* piled together on the sofa or one of us kids belly-down on the floor with chin propped on fist or forearm, a stray foot making contact with those on the sofa, the electricity of family running between us, and eyes transfixed by what was happening on the television screen. The Chinese chef Martin Yan's signature cleaver moved with such speed and dexterity that it literally blurred as it churned out chopped onions and peppers, diced tomatoes, and julienned chicken breasts, and made matchsticks out of cucumbers. Chef Yan explained what he was doing as he went, but he did everything with such alacrity that Dad explained each step to us as well.

"You see how he's cutting the celery, Baitus? The shape of every ingredient affects how it cooks," Dad said, pointing to the screen.

I shifted positions and leaned in to him. I was not yet four on those mesmerizing Sunday mornings of cooking lessons and closeness.

Often the morning's food tutorials inspired my father, and it was he who made Sunday lunch or dinner. An enterprising lawyer who was a slave to his clients and burgeoning practice, Dad seemed to always be at the office or on a business trip. Sundays were the one day he was most likely to be at home with me, Mohammad, and my mother, our constant caregiver. When he wasn't at his office in nearby Mozang, Dad traveled for clients to far-off places like Thailand and France, from which he returned with exotic ingredients. While some parents might come home with a snow globe or some other touristic trinket, our dad returned with special salts and cheeses, oils and vinegars, olives and herbs, their unfamiliar odors announcing his return and summoning Mohammad and me to investigate.

In the kitchen, where he presided over the stove and countertops, cooking up something aromatic, there were sizzling or chopping sounds to fill the space between us, instructions to follow, an ingredient or recipe explanation to be given.

"Open your mouth," he said to Mohammad and me as we sat on the bench opposite the stove, from which the simple yet profound scent of garlic and onions sautéing in butter emanated. Internally, we were reluctant because we knew that if he asked us to open up we'd soon find something strange and unfamiliar on our young tongues, but we were so eager for his focus that when we had it, we wanted to keep it. We opened our small mouths as wide as we could.

Suddenly something round and slimy was on our tongues, springing against the roofs of our suspicious mouths: canned button mushrooms, the only kind of mushroom available back then in grocery stores in Lahore. Dad was whipping up a French-inspired chicken with mushroom cream sauce, a flavor profile that was completely foreign to our youthful Pakistani taste buds. We were in love with him, in awe of him, and drunk on his attention. While he was cooking, my tight-lipped father possessed a lightness and ease, an informative affability that I never felt or saw beyond kitchen or restaurant walls.

For the earliest summer holidays of my youth, my parents rented a house in the mountains with their best friends to escape the Lahore heat. Each family drove the seven hours (plus the requisite bathroom and snack stops) in their own car with their household staff up and up and up the winding, perilous road from Lahore to Nathia Gali, a small village in the lush green hills east of Abbottabad.

Those summer memories glisten with fairy dust. The four mothers—Yasmin, Eram, Afshi, and my own—were young and beautiful; their futures, like our holiday, were full of promise. The fathers drove up on weekends, so during the week we were a female-led gang of mothers and kids, of which I was the youngest. Tabinda, Fatimah, and Usman—Eram's children; Zahra and Ammar—Yasmin Khala's kids; Bano, Mikoo, and Boby—Afshi's children; and of course Mohammad and me. These were the people I considered my extended family, more so than my real cousins, because it was with these closest friends of my mother's and their children that we spent the most time, back in Lahore and there in the mountains where we lived together, eating every meal together, bathing together, brushing our teeth together.

During the day, we were entirely outside. We hiked in the forest, climbing walnut and cedar trees that leopards slept in at night. We played in streams; we went horse riding. We explored the markets, where our mothers bought shawls woven from goat hair and sheep wool and embroidered dresses made by the villagers. It was a dream life, those cool months in the mountain mist, when there was always a friend nearby, a small hand to hold, a new game to play, an insect or animal to study, and a lap to rest on.

In the early evenings, we watched movies on VHS tapes. Each family had brought their favorites and bought new ones for the holiday, and we piled together on the sofas, on pillows on the carpeted floor, leaning into each other like puppies while cinematic delights unfolded before us on the screen. Some nights we children chose and some nights our parents did and some nights we managed to watch two films back to back, but the nightly screenings infused our time there with even more fantasy: We lived in a liminal childhood world where it seemed anything could happen.

To conserve power and avoid unexpected outages, the local municipality participated in nightly load shedding and turned off the electricity on our hillside at eight p.m. sharp each evening, and in those first moments, we experienced a blackness so complete and thick that sight itself seemed the illusion, the invention of a dream. There was always an instant of utter silence, the surprise of darkness, sharp as a slap yet soft as velvet, before the mothers summoned light for us with pocketed lighters and big matchboxes that sent up sulfurous sparks and flared in lantern bulbs and against blackened wicks. Sometimes I was sitting near Mo just outside on the porch or in the yard when the lights were flipped off, and in those instants before our mothers lit the house, I'd wait, blinking into the darkness, until my eyes adjusted and the stars shone through like holes in black paper, peeking into another world.

The children far outnumbered the mothers, so bedtime was a nightly battle of wills, and it was a holiday so bedtime was not so strict—but it was also a treat to be reunited with my pillow after a day spent adventuring with my troop of friends. When our mothers thought we'd dozed off, they reconvened in the main room to laugh, tell stories, and act out scenes from their favorite films, which were on heavy rotation. We fell asleep to Yasmin reciting, "Tomorrow is another day," and my mother replying, "Frankly, my dear, I don't give a damn," as they play-acted those famous last lines from *Gone with the Wind* to each other. As sleep tugged at my eyelids, the make-believe world of film and our fantasy-like summer blended together. I wasn't sure if I was the little girl staring up at the tiny perforations in the night sky or if I actually resided there, in another dimension, peering down from the faraway holes at a mountain house full of laughter and expectation.

In those early days, there was not yet anything to be afraid of. Even the dark was only momentary, with the blackness interrupted by a star, a lantern, or a dream.

chapter 6

SHEDDING SKIN

———

Farezeh

———

Ashtar and I fell into the rhythms and roles of a normal Pakistani marriage. He worked hard at his law practice, and though he, like many new fathers back then, was never a hands-on dad who changed nappies, he was a great provider.

When Fatima was about three, we bought a plot of land in Lahore's Defense neighborhood, one of the city's most desirable areas, and began building our first family home. While Ashtar worked, I supervised the construction of our would-be dream house, but as the structure began to take shape, the family that it was meant for began to show signs of fracture. In the commotion of having two young children, it took me longer than it might otherwise have to discover just how far Ashtar and I had drifted from each other; we were far past our usual distance. Also, perhaps as a result of my persistent naïveté, it had never occurred to me that *Ashtar* might be the one to walk away from our marriage. Indeed, though I wasn't deeply in love with him, I didn't consider that *he* might feel the very same way, or that my dispassion might push him to desire and seek out something I couldn't provide.

It couldn't have helped that his thriving business meant moving in circles where many men indulged in extramarital distractions, making messy marriages seem unremarkable. Nevertheless, it became unbearable, and I felt it might be good to separate, to consider whether we could possibly find a way to come back together and make our marriage work. My girlfriends, who had comforted me endlessly during this time, helped me conceive of a plan: I could go visit my sister Tammy in Texas, a temporary separation period to give both Ashtar and myself time and space to think. Perhaps he'd even visit us there.

Ashtar did not take the news of my plan well. He was livid and loath for there to be anything that could result in any type of scandal for him or his family.

"You'll never survive on your own," he mocked, fanning the flames of my insecurity. He was clear with me that if I left to take space and reflect, I shouldn't come back. I didn't really believe that he would make good on his threat, and so I set off with the children, once again, for Karachi. A lawyer himself, he drew up the separation agreement, which read as a cold document, devoid of any signs of the family we had made. Yasmin's husband, Nadeem, who was like a brother to me, helped me understand the paperwork, and without him I would have been even more lost and confused than I already was.

In Karachi, my mother and sister were conflicted. On the one hand, they acknowledged that Ashtar had ruined the sanctity of our marriage. On the other hand, no one in our family had ever divorced, and it was widely frowned upon: What would become of me? Who would provide for me? How would it reflect on all of us? But I'd made up my mind. How could my children grow up to respect themselves if they saw me being disrespected?

Thankfully, Tammy welcomed me, so I packed a few bags

and flew with my children to the States to begin again. I had no idea where life would take me, but I was certain of one thing: I had to find a way to take care of us.

Four months after we arrived in Austin, Ashtar announced he was remarrying. We weren't even divorced yet. Though our marriage vows had not been sacred, he was true to his word that if I left, it was over. He seemed to have deserted the children. He never visited Fatima and Mohammad in Austin, which meant he didn't see them for two years. There was a sense of betrayal I should have predicted but didn't. Mohammad and Fatima suffered as a result, and it's pained me my whole life how this primal rejection has affected them.

I didn't exactly have a plan when I landed in Austin. What I did have were my two confused children, my sister's address, and fresh divorce wounds. Pieces of the life I'd worked so hard to build for almost a decade were scattered in shreds at my feet. I had barely begun to assess the damage before I found myself on the other side of the planet. And let me tell you, if the world had seemed frightening and unpredictable before, it was much worse for a twenty-nine-year-old single mother who had no idea what her next step would be.

Tammy had always been my caretaker, and there she was again, making room for me and my children in the home she lived in with her own family. But despite her generosity and care, the fact is that if it isn't one's own home, one always feels like a guest. In wanting to be as light a burden as possible, my children and I tried to occupy as little space as we could. We squeezed into one bedroom. We went out of our way to contribute to the daily chores. Mohammad and Fatima even hesitated to open the refrigerator, conscious that its contents did not belong to them.

I'd only known a life where a readymade path was laid out

for me. Regardless of what I thought of it, everything was more or less taken care of. My life had been like a frozen meal, my choices made for me like components rationed into their sad little sections. But in Austin, I suddenly could define myself. I could make all the decisions without protective controlling wings hovering over me, without watchful eyes that both judged and protected. Liberation was terrifying because I quickly realized that there was a lot I did not know how to do.

I had never had my own bank account. I did not know how to write a check. When I had to get Mohammad and Fatima admitted into school, Tammy came along with me because I needed help filling out the forms. When decisions have always been made for you, learning how to make them for yourself is daunting. I was haunted by the damning predictions people offered to scare me into staying in my marriage. *Fari, you need a man. How will your children survive? Fari, don't do this; it will end in disaster. You don't have the ability to take this on! See you in six months . . .* These voices nagged at me, swirling and stoking my insecurities. I was afraid, and in private moments away from my children I let myself weep, but I knew what I had to do.

I sensed Mohammad and Fatima's displacement instantly, perhaps because it reflected my own. They yearned for the security they'd grown up with until this point and were unsure of what their place was. I saw it in the way Fatima clung to Mohammad, and I saw how cautiously Mohammad tread the new waters to cope with his own disorientation. They had questions in their eyes and I was struggling with the answers. My marriage had grounded all of us. Now our roots had to be replanted in new soil, where everything was foreign.

One night after dinner, my brother-in-law suggested I take advantage of the fact that we were in a university town. *Go see some of the colleges, Fari,* he told me. *You might find something there.*

Me? Go to an American college? It was a lofty dream, made even more unreachable because of how small I felt.

Still, I brought home a leafy course catalogue from the community college, and as I thumbed through it, something caught my eye: "Child Development." I looked at the course outline and immediately heard my mother's words: *You cannot handle your children on your own.* A radical idea came to me: What if this course in child development told me what I needed to do for my own children?

I enrolled immediately.

I couldn't believe I was someone who could go to an American college. That wasn't the skin I had been brought up in. I was a nobody. I wasn't supposed to be good enough, and yet that's not the impression I seemed to create in my peers or professors.

I'd always been terrible at math, failing the subject at every turn in my school years. So naturally, I was horrified when I found out I had to take a compulsory quantitative course. In an attempt to lower his expectations, I sheepishly told my professor that I was awful at numbers, the fear of disappointing someone far outweighing my motivation to at least try. He did not bat an eye. Instead he said, "You are such a smart person. You can do this." And apparently, sometimes that's all it takes. Someone believes in you, encourages you, and empowers you with their conviction that you can do it . . . and then you can. Someone sees that there are untapped gifts and talents, which make you worthy of that faith and belief.

My teachers and fellow students were interested in me and what I had to say. Everything that was ordinary about me in Pakistan made me fascinating to my professors, who wanted to learn from me. Like I had something unique to offer. Like I was special. It made me feel valued and validated.

I cautiously began to believe the impression my professors

had of me. Maybe I *was* a bright, self-reliant woman who could go to college, who could work, who could raise and provide for her children. What if the worst fears and assumptions about me weren't actually true? What if I *could*, in fact, do this alone?

I began watering the seed of self-confidence in me that had only ever seen drought up to this point.

Little moments began to quietly build me up. I got a driving license, actual proof that I could be trusted to find my way. I could navigate the city of Austin, go to a large grocery store and find what I needed. I developed an ear to understand the Texan twang, no longer asking cashiers to repeat themselves. I could confidently walk into a bank and know exactly which counter I needed to go to. Everything I had always relied on a man to do for me was becoming second nature.

In the evenings, I went for long walks on my own, exploring the streets with just my thoughts for company—the same isolation I had resented in my marriage, I suddenly recognized as freedom and relished. I didn't need anyone's permission, and my schedule was my own. These unexceptional moments were seminal for me. The environment of encouragement and new experience of seeing myself as others did—strong and focused and capable—incubated me. It was a rebirth, and the same world that had crippled me with fear now seemed a veritable playground of possibilities. There is nothing more empowering than knowing— no, *believing*—that all you really need is you.

Drop by drop, the glass began to seem half full. And I, thirsty so long for liberation, drank it up voraciously.

But my children were still finding their bearings. How could I make things easier for them? How could I gently reassure them that they were on steady ground again? I took these questions directly to my psychology professor Dr. Evelyn Brown. I hung back after every class, sharing my fears and hopes for my children, wondering at things I could do to help them navigate the vastness they must feel.

One afternoon, as I began to talk about my children, my professor stopped me, and said, "Today there will be no discussion of your children. Today we will talk about *you* instead."

I didn't know where to start. Why talk about me? I was fine; it was my children who needed help.

"It's great that you are feeling strong in yourself, Farezeh," she began. "Because you are the essential element that can make your children strong as well. Your outlook, your feelings, everything that you project, has an immense impact on your children."

"Okay," I stammered. I'd suspected this, hadn't I? Somehow my instincts had led me out of a marriage in which I felt incidental and unseen and across an ocean and eventually to the classroom that I found myself in, feeling more confident than I could have ever imagined.

"If you want to help your children, you must first help yourself."

She gave me strategies to help us acknowledge our feelings with each other. Every night for a little while as we went off to bed, Fatima beside me and Mohammad on a mattress on the floor, we went around and shared two things with one another: one thing that made us feel happy and one thing that made us feel sad from that day. Through this, I could help us all bring to the surface things that might instead be swallowed as secrets, causing silent suffering.

She had another interesting suggestion: to engage the kids in a weekly activity. It could be anything, she said, so long as we did it together. She said it would help us strengthen our bond and bring back security and predictability into their lives.

I wondered what it could be, and my daughter gave me the

answer. Fatima's kindergarten teacher began to give her class a weekly assignment. Fatima would come home with a pictogram of a recipe—a cupcake, a fruit cup, sometimes a sandwich—to make on the weekend. Fatima anxiously waited for each recipe and excitedly waved it at me when she ran from the school bus on Fridays. I saw how much it meant to her, how it comforted her. I took my cue from her and decided that Mo, Fatima, and I would cook together every weekend.

Quickly Fatima outgrew the pictograms and started borrowing cookbooks from the school library. She picked a recipe, then nudged me to take her to the grocery store, where we bought the ingredients she needed. I watched her marvel at the food chemistry as cakes rose in the oven, as spices sizzled in the pan, and as vegetables changed color. She was so eager to be in the kitchen, to learn how to do more, to eat new things. At the age of six, Fatima began ordering calamari at restaurants and writing about her cooking experience, diligently checking how she could make each recipe better the next time. Her first love caught her from the freefall that her father's absence, her shift to Austin, and her new surroundings had pushed her into.

As our lives began to be rearranged, I felt something inside me rearrange itself too. I had an outline of who I was, and I was coloring it in.

But this is not to say all was easy. Money was an issue, and no matter how much we cooked or how many techniques I learned in my child development class, there was no substitute for a present, loving father and husband. My studies and school experiences were, at best, a tonic for the deep rejection my children were mired in by their father's departure and swift second marriage.

I knew I had to wear all the hats then. The Mother hat. The Father hat. The Friend hat. The Protector hat. And when I learned in my college classes that children ought to be involved in decisions affecting them, that's where I took Mo and Fatima. They had to be made aware of the consequences of each decision so that they could take ownership of who they were and the choices they made. And all of this created an openness among the three of us wherein I made it clear that they could bring anything to me, that the only thing that mattered was honesty.

chapter 7

FIRST RECIPES
AND LUNCHABLES

——

Fatima

——

YOU CANNOT IMAGINE THE STRANGENESS OF TEXAS AFTER Lahore. It felt like standing on my head, which I could just about do if Mohammad held an ankle. From the mundane details—the fast food, the vivid packaging, the pervasive scent of fresh-mown grass—to the most fundamental fact: my family was a new shape, a table missing its fourth leg. My father had vanished from our lives.

Before we left for Texas, he hadn't been home much. When I asked Mom where Baba was, the response was always the same: "Fatima, he's working." Yet even as a young child I'd felt his existence through little manifestations that spoke of his recent presence and predictable return. Change on the side table by our front door meant he'd emptied his pockets when he'd arrived home from the office or a work trip. The dull whir of the electric shaver behind the bathroom door meant he was readying himself for a day at the office. The sound of the telephone ringing in the kitchen in the evening, my mother's quiet answer, the gentle click of the receiver back in its cradle—these signified his temporary absence. I always assumed he'd reappear at some point because he always had.

I don't remember ever seeing my parents fight, so our sudden move to the other side of the earth without my father was disconcerting. Mo and I had no inkling of what was brewing, then a little bit of information, then a quick trip to stay with Nano in Karachi before being called to Lahore only to find our family disassembled. Our home was no longer "our home," and we went instead to Yasmin Khala's, where we were reunited with our mom. Finally, we were told that our parents were getting a divorce, which we'd suspected . . . and that we were moving to Texas.

After an awkward and confusing few days, we said our final goodbyes to our father at the Lahore airport. Mo's small nine-year-old hand held mine, and Baba gave each of us a thin gold chain necklace and said, "I'm only a phone call away." But what does that mean to a nine-year-old and a four-year-old? Kids don't like to talk on the phone, and their reality is what's in front of them, which our dad most certainly was not. On the plane I suggested that since the necklaces were made of real gold, Baba must really love us, as we'd never been given jewelry like this before. Mo just shrugged and turned away from me toward the window.

My Tammy Khala, her husband, and their two sons lived in a two-story brick house with a deck that overlooked a creek in a pleasant neighborhood in Austin. At my khala's house, my mother and brother and I slept together in one room, a happy arrangement, as far as I was concerned, as they were the two people I most loved to be near. The strangeness of this new American life, its sounds and scents, the very air that pumped through it, were less frightening because Mom and Mo remained close by at almost all times. Sometimes I woke up in the night, startled by my surroundings, but could see from the night-light's glow that Mo was right there, breathing quietly, asleep nearby. I tiptoed out into the hallway and saw light from the kitchen and found my mother there alone, up late again, sipping cold coffee, with textbooks and notepads strewn in front of her, brow furrowed. My mother had gone back to school to get a degree in education. I rarely found her in bed asleep when I woke at odd hours in the night. She was always studying.

In this affluent white suburban community, our new life was a thin pie slice of the American fantasy, though of course our fatherless unit was anything but normal, and the fact that we lived together in a room in a house that belonged to another brown family made us even less the American ideal. Still, although ours was now a three-legged table, we balanced quite sturdily.

Kindergarten was odd. There was a little Indian boy named Keyshef, but other than that, everyone in my class was white. Two little girls in my class teased me.

"You're Asian," the little girls told me, saying it in such a way that I immediately understood it was a bad thing, which they immediately confirmed by saying, "Our parents told us that's bad."

They forbade me from swinging on "their" swing set. Keyshef wasn't allowed either.

"You're dirty," they explained. "You can't touch the same things as us."

In Texas, I realized for the first time that some people hated me simply because of the color of my skin.

Sometimes I looked up from my desk to see Mohammad's profile on the other side of the classroom door. He checked on me periodically, and when we rode the school bus home together, I debriefed him on the perils of my day, until he was big enough to ride his bike to and from school and I was left alone with my thoughts. I'm sure he was experiencing prejudice as well—he told me that on his first day, when the teacher tried to pair off classmates in the buddy system, no one in his class raised their hand to be his buddy—but Mo seemed to take everything in stride. If someone picked on him, he never showed that it hurt him, and so I tried to do the same.

Baba called us occasionally. When he asked to speak to us, my mother or aunt came to get us, if we were awake. Mohammad was wary of him because he'd hurt our mother so much, and I looked to my brother for clues on everything. I was different during those years in Texas. I took every step tentatively, as if the earth might crumble and fall away beneath me, leaving me like a character in a cartoon who had run off the edge of a cliff. To combat my fear of free fall, I carefully stepped in the imprints Mohammad's feet had pressed into the ground ahead of me, as much as I could. I mimicked his swagger. I longed to be big enough to ride a bicycle beside him.

One Sunday morning the phone rang in our house and Tammy Khala answered it and handed it to my mother. Mom spoke briefly and tersely to the person on the other end of the line.

"No, Ashtar, I will not tell them for you," she said quietly but forcefully into the telephone. "They're right here. You do it yourself."

My mother lowered the receiver from her ear to her side and called to Mohammad, who walked toward her and took the telephone.

At first Mohammad put on the happy, needy tone that we'd grown accustomed to using with our father when we spoke to him and told him that we missed him and asked him when he was coming to visit, but then Mo turned his back to the room, turned his back to me, as if to shield me from something ugly on his face. My mother, who had been standing in the doorway, half in and half out of the room, disappeared from sight down the hall. I looked back at my brother and his head fell, so that his chin must have laid upon his chest. His voice was mechanical and muffled for the rest of the short conversation he was having, of which I heard only his part.

"Uh-huh . . . Okay, but . . . Oh . . . Oh . . . But, what does that even mean? . . . Oh . . . Okay . . . Oh . . . Okay, bye." Mohammad lowered the receiver from his ear but kept it clasped in his right hand by his thigh for a minute without moving.

"Mohammad, what did Baba say?" I asked. "Mohammad!"

He replaced the receiver carefully, quietly, and then slowly turned to me. It was only us in the room then.

"Baba's gonna get married again," he said, his face totally composed, but his black fringed eyes shining.

"What are you talking about? He can't be married to two people at once!" I explained to him, trying to reassure the both of us through my growing panic.

"Well, he must not be married to Mom anymore then," he said softly. And then he ran out of the room, out of the house, and toward the woods that circled the property. I watched him from the big bay window as his back disappeared between trees.

So that was it. That was how we found out that there was no going back to life before Texas. It was official: *That* life—*our* family—was over. We stopped calling him Baba and refused to speak to him from then on. Mohammad did a good job of pretending he didn't much care about him, and so I did just the same. He asked Mom a lot more questions about their separation, insisting she explain things to him as if she was a teacher and he was a pupil. He wanted the technical explanation for how their marriage had dissolved. He wanted to understand the science behind walking away from a family. Mom assured him that just because he was remarrying, it didn't mean he wasn't our father anymore, that the only thing that was changing was that he and my mom weren't married. Mohammad asked whether this meant that the woman he was marrying was our new mother, and my mother assured him that she was not.

"He'll always be your father," my mother said. And we waited, without admitting that's what we were doing, for him to come to see us, but he never appeared.

I was more caught up in the practical aspects of life without my dad. At Halloween, all my classmates' fathers came in to help carve pumpkins, and when Mrs. Ricks realized that no one was coming for me, she made me sit with another little girl and her father. I looked pathetically at the tall fair-skinned father holding the sharp kitchen knife half stuck in a jack-o'-lantern's eye socket. This stranger half-heartedly beckoned me toward their island of newspaper, their pile of slimy seeds, and I felt sick to my stomach as I knelt near the white American dad and his white American little girl, pretending to be together with them but so obviously separate.

I was angry when I got home from school that afternoon, humiliated by my loneliness, my obvious sense of lacking. I thought spitefully of the teacher waving me toward my classmate and her father. If families were so replaceable, why couldn't we find a man here to replace the one we'd left behind? A few days later at the mall when I was with my mother getting a new pair of shoes, it occurred to me that since in America you could buy almost anything, perhaps we could purchase a new dad for me and Mohammad. When I asked my mother about it, her lips tightened and she turned partially away from me before responding.

"No, Fatima," my mother said with wet, reddening eyes that met my gaze. "That won't be possible." I promised myself to spare her any more pain: I wouldn't ask again.

Even though I was hurt by my father's disappearance, I understood that my mother was also suffering, and neither Mo nor I wanted to give her any more to worry about. Though I did ask Mo if our dad might still come visit us, and if he did, whether he'd bring his new wife, I didn't talk with my mother about how Dad's disappearance made me feel. Actually, I am not sure I felt anything I could articulate other than bewilderment. Instead, at my aunt's house, where my little cousin was infuriated by my young presence and having to share with me and adapt to another kid around, I tried desperately to disappear into my own world of books and food.

I pored over the recipe card for "ants on a log" that my kindergarten teacher had sent home with us for the weekend, meticulously spreading peanut butter over a crisp rib of celery and picking only those raisins with a stem to line up like soldiers on my midafternoon snack. I was thrilled with my accomplishment, with the joy of being able to share something I had created with my own hands. Even though these simple assemblages couldn't have been more different than the traditional Pakistani food—recipes like dal, chawal, and shami kebabs—that I was used to watching my mother or aunt cook and that I loved to eat, I recognized a sameness in the process: the collecting of ingredients, the following of instructions, the gathering at the table to enjoy the pleasure of the result. I loved the sense of order that could be derived even from those simple and cartoonish pictorial recipes. Soon I discovered that there were cookbooks in the library at our public school and that I was allowed to take out one at a time whenever I wanted. Though I was only beginning to learn to read, I took them out and lay on my belly in our room, fanning through the pages. My mouth watered and my eyes widened as I examined the photographs.

I was literally a kid in a candy store: America was a bizarre wonderland of processed foods. Cereals so sweet they made my teeth itch, Lunchables, Twinkies—you name it, I wanted to try it. Even something as uninteresting as sunflower seeds became intoxicating to me when my brother offered me the ones he'd snuck into his pocket in homeroom. I became obsessed with food in all its forms, associating it with family and the fun of sneaking naughtily into the pantry to eat my grumpy cousin's Lucky Charms.

On the weekends, while my mother studied on a picnic blanket beneath an enormous pecan tree, Mohammad and I ran and played in the local park. I knew Mo would have saved up the fifty cents that Mom gave him each day to spend at lunch. I knew that if I begged him long enough, he would always give in and buy me an ice cream cone. He always placated me. And he always protected me.

chapter 8

TUTORING AND TEMPTATION

———

Farezeh

———

Iн 1995, WHEN I FINISHED MY DEGREE IN AUSTIN, without any money, there was no viable option but to return to Karachi and to move in with Mummy and my sister Saby. Mohammad, Fatima, and I moved into the second-floor apartment of a duplex in Shamshir, which was in a tucked-away part of the Defense neighborhood, near to Khadda Market. It was a far less tony neighborhood than the one I'd grown up in, but no matter: As a single mom and divorcée, I was less tony too.

I moved from one sister's home into my mother's. The Tanzeem house was still being leased out to provide my mother with some income, as it had been for the last decade. Once again, the children and I shared a room, which offered some healthy consistency from Austin and made them happy. Mummy and Saby's presence offered us a sense of safety and nostalgia. The problem was that while all this was familiar to me, I was no longer comfortable with it.

I returned to Karachi a changed woman. I had a purpose. Ideas. Skills. A new confidence that I had carefully nursed and wanted to pour into my children. My parenting style and my views on education and the world had grown so much. I was no longer the naïve girl who did not know how to pay utility bills.

The society I returned to, however, had not so much as moved a muscle. Everything was exactly as I had left it. The same prying eyes and hungry ears were seeking out juicy gossip to satiate themselves. The same judgmental gazes, the same hypocrisy, the same social cage seemed to appear around me. A young, divorced mother was ideal prey. That laser-sharp scrutiny can be targeted and deeply damaging, and what it went after most ferociously was a woman who seemed to have realized her self-worth.

Once you experience what it is like to be in the crosshairs of scrutiny, you can't help but want to protect your own from it because of how debilitating it can be. And this is why sometimes those who love us most—in their attempt to shield us—scrutinize us even more. If they can weed out all from within our homes that might set off the rumor mills, then there would be no reason to fear being crushed by the invisible but powerful social pressures and judgments. It showed in the ways that my mother and sister exerted limitations and control on me. I, a woman who was now into my thirties and was single-handedly responsible for the lives and well-being of two children, had a curfew. From walking the streets of Austin alone at night, I suddenly had to tell my mother where I was going whenever I stepped out of the house. I was questioned about who, why, and how I was meeting just about anyone. In the new life I was building, I wasn't meant to be answerable to anyone, or seek permission to exercise my choices, and yet under my mother's roof, I certainly was.

I was still young and men presumed that since I was divorced, I was available. I was propositioned by married men relentlessly in Karachi, and being inundated made me feel unsafe and fed into my self-doubt as a single woman in Pakistan with two small children to care for. *Could I actually manage without a husband? Without a protector? Without an enabler?* I was raised putting men up on pedestals—as Mummy had with Agha Jani—as superior, smarter, stronger, and my anxiety about going it alone reared its ugly head upon my return.

Of course, I was in the line of fire for ending a marriage—that was clear and to be expected. But the stigma leaked even into Mohammad and Fatima's lives.

Mohammad returned home from school one day visibly upset. After I pried it out of him, he told me that his teacher had called him a liar. When I asked what had made her do that, he told me that he hadn't gotten his spelling test signed by me (I had been unwell, and he didn't want to disturb me so took the paper back without my signature). He had scored 19 out of 20—a stellar grade he would have no reason to hide from me. She made him stand up in the middle of his class to make an example of his noncompliance. When he explained why his mother had not been able to sign it, she dismissed his excuse and demanded to know why he didn't take it to his father instead. He shrugged and said, "I don't have a father here." *My parents are divorced,* he told everyone.

His teacher could not even fathom that she had a child of divorce readily admitting to it in front of everyone in her class-room. She called him a liar, for telling the truth. And for some-one who had been raised to always tell the truth, this was a humiliation his eleven-year-old self could not and should not have known how to handle. But this is precisely the burden you are forced to carry when you deviate from the conventional—she shamed Mohammad as if he were part of the problem.

In Austin, I was taught to tell children of divorce that fami-lies can look different and that's okay. We saw many examples during their time in America: same-sex parents, adopted children, interracial families—the list went on. Divorce was commonplace for the children Fatima and Mohammad befriended in their school in Austin. It demystified it and made it something they were both up front about, sharing that their parents were divorced without hesitating. But whenever they did in Karachi, they were made to feel like they were accidentally confessing to a crime.

One day, Fatima, then in third grade, brought home a book from the library. I read these books to her when it was time for bed, and she was particularly excited about this one. I felt like she was imposing an early bedtime on herself that evening just so that I could get this book going. Without noticing much about it, I picked it up and started reading. It was about a girl who had moved cities because her parents divorced, to a new neighborhood where nobody knew her, and how this girl was always alone in her new school; how empty the packed playground felt, how she didn't have any friends. There was a part in this book that read, ". . . and no one understands." Fatima looked at me and said, "I feel that too, Mom. No one understands. Even when I try to tell them, they don't get it."

When Fatima shared the fact that her parents were divorced with her friends, they asked her *Why?!* and she never had an answer. I felt my daughter trying to find the vocabulary to express her experience with me, to try to articulate things she didn't yet understand herself, and this book was a way for her to do this, and it gave her some comfort knowing that she wasn't alone in her feelings, even if the only one she could relate to at that point was a character in a storybook. I felt her pain, and it spurred me on to publish an article in a local paper about divorce, its impact on children, and how to address these issues in our society. I felt some of the pain my children felt was exacerbated by the mindset that surrounded us; my article was an attempt to create some change.

I was resolute about putting my degree to work and began carefully laying the foundation for my new career. I gave private lessons to children at a local school, tutoring there from noon till nine p.m. every night. I worked hard and saved money by living with Mummy and Saby in the Shamshir house for a year and a half.

I got myself a job teaching preschool at a small mainstream school, which had the added benefit of offering a tuition cut for my own children to attend, and I enrolled them immediately, grateful they'd have a sense of community. The school's owner knew from my job interview that I had a background in child development and that I was trying to make money to support my two kids, so she began referring children with learning difficulties to me for tutoring to make myself some extra income. In the afternoons, after I came home from teaching preschool, I started tutoring and worked from two thirty to nine p.m. My degree had given me the tools and strategy to know how to help them, and the children soon showed positive results in school. I began building a name for myself. As word got around, parents and their children started coming out of the woodwork to seek me out for the support their children needed. I started to realize that there was a real need in my city that couldn't be fulfilled by mainstream schools. That was the beginning of Spellbound, my own educational center for students with learning difficulties, which I launched in 1997.

Bit by bit, I inched closer to my goal of becoming self-actualized. Bit by bit, I proved wrong the naysayers and doubters, the alarmists who wanted to keep me caged up. I showed that I *could* get a job, that I *could* start a program, that *I could be an independent woman* and provider for my children. A year and a half after returning to Pakistan, I had saved 4.5 lakh rupees (about $10,000) and could afford to move Mohammad, Fatima, and me out of Mummy's house. I wanted my kids to have a sense of ownership, to finally have a home of their own, and found us a modest but appealing three-bedroom townhouse in Clifton, walking distance to Fatima's school and to Spellbound. The children were delighted; we were back to Us Three. I bought them bicycles, which they rode to Spellbound as I walked with them. They played in the park while I worked. After work, I took them home and we prepared a meal together.

I wanted stability—to have enough money to pay my bills and look after my responsibilities. These were my goals. I had no support from anyone, so I had to build my own life and stand on my own feet. By the time I got Spellbound off the ground at the age of thirty-three, the negative voices, the discouragement and ensuing self-doubts, the fear stoked by so many who had told me not to leave my husband—all of this that had weighed on me so heavily began to lift.

I stopped listening to the narrative that I was an unimportant and second-class member of our family and I finally saw that I was worthy and capable, that I was at long last a self-sufficient woman. I carried with me a quiet pride, a careful confidence, the sensation of which was like catching a glimpse of one's reflection in a pretty new dress: I liked what I saw, but I nearly didn't recognize myself. Finally, the great risks and sacrifices I'd made, and forced Mohammad and Fatima to make with me, were paying off. I don't know if it was a fair trade per se— I didn't think it "made up for" the pain we three had waded through to get to this stage, but it was a defining time for me as an individual, a new chapter, and my kids were happy.

chapter 9

TEPID MILK AND SILKEN SALMON

———

Fatima

———

UPON OUR RETURN TO KARACHI, AFTER SPENDING two years in Texas, Mo and I felt more American than we did Pakistani. Little bits of the States had wedged themselves indelibly into us. From friends to food, when it was time to leave Texas, Mo and I bemoaned what we were leaving behind far more than we rejoiced over what we would get back upon our return to Pakistan. Seeing Nano and our family friends were reasons to celebrate, but these were the only ones we could think of; the rest was too abstract.

I had lived nearly half of my six-year-old life in America, and in Pakistan, everything seemed strange in ways big and small. We moved in with Nano and Saby Khala. The house was on a corner, close to the road, and another family lived on the ground floor, but it felt immediately like home thanks to Nano and her scent of cold cream and mothballs, the carpeted rooms and the chests of drawers and the biscuit tins that were filled with Nano's eccentricities, through which we were constantly rummaging.

Upon arrival in Karachi, Mo and I both discovered that we'd

lost a lot of the Urdu that had once been second nature. While we were in Austin, there'd been virtually no religion integrated into our days, but in Karachi, our Nano, who practiced regularly, became our religious guide. She invited us into her religious routines and rituals without imposing them upon us. With her gentle mentorship, the holidays and rites became a source of wonder. For Muharram, the first month of the Islamic calendar, we accompanied Nano to the local Imam Bargha, where Shias congregated to mourn the death of the Prophet Muhammad's grandson, Hussein Ibn Ali. The colors, the chanting, the scent of burning oud mingling with daigi biryani rising up from its massive pot, or chickpea stew handed out free of charge—these elements were intriguing and made us hungry for more. But there were also elements that frightened us, such as the self-flagellation and when the chanting went from sonorous to thunderous.

Mohammad was horrified (and, therefore, so was I) by the taste of Pakistani milk: tangy, sour, and always too warm; nothing like the round, silken texture of cold American milk straight from the fridge. We were back in our native country, but Karachi was new to me, so I did what I always did when I was confused or afraid: I followed Mo's lead. If Mo climbed a tree, I climbed it. If Mo walked the plank on our neighbor's wall, I walked the plank a few feet behind him. If Mo lay prostrate on the ground beneath a parked car to fish out a meowing kitten from under the bonnet, so then did I. Thanks to my grandmother, there was a house rule that I had to wear three dresses per week, which meant that my legs were exposed—to bugs, to rusted fenders, to gravel when I tumbled—while Mo's were protected by the thick armor of his denim uniform. As far as I could tell, dresses were handicaps, but I wouldn't let them get the better of me, so it was greasy fingers, bloody knees, bruised elbows, and a sweaty brow that made up *my* uniform, more so than any frills. When I cut myself, Mo obligingly blew on the wound. When a branch was too high, he catapulted me up to it from his shoulders. I was his shadow and he was my idol.

Our daily routine was simple: We got up early and forced down cereal with cheap, gag-inducing warm Haleeb milk for breakfast, then went to school, if you could even call it that. It was in an old converted house and felt unsubstantial and slightly ridiculous after Austin's sprawling midcentury building with a playground, soccer pitch, and baseball diamond unfurling around it. We never had much money in Texas, so Mom bought us our clothes from bargain bins, sources of perpetual embarrassment there when snooty kids teased us for wearing imitation Adidas or fake Abercrombie & Fitch. But back in Karachi, our new classmates didn't know the difference, and anyway, our worldliness and knowledge of Backstreet Boys songs made us cool and desirable. Playdates weren't really a thing in Pakistan, especially not with a working mom, so after school we came home, had lunch, and did our homework. The rest of the day was ours to fill.

"IF SOMEONE LIVES THERE, how come we never see them?" I asked my brother for the umpteenth time about the enormous stone house next door, which was the subject of many ghost stories and local legends.

"Because they don't want to be seen" was Mo's answer, as he traced shapes in the sandy dirt by the bottom step to the entrance of our house or searched the wild sweet pea plant that grew outside the house for fresh pods. "But if you look long enough at the top-floor windows, you'll see a shadow or them peering through the curtains."

"I've never seen anyone up there!" I said adamantly, guessing at my brother's fib.

"Oh, they're there. You just have to watch carefully for them."

I stared and stared, trying to see something, anything, moving near that house other than the birds, trying not to blink, until Mohammad interrupted me by poking me in the ribs and then taking off across the yard. I dashed behind him as fast as my little legs would take me, until we were both panting at the edge of the large empty plot adjacent to the Shamshir house, a swathe of untended land that was our de facto playground. Like many uncultivated expanses in third world countries, the undeveloped plot beside our house was used by many as a dumping ground, but that meant it was rife with things for us to explore. Household trash, industrial trash, abandoned appliances, stray cats and dogs, cute little mice, big ugly rats, and, during the yearly bakra eid, the macabre remains of animals that had been ritually slaughtered.

For Eid ul-Adha, or the Festival of the Sacrifice, when we celebrate the prophet Ibrahim's willingness to sacrifice his only son to God and God's merciful offering of a lamb instead, a cow was slaughtered in our yard. Mind you, it wasn't just a random cow that showed up on the day of the festival. No. The cow arrived days, even weeks, beforehand—plenty of time for us to feed and befriend it before we had front-row seats to watch its execution in the name of religion. The night before the actual holiday, Nano made a saviyyan, a vermicelli milk pudding with cardamom, coconut, reduced milk, and almonds, which cooled on the counter overnight, and then in the morning, when it was cool and inviting, the butcher arrived on his rounds and Mo and I looked on as he strung up the ropes and said a prayer, and then the gentle-eyed animal's throat was cut—*from the North Pole to the South Pole,* he used to say as he did it, and, of course, *Bismillah Allahu Akbar,* the essential phrase uttered in order for the meat to be halal. We were encouraged to watch. We observed as it bled out, as all halal meat must, as it was hung, skinned, and chopped into pieces our Nano would use for many an upcoming meal. She relished the whole process, our delicate, ladylike little grandmother who loved flower arranging and Chanel No. 5. She collected the blood as it drained from the slit throat and mixed it with water to cool it before fertilizing her garden with it. After the animal had fully bled out, the butcher skinned and processed it, our meal for the very next day.

Our neighbors also participated in the bakra eid, and it was common for the discarded organs to be tossed into empty lots, like the one next to our house. Acid green bile sacks, pale veiny lungs, and a tangle of intestines were identifiable from a distance thanks to the tornado of flies that gyrated above them. Officially, Mo and I were not allowed to explore this playground of detritus, but we often opened our gate and crept into the plot to rummage through all the flotsam looking for a diamond in the rough.

Most often, it was me and Mohammad and Niall, the elder of two kids who lived on the ground floor of our building. One of our trademark capers was walking the boundary wall around the Shamshir house. More than once, my mother glanced out the window from where she was tutoring and saw Niall and Mo walking the twelve-foot-high six-inch-wide wall with a much smaller, skirted silhouette behind them (me). This incensed her, naturally, as had we fallen, any one of us could have broken our neck, but the part the boys were reprimanded for was allowing me to follow, not for doing it themselves.

"Mohammad, you cannot allow your sister to follow you everywhere you go," Mom chided Mo. "She's far too little and it's completely inappropriate for a girl her age."

Indeed, I was quite tiny, and at first Mo might try to shake me, but I soon showed him that my will was stronger than his long legs; I would not be left behind. Mo gave in easily rather than testing whether I'd make good on my threats to tattle if he excluded me from a particularly risky activity. Even at seven, I despised the idea that anything should be off-limits to me because I was a girl. I knew this was typical of Pakistan, but I considered myself practically American, so I wasn't having it, even then.

As for Mom, she was torn. Her conflict about the imbalanced cultural expectations, which are far more severe on women, was obvious. On the one hand, me being female was an almost automatic pretext for me being fragile and needing protection. On the other hand, Mom had liberated herself from so many of these ingrained cultural norms during her time in the States, and she balked at these inequalities as well. Mom told us that if we believed in something, we should not be bound by the dominant norms. So though she told Mo off for letting me follow him, she turned a blind eye to many of our escapades, not wanting to hold me back just because I was a girl. She encouraged me by never actually stopping me, but she also had her own watchful mother looking over her shoulder, judging how her granddaughter was being raised. That, compounded by my domineering, tomboyish khala, made my rebelliousness all the more risky. Living in such close quarters to our traditionally minded Nano and our formidable khala made it difficult for me to mimic Mo in every way, for fear of judgment, and some underlying concern that I'd forever be unladylike, but mostly we prevailed with our mischief.

During the monsoons, heavy rains flooded the streets around us and created gushing torrents where dusty alleys had been the day before. We sailed paper boats down these seasonal rivers, and potholes became mysterious pools of which we had to measure the depth by jumping in. We ran out to play in the rain, knowing that within the hour the electricity might fail and not come back for hours or even days. We rationalized to our elders that wet clothes would keep us cooler during the sweltering Karachi nights.

A few months after we returned to Pakistan, we saw our father. He was already nearly two years into his second marriage by the time we were reunited. He hadn't had more kids yet, but he'd begun an entirely new life. The encounter, in the formal drawing room of the Shamshir house, which was full of Nano's Chinese chests and Japanese folding screens, and which we never used except for special occasions, was not an easy one. My mother scrubbed us in the shower and dressed Mohammad and me in brand-new clothes that were literally unworn, and therefore itchy and stiff. When we were told to go in, our father awaited us, but he wasn't alone. He'd brought a client along. It was incredibly strange and awkward, and I watched Mohammad for clues of how to behave, but he looked just as nervous and confused as I felt. Why were we so dressed up? Why was it so formal? Of course, I understand now that this was my mother's way of making a good impression, of saying, *We don't need you. We are fine—better than fine—without you,* which I guess we were, but it was still so strange. We hugged once. He gave us a video game and his email address. When it was over, I asked Mo why we couldn't just be alone with Dad, but he just shrugged and looked at his feet, so I did the same.

Dad came to Karachi for work a few times a year and would contact us and usually tack an extra night onto his trip so that he could take us to dinner. We met him at the fancy five-star hotels at which he stayed. We'd go up to his room and hang out for a bit, finding ourselves with little to say, and then Dad would ask if we should go eat. We'd walk to the hotel's upscale restaurant or go to someplace that he liked or had heard good things about nearby, and almost always they were "special occasion" restaurants that we got to go to simply because we were with Dad. The smells hit us when we walked in the door and by the time we had napkins on our laps and menus in our hands, the mood had shifted and we'd found something to talk about: what to order. *Wow, what's this?* I'd say. *I want that!* Mo chimed in. *Let's get both!* Dad offered, and then something like: *Have you ever tried lobster?*

Everything was on the menu when we were eating out with Dad, and just as he had when we were little, he pushed our palates and encouraged our experimental and ever more extravagant tastes. One night we were at a Teppanyaki table, eating chicken and beef and prawns that were grilled right in front of us, when Dad asked if we'd ever had sushi.

"What's sushi?" a twelve-year-old Mo asked.

"It's raw fish," Dad explained. "It's Japanese cuisine, just like Teppanyaki, which you both love."

"I'll try it!" I shouted before the opportunity could pass.

A few minutes later we had slices of fuchsia tuna, stripey salmon, and pale pink yellowtail laying over little rice rafts in front of us, with a tiny porcelain bowl of soy sauce, a mound of green wasabi, and a pile of pickled ginger. I was breathing through my mouth to try to avoid what I assumed would be wafting up from the plate: the smell of the fish stalls at the market. I looked at Mo and he looked like he might be sick onto the little wooden block that held these uncooked but very pretty treasures. Dad explained what I should do: *You dip each piece in*

the soy sauce and then eat it. I saw an opportunity to impress Dad
and my brother in one fell swoop. I used my little fingers to lift
the raw salmon, slide it through the soy bath, and shove it into
my mouth. It was an utterly bewildering sensation for me to
have such a different experience in my mouth to what I was
expecting. It was like when we were very little, before Texas,
when Dad told us to close our eyes and open our mouths and
he'd drop pickled bamboo or heart of palm or a Greek olive in
for us to taste. The salmon was silken on my tongue, with just
the slightest hint of heat riding on it from a light kiss of wasabi
on the underbelly of the slice, tempered in my mouth by the
floral flavor of the rice. The rice alone was so different from the
rice we ate every day, moist and pillowy and laced with a hint
of something slightly sweet and bright. I chewed a couple of
times and then couldn't help but swallow this mesmerizing
combination of three simple ingredients.

After enjoying the taste so much, I was no longer nervous
about the smell and inhaled deeply. There was nothing fishy
about the air above these edible jewels. One bite and I wanted to
eat sushi all the time! After seeing my reaction, Mohammad had
gone for it too, and found that sushi was extraordinary. At
home, Mo and I recounted our gastronomic adventures to our
mom, and though I am sure our expensive escapades with our
father may have made her feel a bit shabby, as she certainly
couldn't afford to take us to some of these meals, she always
took the news gracefully, glad we'd spent time with our dad. I
had several epiphanies the first night we went to a sushi dinner:
one was that I was game to try anything; two was that food
somehow magically created a way to communicate with my
father—a language where there had been fraught silence; and
three, that when it came to food, he'd never say no to us.

At least once every year, Mohammad and I went to Lahore

under the auspices of visiting our dad. I say this because at least for those early years after we returned from Texas, we did not actually stay with him and his new wife. I don't think that we were explicitly not invited, but it was obvious that it would be an uncomfortable setup on all sides. Naturally, being back in the F.C.C. house, which was once our own home and now belonged to our stepmother, whom my mother had never even met, and eventually a new family (our half siblings were born in 1997 and 2001), would have been a recipe for unease in every direction. Instead, we stayed with our chosen family: Eram Khala and Afi Uncle or Yasmin Khala and Nadeem Uncle, my mother's best friends and their husbands, and their kids, who were our best friends. One year, in the afternoons during our visit, we were dropped off at our dad's office for a couple of hours to spend time with him. Sometimes his dad (our granddad) would meet us there too. It never felt cozy or natural . . . how could it? We weren't temp employees, we were his kids, in from out of town, having a "playdate" with our father in his legal offices.

Eventually my father did want us to stay with him in Lahore, but after years of staying with our beloved khalas, their kids felt like our favorite siblings and cousins more so than our baby half siblings did, and it was hard to revert back to Dad. At one point, my father was appointed an advisory role in the government, a job that necessitated that he move to Islamabad. For the first time, Mo and I were invited to go too, and to be a part of our dad's home life. I had always felt uncomfortable around our stepmother. The idea of being with them for an extended period of time, without having our adopted khalas a phone call away to rescue us, frightened me. Mo, however, was up for the adventure and went to Islamabad with them. When he got back he reported that things had thawed a bit, that our stepmother had become friendlier and it wasn't so tense anymore. I never experienced that easing; our energy was always strained.

After our two years in Austin and the spell at the Shamshir house, we—Nano, Saby Khala, Mom, Mo, and me—finally moved back into Tanzeem and spread out among its grand configuration. Seventeen years had slipped away since my grandfather's passing and much of the house's luster had been buried with him and dulled by renters, but even seeing it as a shell of its former palatial glory, I fell in love with it instantly. To me it was an endlessly fascinating source of mystery and joy that contextualized who I was. It provided a backdrop not just to my young eight-year-old life but a map to my mother's identity. She was like a universe next door to mine but visible only through the telescope of her stories, the lens of her perspective, and the Tanzeem house was rich with clues. The indelible energy of generations past was everywhere, a child's utopia, rife with unexplored space.

There was a graceful mahogany banister, itching to be a slide, winding upward as soon as you entered from the grand foyer. To maximize speed and slipperiness, we wore soft pajama bottoms, socks, and a hint of talcum powder, if one was feeling particularly daredevilish. It's a miracle that we never cracked our skulls and ended up in the emergency room from the countless attempts to speed down the banister and land in a stylized pose for judgment from onlooking cousins and visiting friends.

The basement was expansive with old paint cans and turpentine, antique furniture on its last legs (literally), and odds and ends to be sniffed and explored. Relics of my mother's childhood remained: the concrete basement walls were covered with English words that my youthful mother had taught the domestic staff's children during daily "school" sessions, early harbingers of her new degree in education. Many a hot, hazy afternoon was spent in the cool basement, scavenging for interesting scraps with my friends, stomping on silverfish nestled between dusty rolls of old carpet. We made up terrible song lyrics and strummed a badly broken four-string guitar from my uncle's college days, which we'd found between sheets of plywood and tarp.

And then, of course, there were the sweltering market visits with my Nano. There were the early evenings doing my homework in the kitchen, watching as Qadir cooked us supper. I begged Nano for culinary lessons, the better to know her secret way of winning people over through their taste buds, of showing affection.

"Teach me your khowsuey, please, Nano! Teach me your aash," I begged, referring to her famed version of a Burmese noodle dish with aromatic coconut broth, succulent chicken, and a dozen essential condiments, and the Iranian noodle dish with layers of minced meat, chickpeas, and yogurt for which she was renowned.

"Fatima, first you must learn the basics, the building blocks," she told me. "Let's start simple. I'll teach you to make mayonnaise."

I'd take what I could get, and anyway, there's magic in mayonnaise—how it goes from golden liquid to opaque solid, clear oil to creamy, jiggly yellow-white spread.

"It's a trick of temperature," Nano told me. "All the ingredients must be the same temperature for it to work best." She lined up the oil, the egg, the mustard, and a halved lemon on the counter.

I watched as she spooned the mustard into the big mixing bowl, cracked the egg on its lip and separated the yolk from the white (this alone was spellbinding, and I was desperate to try). Then she broke the yolk into the bowl, added a big pinch of salt, squeezed in lemon juice, and began to whisk, while slowly, ever so gradually drizzling in the golden oil in a thin but steady stream. I watched the way she gathered the thickened part with each turn of her whisk, coaxing more oil into its opaque sturdiness.

"If you add the oil too quickly or you add too much of it, you'll break it," Nano explained while pouring slowly.

"Break it how?" I asked, furrowing my small brow at the viscous contents of the bowl . . . wondering how a thick glob could break.

"Breaking a sauce means it will change back into a liquid from the thickened solid you've created," she explained.

It seemed impossible that *all that oil*—a full cup for every egg yolk—could disappear into the growing jiggle of mayonnaise. *Surely another drop of oil will break it,* I thought. But Nano knew the measurements by heart. She knew the limits and she knew that she could make more than a cup of fluffy mayonnaise before it would break, and she always stopped right before this point and added a few more drops of water "to set it." I wanted that confidence and told myself that it would someday be mine.

I remember thinking it was such an amazing thing, that I could actually make something with my own hands. Nano taught me to make buns in the shape of bears with peppercorns for eyes and cloves for buttons that we wrapped in red cellophane and I gave as gifts to mystified friends. I worshipped her for sharing her secrets with me, for teaching me the language of the kitchen.

After dinner, Nano often put us to bed, telling us biblical legends as bedtime stories. The tale of Musa (Moses) with his miraculous infancy, his splitting of the sea, and his time in the wilderness; the tales of Isa (Jesus), Nuh (Noah), Ibrahim (Abraham), of Muhammad, of Ali (Muhammad's nephew)—these epic stories were our fairy tales, replete with fantasy, miracles, drama, and, of course, some sort of moral messaging. We plied her with questions afterward—*But why did he need to put his hand under his armpit to make it glow?*—and fell asleep imagining children with extraordinary powers.

I couldn't help but wonder why Nano never married again despite the many eligible suitors who waited the appropriate amount of time to make their intentions known. I idolized and adored her and wanted her to be admired and cared for, and so I asked her why she never accepted another proposal. She fussed with the edge of my sheet quietly, and after a minute she began to speak.

"You know that wonderful record that I sometimes play for you by Mehdi Hassan, Fatima?"

"Yes, Nano," I said, with the sense that something important might be coming.

"Well, he was a friend of your grandfather's and mine, and on our twenty-fifth wedding anniversary, he sang in this very house. He sang 'Zindagi Mein To Sabhi' at your grandfather's request. Can you translate that?"

I hesitated. My Urdu was still quite rusty after our two years in the States.

"It means 'Everyone loves in their lifetime, but I will love you even after I die,'" Nano said with tears in her lovely eyes. She shrugged her shoulders slowly and shook her wispy white head. "He was the love of my life."

And to that, how could I respond? I hadn't known my grandfather, and I was just a little kid who hadn't known a love like that. The closest thing I could imagine was how much I loved my brother. Upon consideration I realized that no one could replace him—no one could ever take his spot in my heart, so, in a way, I understood Nano's point.

chapter 10

HUNGER AT THE MARKET

———

Fatima

———

WE OFTEN ACCOMPANIED OUR MOTHER TO THE market to go grocery shopping, which I already understood as the first phase of every meal. We sat in the back of our rickety, dinged second-hand white Suzuki Khyber and drove to Khadda Market with my mother playing a Stevie Nicks tape, singing along loudly to "The Edge of Seventeen."

As soon as we pulled up to park, I heard a sharp rap on the window and my head snapped up. Large brown eyes, the same size as mine or Mo's but seeming larger because of the sunken cheeks beneath them, appeared framed in our windows. A million miles between a centimeter of polished glass. The children put their hands out for money and then motioned to their mouths. The universal sign of hunger.

"Hello, hello," my mother greeted them good-naturedly, as she and Mohammad helped my seven-year-old self out of the back seat of the car. "How many of you are there?"

"Well, us two and our cousins," a child said sheepishly.

"Go round them up," my mother told them, and off they ran, disappearing into the jigsaw of parked cars and crowds and child-size crevices between overflowing shops. Sometimes they whistled to get each other's attention from afar, and suddenly there were eight, twelve, fourteen little and not-so-little people around us, shabbily dressed, hair uncombed, faces unwashed and thin.

My mother looked around her for the closest dhaba, a simple little local eatery serving big vats of food, where cabbies and market purveyors all buy cheap, good meals.

"We've got fourteen kids," my mother told the proprietor. "What are you going to give them and what is it going to cost?"

The proprietor made up big plates of daal, curries, and fresh naan for the kids, one plate for each, and named a price for my mom, usually around thirty or fifty rupees, which included Cokes for everyone. She paid and waited for all the children to be served their food, while my brother and I watched the kids our age laughing, poking each other in the ribs, playful and relaxed for a moment now that they knew their next meal was coming soon and that it was to be a fresh one and not foraged from a trash heap. I watched as this band of beggars' mouths watered, and instead of getting hungry myself, I felt my small throat go dry.

Certainly, I was not immune to the seductive scents of Pakistani comfort food being readied for consumption. My mouth watered as I smelled fluffy biryani warming on the stovetop or shami kebabs for dinner at home, but seeing these hollow-cheeked kids so giddy and ravenous, I realized I'd never truly known hunger. Though I knew that money was hard earned, not only could my mother always feed us, but she had enough to feed this small army of street kids. Fifty rupees is all it took, and every Sunday we were fifty rupees lighter and those little boys and girls had full bellies for once.

Not knowing how or when, I made a promise to myself that I would feed people.

chapter 11

THE CHORUS

———

Farezeh

———

Mᴀ CAREER WAS BEARING FRUIT AND, WITH THE funding in place, I was looking to expand my learning support center. At the suggestion of a friend, I reached out to a real estate broker to help me find the right place, and when the owner of the realty business showed up for our meeting, I was pleasantly surprised by the man standing opposite me: tall and handsome with salt-and-pepper hair, a gentleman named Imtiaz. In the weeks to come, we found excuses to meet. He appraised the Tanzeem house for a potential sale for Mummy, offering to help without charging commission, somehow making an emotionally daunting situation feel more secure. He invited me to a party, and though I didn't feel ready for romance, I found myself leaning on him for support more and more. He, too, was a divorced single parent. Years before, he'd even read the article I'd written about the stigma of divorce, and praised me for having written it. Our connection blossomed.

Finally, in August while my kids were staying with Eram and Yasmin in Lahore and spending some time with their dad, Imtiaz and I went on our first official date. He was only the second person I'd felt strongly about since my marriage ended. Un-accustomed to the freedom of living on my own *and* not having the children at home with me, one date became two; two became ten. Imtiaz was very sure about what he wanted: he wanted *me*. In late August, after just two romantic weeks together, Imtiaz asked me to marry him and, almost reflexively, I said yes. No sooner had I agreed than he began to push me to set a date.

I'd fought so hard for my freedom, for my independence, for my sense of self. I'd broke all the stereotypes that had been drilled into me and I had become *someone*—someone who could stand on her own two feet. Why, then, did I wander willingly but without deep consideration back into the marriage pact? Was I trying to re-create the idea of a love-based union that I'd observed in my parents? Or were the childhood warnings and cultural dogmas of a woman being incomplete without a man controlling me once more? When had I again begun listening to the negative voices telling me I wasn't enough, that I needed protection and that I needed a man to keep up appearances? It's extraordinary how the message of self-doubt is transmitted: At first it's a passing thought, a tickle of hesitancy that one brushes aside like a stray hair. Then, bit by bit, the small voice becomes chatter, a radio on in the background, constant but ignorable. Then one day the buzz, the babble, has become a chorus, a many-throated monster that controls you with its endless bleating, its vile voice: *I AM NOT ENOUGH. I AM NOT ENOUGH. I AM NOT ENOUGH.*

The truth is that in our Pakistani society, for many women, marriage is license. Marriage, in some perverse way, is permission. It is so well understood and widely accepted as some sort of means to a more free and fuller life for a woman. A husband offers a life untethered to your parents, protection from slander, from being destitute, from prying eyes and hungry mouths. A husband makes a home, brings stability and safety, and takes charge and ownership of his brood. I suppose this is what patriarchy does when it is drilled in from every angle, from the chatter at chai time with the ladies, to the relentless advertising: soap, Coke, tea, milk, butter, biscuits, real estate! Every ad pumps out the same images and ideals: the happy little nuclear family, with the man at the center, the anchor for the house, the provider, the protector. I was blinded to what I was capable of and could only zero in on what I didn't have.

I looked around at my life, and the pieces were coming together nicely: I had my own house. I had an open and beautiful relationship with my children. I had a meaningful career that showed new promise every day.

But I was missing a partner in a society that saw only that deficiency and disregarded everything else. A husband was the missing ingredient that no one was letting me forget.

And then, as if on cue, a tall, handsome man—one who physically resembled that archetype that had been so ingrained in me—entered the picture and told me that I was lovely, that I was beautiful, that I was smart, that I was a good mom. The things we need to hear because we've been taught we need to hear them. The little girl inside me who was told to say please and thank you and to chew with her mouth closed and to keep her eyes lowered and to cover her shoulders, the little girl inside was suddenly thankful, because there was a reward, a reasoning for all the rules. And it was a relief.

That relief was only strengthened by how Imtiaz was with his children. He had taken the sole responsibility to raise his daughters—a rare phenomenon among single fathers in Pakistan, even more unusual in that he proactively wanted custody of his girls.

When the kids learned that I had met someone special and

was going to remarry, they couldn't have been happier for me. Both Mohammad and Fatima repeated again and again as the October wedding date drew near: "Mom, we are so happy for you. You deserve to be loved, Mom."

The narcotic of convention still haunted me, and I let its familiar haze envelop me—my naïve idealism seemed to push me into this next phase with blinders on. I figured that it made perfect sense: two homes, Imtiaz's kids without a mom and mine without a dad, both wanting what the others have, the missing puzzle pieces finding their home together. I was so taken with the fumes that even when I saw the smoke, I chose to believe there was no fire.

Imtiaz had two daughters, Saadia, thirteen (Mohammad's age), and Sarah, eleven. Fatima was nine. I asked Imtiaz, "Are your girls okay with this?" and I believed him when he said yes. It's not difficult to see why he said that in hindsight. At that time, his daughters never spoke openly in front of him or shared how they truly felt. They had their own private battles to contend with. They were, or had learned to be, different people with their dad.

By October, I was remarried and I began to fold my family into the three-bedroom apartment in Sea View that Imtiaz shared with his two girls. I was determined to pick up the pieces of two broken families, to glue them together however I could to build a unit. It was going to be everyone's reward for all the pain we had undergone. It was going to give our suffering meaning. And I placed this responsibility on myself and began shoring up all my energy to carry that weight. I figured, we just need a chance, a little time to readjust and calibrate to our new and better lives. Very quickly, however, I was completely overwhelmed.

Mohammad, newly a teenager and the only boy—a distinction that knows no limits—got his own room and began to drift toward independence. Fatima, who had always been his shadow and mimic, was cordoned off with the other girls, her new sisters. Saadia and Sarah, who formerly each had their own room, were put together with Fatima—a source of great indignation for them. Imtiaz forbade his girls to wear Western clothes in favor of our traditional garment, the shalwar kameez, so Fatima was abruptly not allowed to wear the tomboy clothes that had become her second skin and that echoed her brother's style. Fatima started to recognize a new normal creeping in: that privileges afforded to her brother were off-limits to her.

Both my children quietly protested these new rules—Mohammad on behalf of his sister—but we had made a deal to integrate ourselves as best as we could, reasoning it would give us the best shot at shaping ourselves into the family we had always wanted. I soon realized that I had married an extremely conservative man, the antithesis of my ever more open-minded identity. Sensing his preferences, I voluntarily discarded all of the clothes I felt showed too much skin. My shirts and jeans became extinct, along with my sleeveless kameez.

Fatima and Mohammad hatched a plan soon into the new marriage: They would call Imtiaz "Dad"—to elevate his status, give him a sense of ownership, and to proclaim and make public their acceptance and commitment to our new family on a daily basis. It was a subtle but powerful play, and I told them how proud I was that they could be so mature and thoughtful. Mohammad shared with me later how for Fatima, at her young age, it was a confusing and conflicting maneuver. She did not understand what it would mean for her real dad, her Baba, whom she longed to spend more time with, the only one she associated with occupying that esteemed position in her family tree. For Fatima, this dilemma and challenge so early into this new configuration was just the beginning of far tougher battles to come.

While my children were delighted for me and to have a new father figure in their lives, my new husband had a side to him that I was dumbstruck by. His anger and rage would send his tongue lashing out some of the most cruel and degrading language I had ever heard. His dark side was noxious and corrosive, a poison for our new and still very fragile family.

Imtiaz's two daughters also had emotional outbursts. They were perpetually upset—temper tantrums, tears, violence, and aggression; they lashed out daily. I was beginning to understand where this all was coming from, and instead of my limbic system compelling me to "fight or flight," it had me in a nearly catatonic "fright" state. My actions and reactions became automated, and the crescendo of alarm signaling impending doom became background noise. We had to make this work; this was meant to be the happily ever after.

I saw only the two girls struggling with their new circumstances, and I leaned in to my tendency to fix things by going into overdrive to take care of Saadia and Sarah. I wasn't merely going to break the archetype of the evil stepmother; I was going to mother them like they were my own. I tried constantly to please them. *My kids will be fine,* I told myself. *They've received so much of my love and are better equipped to survive without my attention,* I reassured myself when I worried that I wasn't giving my own kids enough. I could barely stay afloat, and every wave of my newfound problems threatened to take me and this entire thing under. Perhaps they sensed this, because Fatima dared not complain to me about anything, and Mohammad chose to be as nonexistent as possible.

Whatever I tried with Saadia and Sarah didn't work. If anything, it frustrated them even more. I loved my new husband, and despite his rages, I knew he loved me as well. I felt certain that we wanted the same things for our children and for each other, so I fought for us. I buried my reservations, doubts, and fears and doubled down on my commitment to make it work. *It's my duty to solve this,* I told myself, as any mother instinctively tries to when their children are suffering. And I truly saw Saadia and Sarah as my own daughters. I could not stand to see what was happening and was hyperaware of how this could lead to yet another broken home. I was not going to let my family suffer that again.

Cruelty was normalized in Saadia and Sarah's family, internalized by them and exhibited only in painful fits that they kept hidden from their father. And when it had nowhere to go, the youngest of our unit was the perfect scapegoat. I knew that little Fatima was getting less of me, but even at only nine years old, she bristled at my concern. "Don't worry about me, Mom," she told me. "The girls need you more; they're having a hard time." She never wanted to be any trouble. Fatima was being shortchanged, pushed into the periphery and deprioritized as a dubious reward for just how together and remarkable she was.

Fatima never once told on her new siblings or complained. Instead, she became withdrawn and quiet. An avid reader, Fatima spent hours alone frolicking in the fantasy and adventure of her books. I thought she was fine. After all, what young child has such mastery of her emotions that even her own mom can't see what's happening?

It wasn't until I stumbled upon Fatima's journal that I learned of her sisters' taunts. It flooded me, to see how rejected she felt. How small she was being made to feel. How little she had in this new world that my decisions had landed her in. Every word of her anguish gutted me like a knife.

The girls called little Fatima cruel names, like so many children do on the playground every day. They didn't include her and locked her out in the sweltering heat after school. Perhaps Fatima was the symbol and embodiment of their newly imposed oppression. I'd return from work at five p.m. and would find Fatima dehydrated and in sweat-soaked clothes in the lounge off their room where there was no air conditioning. Yet I didn't confront them because I was too afraid of upsetting the applecart. I rationalized that I would be more present for Fatima, and that would help make her feel more supported. If I took this to Saadia and Sarah and squared up with them, their mother would pounce on this as her gotcha moment, finally having evidence that I was in fact the evil stepmother, the one who was only interested in her own daughter's interests and not theirs. I could handle this, I told myself.

But the cracks that had formed were determined to spread and widen. Though our family had grown, it had also fractured. Both Imtiaz and I were working full-time and relying on our cherished Qadir, who had been with my family for three decades, to prepare all meals, and Zaman, Imtiaz's loyal driver and henchman, his lackey meant to serve and protect us, to ferry the children to and from school. Mohammad was aloof—a teenager struggling against the rules, who retreated from the family drama and looked for any escape he could find. No one seemed to notice that our smallest one was falling through the cracks. Well, that's not entirely true: One person noticed.

They say of relationships and families that one never knows what goes on behind closed doors. There's much truth to that, but there's also an exception: when the *one* is on the inside and is privy to the inner workings or fissures of a family. We had a predator in our midst and he was hiding from us in plain sight.

chapter 12

A PROMISE OF
ICE CREAM

—

Fatima

—

I LIKED MY NEW STEPFATHER IMMEDIATELY. HE WAS strict and principled, but this made sense given his Pashtun Afghan origins. They are very proud people, very serious, and he grew up disciplined, with strong family values and a clear sense of duty and patriarchy, which he stepped into early as his father died young. He'd taken care of his four siblings—an unfair, burdening responsibility, but he never shirked it. I sensed that he was a good person, that he truly wanted us all to be happy together.

I was glad my mother had found a man who was so committed to the people in his life; I thought that we were becoming a part of his flock, and a bit of me wanted to be cared for with that same unflinching allegiance. But an immediate loyalty did not extend to my new stepsisters, Sarah and Saadia. Their tempers were like trip wires, impossible to navigate and clamping down on me like vicious traps. I saw my mother struggling to hold it together—a new family bound by the flimsy floss of a short courtship. My new sisters immediately cast Mom as the evil stepmother, even though she was extremely patient with them and bent over backward to try to appease them.

I know I annoyed my new sisters—the baby always wanting to be included in their games and secrets, begging for ways into their world, their private language of eye rolls and inside jokes. Mohammad suddenly seemed so grown up and withdrawn, and without him to follow, I longed for the girls to embrace me or at least let me tag along. Yet the more I tried to win them over, the more I seemed to disgust them. While this hurt, it hurt far more when they realized that I was being terrorized and abused, and did nothing to stop it.

At first I'd been relieved when our school schedules dictated that Zaman, my stepfather's longtime driver and right-hand man, deliver us home from school in two separate trips. I missed studying my new sisters for clues of how to be cool and trying to win them over, but I also enjoyed the peacefulness of being in the car without them in the afternoons. It was a relief not to be picked on, frankly, and Zaman let me choose the cassette. Before long, however, the time alone in the car with Zaman took an insidious turn.

On the stifling afternoons when he was driving me home from school, he maneuvered me through my greatest weakness: food. He began by offering to stop for ice cream to win my trust. Then, when back in the car, Zaman made me climb onto him and steer the car from his lap. He called it "teaching me how to drive." I had just turned ten years old. Day by day, he began to move his fingers higher and higher up my small dark legs toward my school uniform skirt. Soon the ice creams became my dangled reward for sitting on his lap, one that I no longer wanted.

When it started, I was too terrified to scream. The longer it went on, the bolder Zaman got, moving his fingers past my panties, touching places I hadn't even known I had. His pants were suddenly undone and pulled down, and he held my little wrist and forced me to stroke him through his shalwar. A few days later, the routine escalated, with nothing between us, just his skin against mine, looking for my seams. It was beyond what I could understand or define, and something I tried to will myself to forget.

Zaman had been observing us all: my stepdad, who expected my mother to look after the four children; Mohammad, who was becoming a teenager and distancing himself; my sisters, who were excluding me; and my mother, whose belly was growing. The spindly string that held us all together became much sturdier when my baby brother, Bangu, was born. We may have had our differences, but in that one thing we were united: The baby was perfect and we loved him endlessly.

Zaman was cunning: He saw the adoration we put on little Bangu, how our devotion to this tiny squirming, squeaking bundle bonded us, and so he included the baby in his machinations to get me to do what he wanted.

"If you tell anyone, I'll hurt the baby," Zaman hissed into my ear on his tobacco breath when he was finished with me. I feared my siblings' and my parents' judgment, but nothing terrified me more than the idea of Zaman hurting the baby. "I don't *want* to hurt him," Zaman said many times, "but if you don't give me what I want or if you tell anyone what we do together, then you understand that you will make me kill him."

I understood the threat and I stayed silent.

One night, during a blackout, Zaman once again approached me to bend me to his will. It had happened so many times by this point that I understood what was expected of me: to do as I was told and to participate. But whether it was the physical pain of him trying to rape me or the fact that he'd threatened to murder my baby brother, on that black night I finally found my voice and I screamed. I ran and locked myself in my dad's room and shouted for Qadir to call my parents, who were out for dinner.

"Call Ammi and Abbu!" I screamed through the door at Qadir. Of course there had been other nights when our parents were out when we asked Qadir to call them, but this was different. This was a real emergency. I pleaded through tears, and though I never told him why, Qadir eventually gave in and called them. They were already on their way home, thank God.

When my parents arrived home, I didn't tell them what had happened. I couldn't face the disgust I was sure would overcome them when they found out what I had let happen with Zaman. I had resisted, but when I thought back on it—the many episodes over so many months—I felt sure I could have fought harder. It was certainly at least partially my fault.

It was a secret so filthy and sharp that it was lacerating me apart from the inside, infecting me. A few days later, I summoned the strength and confessed to my sister Sarah. I suppose I hoped that it would immediately all be over once I told her—as if uttering the truth was powerful enough to unshackle me or that she could somehow fix everything, but actually it took a few painful days for her to repeat the information. Sarah told Mohammad and Mohammad told Mom.

I heard my mother wailing, and then her footsteps as she came running toward our room, opening the door with a frantic, wild look in her eyes. She grabbed me up as if yanking me back from in front of a speeding car and clasped me in her arms, nearly crushing me, and asked me, "My darling Tatu, what did Zaman do to you?"

I thought I might be sick to my stomach. He did everything to me. How am I supposed to tell my mother that a fifty-two-year-old father of four—who my stepfather trusted blindly, who was meant to be a part of the family—molested me? I didn't really understand much about sex; I knew something bad had happened to me, but I didn't know *how* bad it was. And while my mother rocked me in her arms weeping, I thought, *What if it wasn't so bad? Why then have I done this? Why have I told anyone? Why have I caused so much distress?*

My mom took me to her room and gently began asking me questions, trying to ascertain what had happened to me.

Did he touch you here? Did he touch you there? Did he do this? Did he do that?

With every question and every affirmative response, I felt sicker, even more confused, and very, very guilty. Certainly this was my fault.

Soon the police arrived and Zaman made a pathetic attempt to evade them by threatening to jump off a second-story balcony in Mo's room, which would have resulted not in his death but probably a broken leg. Through the door, Mo persuaded him not to jump and eventually to open the door, on the other side of which the cops were waiting to arrest him. It turned out that he had also stolen tens of thousands of dollars' worth of my mother's jewelry.

This man had caused ruin to our family. It felt like he had come into our lives, taken what he wanted, and left, absconding with my innocence. I suppose he was sitting in a jail cell somewhere, but it felt like he got away with it because he just disappeared.

I realize now that Zaman was watching us, always watching, and that I was the little minnow that was separated from the school of fish. It was terrifying to admit what was happening, and I felt that if I did, it would break our newly formed and delicate family apart. I felt like confronting Zaman was confronting my stepfather, because Zaman had come into our lives with our stepdad. I thought it would break my mother's heart to know what Zaman had done to me. About that last part, I was right. Zaman's abuse had not only terrorized me, but had traumatized my family.

I hadn't consciously identified it, but a pattern was emerging: men, apart from my brother, were not to be trusted. My father had driven my mother away and seemed not to mind being a bit player in our lives. My stepdad never addressed what had happened, how I'd suffered at the hands of Zaman, his guy, and he certainly never apologized. I didn't want to dwell on it, but I was nonetheless furious with him, first for not protecting me and second for not acknowledging what had happened. This anger manifested in my avoiding all physicality with him. I no longer could let him run his hand through my hair or put an arm around me.

I had been glad to have a father again. But now he represented my abuse and my mother's distraction and encumberment. The autumn that my mother remarried, she brought Imtiaz with her to our annual sports day at my school. It had always been a great source of pride to me that, like me, my mother loved to run and could out-dash the other parents in the student-parent relay races. That year, when she tied her left leg to my stepdad's right leg for the three-legged race, he slowed her down. It felt like a metaphor for everything I was going through: We'd been better off when it was just us three, without Imtiaz, his angry daughters, or his duplicitous bodyguard. But of course it wasn't up to me. It's never the choice of the children of divorce who become their new parents.

In that first year and in those that followed, I accepted that I was his daughter, tied to him by my mother and by our new baby brother, but I also recognized that I was separate, different. I stood up to him in ways my sisters didn't, talking through my perspective and rationalizing why I believed something was fair or unfair. I mediated between my sisters and him when his sense of patriarchal authority had gone too far or was misguided. It had never occurred to my sisters to stand up to him, and I think my solidarity helped them realize they too could speak their mind, albeit respectfully. I was reverential, but I tried to give him permission to let down his guard a bit, to resist policing us women, as we really didn't need it. The sense of duty that made him loyal also made him shortsighted sometimes, and I wasn't afraid to go head to head with him, which paradoxically warmed him to me—the littlest one. I also understood that I needed to appear healthy and normal, that my mom needed that from me to make her marriage run smoothly and to be able to focus her attention on baby Bangu, and so I did.

My mother had so much to worry about other than me. Her baby brother, my Mamu (maternal uncle), who had always been a bit of a hellraiser, fixing up pickup trucks with Corvette engines and the like, let his daredevilish ways get the better of him and was in a horrific car accident that left him in a coma for eleven months. Nano and my mother were with him constantly, praying for his survival—an answered prayer. Mamu survived, but as often happens, chaos is left in the wake of illness. Loan sharks from whom my Nano had borrowed to keep her house and life afloat came slithering out of the woodwork to collect.

If my grandfather were still alive, he would have fended off these insidious men. If my grandfather hadn't died, we wouldn't have needed loans to pay for Mamu's medical care. Hell, if my grandfather had lived, Mamu wouldn't have been allowed his shadowy existence—he would have had a real job. If Mamu had

had a real job, he wouldn't have had this accident, and my mother would not have given up so much of her career to be his caretaker. If, if, if.

Nano had to sell the Tanzeem house. Between the mountains of hospital bills, ongoing treatment, and Mamu's questionable life choices, my mother's and then my childhood home was signed away to a family that promised to keep the original structure of the house intact, but no sooner had the ink dried on the deed than a bulldozer demolished and flattened the entire plot. With Mamu's accident and ensuing infirmity and the consequent destruction of the Tanzeem house, yet another veil of childhood was lifted. As with my driving lessons, I was forced to confront the unfairness of life, the propensity for the immoral to take advantage of the weak, one of which I never wanted to be.

chapter 13

THE FIRE INSIDE

———

Fatima

———

WHILE LIFE AT HOME WAS HAUNTED BY WHAT WAS left unsaid, school was my haven. My time in Texas gave me a sense of distinction and was a point of interest to my schoolmates in Karachi. Whereas my transition into elementary school in Austin had been cold and cruel, at Karachi Grammar School, I had my pick of friends. I loved school and enjoyed excelling in it, doing my homework and acing exams. Karachi Grammar was progressive, but also steeped in its colonial past. Though thanks to my stepdad I could no longer dress like my brother, I could still be a tomboy when it came to playing sports. On the track field, I felt independent, exhilarated with a competitive zeal that I carried with me even when I wasn't sprinting. Although our meets and matches were competitions with other schools, I always felt like my greatest challenge was competing with myself: beating my own records, exceeding my own expectations. Even when I won, which I managed often, I was never satisfied. I felt a momentary gladness for having done my best and succeeded, but then a sense of being unfulfilled seeped back in. Perhaps I was chasing a phantom on the field: perfection, which, if caught, I imagined could make me feel whole again. The trophies or medals were meaningless to me. Perhaps I didn't want to rest on my laurels because I wanted to be the best in a forum that I had not yet identified.

One day during relay races, I'd gotten us into first place, but the third runner on our team dropped the baton. A girl in my year, Zainie, who I liked but didn't know well because she was not in my class, was the last runner, the anchor, and she had no chance of winning the race thanks to our teammate dropping the baton. I was shocked to see her crying after the race, horrified that she felt so sad about losing when it wasn't even her fault, so I went up to her and took one of the first-place medals from around my neck and put it around her neck. She looked at me through tears and we exchanged small smiles. Zainie would go on to be one of my closest friends for life.

My school friends became like family; our small group of five was inseparable. Though each of us was distinct, we were all overachievers who got excellent grades. When I finally admitted to my girlfriends a little bit of what had recently happened to me at home, I was astounded to find out that they each knew someone else who had been inappropriately touched. I began to realize then that not only was I not alone in my exploitation, but many, many Pakistani girls were victims of lecherous adults' perversions and damaging behavior. My mother had cautioned me to stay near her at the market and to be careful not to let strangers brush up against us in crowds, and I had thought it was to protect us from pickpockets, but as I heard my friends tell me of wandering hands that had reached for other young girls in public and in private, I realized that the wider world was just as unsafe as the prison of my driving lessons had been. I vowed that the next time someone touched me, it would be because I wanted them to. It would be my choice.

It felt phenomenal to scream to my teammates on the field, to root for them at the top of my lungs from the sidelines. No one around me knew the pain and anger that I was working through under the guise of cheers and "Over here! I'm open!" The ritual physicality of sports was healing me, giving me a playful canvas on which to unleash my pent-up rage. On the athletic fields, I wasn't self-conscious about being a little bit tough, for being loud, for being fast, for having strong legs and energy that elsewhere might be considered unladylike. Makeup and dresses are not welcome on the soccer pitch or track circle, and so I felt I could be myself: no less female, but not overtly so—not female as a kind of show, not having to prove my femininity with arbitrary outward signs. I sprinted and did several field sports: javelin, shot put, and long jump. I played volleyball and netball; I swam. Perhaps sports were the way that I was subconsciously preparing for my eventual escape from Pakistan. Perhaps I knew that I needed to be physically tough to survive in the wider world that awaited me beyond the prim, secluded society of ladies from which I came. Perhaps I just relished the minutes of extreme physical duress that seemed purposeful, that had a predictable outcome.

Winning for me wasn't about victory, but rather about setting a goal and achieving it, and achieving it made me feel good and like I had some sort of control . . . if only for a second. I threw myself into school plays, finding that I loved to perform, again in a forum where the outcome was predetermined. In theater, you know how a story will end. You know when the audience will laugh, when they will lean forward in their seat—at least, if you're doing your job right, of course, and I loved this sense of power and predictability. I loved playing the ham by becoming a character, making people laugh.

When I wasn't on the sports fields or on a stage, I spent my

afternoons at home glued to cooking shows on our TV. We got
BBC Food and I obsessively watched Nigella Lawson, Gordon
Ramsay, and the hilarious *Two Fat Ladies*. Watching them create
these elaborate dishes that I could almost smell and taste through
the screen seemed like magic. These chefs became my superhe-
roes. I watched them religiously—even during Ramadan, when
everyone was fasting and my sisters, drooling with hunger,
begged me to turn off the programs, I couldn't stop. Then,
when out of my family's earshot, I uttered culinary catchphrases
like spells to myself—*A pinch of sugar there . . . Add a little bit of
flour to the pot*—practicing in the bathroom mirror for my dream
of someday having my own cooking show.

One spring when I was eleven or twelve, I was asked to contribute to a fundraiser for my mother's learning center. I turned
it over in my head for weeks. What could I do that would be
cheap to execute and original? I talked it over with family and
friends, but nothing they suggested felt quite right. I didn't
want to resell candy or chuck water balloons . . . I wanted something unconventional and I knew I wanted a food booth. Finally, over dinner one night it occured to me: Fatima's Potato
Stall . . . *Fat's Potatoes!* I'd serve pre-roasted and pan-fried potatoes and ask each customer what "flavor" they'd like. I'd offer
sour cream and onion, creamy garlic, spicy masala, or just plain
salt and pepper. Everyone loved the idea, and it was a great success. Students and their families came up and bought Fat's Potatoes from me. I ran the booth on my own, enjoying the pleasant
chaos of taking orders and payments and putting them in my
"register," which was a can. I suppose you could say that it was
my first restaurant concept.

As in all corners of the world, traditions are followed, patterns appear, society steers its members onto well-worn paths to
keep civilization on a familiar trajectory. I could see how my

future was most likely to pan out if I was passive. I was lucky to be from the wealthier side of Pakistani society, and so I knew that I would finish high school and then go to college, perhaps abroad, and then return to Pakistan to live with my parents and be a member of the flock of young women who get thrice-weekly blowouts and manicures while looking for a husband (or while being pushed toward one by their parents and aunties and cousins). I'd see my friends at the salon and then at the end-less pageant of parties and weddings. The refrain would con-tinue to get louder and more frequent that I needed to find a nice husband, someone from a good family, someone who could provide so that I could have children of my own . . . I would find someone (or someone would be found for me) and we would have a big wedding, and not long after, people would begin to ask when we were planning to have a child, if they'd even managed to hold their tongues that long, and the cycle would begin again. We would hire staff and have a nice house, and everything would be perfectly pleasant and predictable and staid.

Instinctually I always knew that I wanted something differ-ent from the life waiting for me in Pakistan. Intrinsically, I began to realize that complying with this pattern, this preor-dained order of things, would mean sacrificing a part of myself, would mean denying who I really was on some level, but I was able to admit it to myself in a different way after my sixteenth Christmas, when my future began to take shape in a clearer way.

chapter 14

MY A STUDENT

—

Farezeh

—

WHEN FATIMA WAS ELEVEN, SHE STARTED DEVEL-
oping debilitating urinary tract infections. She suffered silently
at first, hoping whatever she was feeling would pass without
anyone needing to attend to her. If they got bad, she would grit
her teeth and bear them—she might become a bit quiet and ir-
ritable, but she never complained. She downplayed her ordeal if
I tried to talk to her about what was happening. Her physical
strength, her determination and ability to conquer a challenge
she set out for herself, like she did in sports at school, were important to her. If she could avoid telling me about it (because
she knew I would worry), she did. Fatima thought she could
overcome pain through sheer willpower, and sometimes she
did.

So you can imagine how bad it must have been when she
eventually agreed to let me take her to a doctor. Most of them
dismissed it as an unpleasant but altogether harmless side effect
of puberty. This nonchalance caused her to double down on her
endurance. Only, that's not how bodies work. Finally, a doctor
discovered what was going on. She had an extra ureter, and she

needed surgery to remove it. He balked at her ability to have borne the pain for so long, asking her why she had let herself suffer like that. I didn't know how to tell him that that was just who my daughter was.

On the other hand, I panicked. I was still haunted by Fatima's hospitalization as an infant and prayed she'd never need to be hospitalized again, until the birth of her child. But here she was again, on a hospital bed, in a gown, an IV dripping into her arm.

When she woke up after the anesthesia had worn off, she was in a lot of pain and could barely move. She searched for the now bandaged wounds her surgery had left her with. Two days of rest later, she started to sit upright on her bed, and hatch a game plan that would ensure she quickly got back to her friends, to her favorite classes, to the sports field, to the kitchen. And so, she pulled herself through her recovery with the discipline of a trained athlete. Her doctors were surprised by her quick progress, and at times would tell her to rest more, to relax more, to accept that she needed to just tune out and do nothing for a little while. Two weeks later, she was back in school.

This was who she was becoming. Fatima could persevere through storms, never even blinking at the bruises. If anything, she cracked a joke about them. It left me awestruck. Fate dealt Fatima with one bad hand after the next. She was still so young, and perhaps that helped, because the things Fati had dealt with up till that point were enough to bend and break someone less tenacious. They only seemed to make her stronger, more determined.

When she wasn't cooking with my mother, Fatima was sprinting on the school's track field, winning medals and trophies. At the end of middle school, she was made the "Junior Victress"—the title given to the best athlete in middle school, and she vowed to win it again as an upperclassman. It was her goal to become captain of Papworth House—one of the four houses into which the school was split—in her final year at Karachi Grammar. I saw the determination and self-imposed responsibility with which she pursued her goals and knew I never had to remind her to do her homework; she relished staying ahead of it all.

So I was caught completely off-guard when I got a call from the school telling me that I needed to come in to "discuss" Fatima. *How strange,* I thought. With Mohammad, Saadia, or Sarah I wouldn't have blinked an eye at this request, but come into school for Fatima? Something must not be right. Fatima aced everything without any tutoring, so I couldn't imagine what they needed to discuss.

It turned out that Fatima and her friends had created a slam book—one of those notebooks that kids and teens make with gossip and dirty jokes and pass around for each other to add comments to. In it were jokes about sex and boys, and hilariously inaccurate anatomical drawings—things they had never experienced themselves but, like all teenagers, were curious, confused, and competitive about. Needless to say, the teachers and senior management at the school found zero hilarity in any of it. For them it was pure scandal.

Had the book been written by boys instead of girls, the whole episode would have been shoved under the rug—which I told the headmaster in no uncertain terms—but because it *was* created by girls, there was a heavy punishment: Fatima and her friends were suspended for three days.

As if this wasn't absurd and unfair enough, the repercussions of suspension lasted far longer than the three-day punishment: Fatima and her friends were forbidden to speak to each other, a stipulation that we parents were expected to uphold, much to the despair of our daughters. A rule of the school was that any student who was ever suspended could never be nominated as a captain or to be on student council—Fatima's dream of being Papworth House captain was destroyed. I tried to comfort her, but she was inconsolable.

By the time three days had passed and the suspension was up, Fatima had come up with a plan. The following term, as Fatima entered grade seven, she approached Mrs. Mancharjee, the fear-inspiring headmistress who ruled the school with an iron fist. *I want to be captain of Papworth,* she explained her goal for her final year at Karachi Grammar, after marching courageously into her office. It was a small school and everyone knew that Fatima was a straight-A student . . . but everyone also knew about her suspension. The headmistress considered Fatima's situation. No one had ever come to her like this before—an act of contrition, taking complete responsibility and stating their goals with such determination. Eventually, Mrs. Mancharjee offered a solution: If Fatima continued to get excellent grades and lead by example right up to her final year, she'd strike her record clean. Fatima promised and was true to her word. Even her final year, when there was a tradition that the whole graduating class skip school together one day in the spring, Fatima didn't go with the flow. She showed up at school alone to keep her pledge. She got perfect scores on her O levels; she got a certificate from Cambridge. She got a 99 in literature and 100 in language. She never listened when people tried to limit her . . . and people around her often did.

chapter 15

AND THEN I COULD SEE IT

Fatima

THE KITCHEN HAD BEEN MY HAPPY PLACE FOR AS LONG as I could remember, and bit by bit, I'd grown more ambitious in my experiments in it. From the first "soups" of water and vegetables that my Nano taught me, to chapati, to dressing up instant ramen with whatever I could find in the refrigerator, to Thai curry from scratch, to making real stocks, to cooking special dishes to bring in to school to eat instead of the school lunch, my culinary repertoire was ever increasing. As usual, I was always on the lookout for ways to outdo myself, so when I heard that a particularly large number of relatives would be in town for the holidays one year, congregating for weddings and parties, I took it upon myself to cook for them.

"How about if I cooked for everyone?" I chimed in one evening as my family was discussing the imminent arrival of aunties and uncles, cousins and in-laws.

Naturally, my family was enthusiastic about my proposal, but as they responded with smiles and suggestions, of course a part of me silently thought, *What have I done?* Cooking for sixty people was no joke. It would also be the first time that I would cook a traditional Christmas dinner—a twenty-pound turkey with all the sides—by myself. I was sixteen and cooking for sixty. But even as I felt a pang of anxiety, I also was one hundred percent certain that I could do it and that I *would* do it.

The prep for the Christmas feast started the day before. I woke up at six a.m., sleepy and groggy, and began to ready the enormous bird, which we'd ordered from Agha's supermarket in Clifton. To go with it, I made cranberry, fig, and mushroom sauces. I made garlic roasted green beans, glazed carrots, creamy mashed potatoes, baked cauliflower in a cheese sauce, penne pasta with fresh tomato sauce, and a green salad with mustard vinaigrette. And because American traditions can only go so far, I added on a stuffed whole red snapper and roasted a leg of lamb. No big deal!

We don't eat dinner before eleven p.m. in Pakistan, especially if it's a party, so I had two full days of prep, but even so, when the guests began to arrive at eight that night, I didn't feel ready. All the adults were drinking, talking, and there I was working in the kitchen alone. But past my aching back and sweaty temples, I recognized there was this buzz in the house, this energy that I could feel through the kitchen door, which swung open often, releasing the fragrance of my concoctions to the waiting guests. People kept asking what I was making. "Shut up!" I'd shout with a sly smile when they stuck their heads in the kitchen. "Get out!" I was utterly focused on the task at hand: making a dozen dishes that should all be ready at the same time. I suppose in my heart I was already a rude chef, or at least that's the image I hoped to project to my extended family waiting like hungry wolves beyond the swinging kitchen door, not the nervous teenager that I actually was, hands shaking when they weren't busy basting the bird, tossing the green beans, and whipping the mashed potatoes into a buttery billow.

My Itrath Khala, who was in charge of the desserts, gave me an apron that she'd saved for me, and an irrational delight and sense of importance came over me as I tied the strings behind my back, a giddy glee as if I were putting on a superhero cape. In that instant, I felt strong and like I knew just who I was, even if my knees felt like jelly with jitters and fatigue. When I'd wiped the edges of platters with damp cloths the way I'd seen the TV chefs do it and I'd made sure each vessel had a serving utensil propped on its rim, I put on a red nose and antlers like Rudolph, a festive face to hide behind, and as soon as they were on, my mom shouted, "Food is served!"

Everyone spilled into the dining room, where the table was literally covered by the dozen dishes I'd prepared. When my family caught sight of the array, the big golden brown bird, the whole stuffed fish lying on a bed of herbs, the impressive lamb's leg garnished with rosemary, and plate after plate of side dishes and sauces, the boisterous stampede of party guests quieted, and they hovered, eyes wide, licking their lips, as if they were contemplating a miracle.

I'd sidled into a corner, feeling awkward and unsure of myself, my heart beating wildly. I couldn't believe I'd pulled it off and done it all myself. The table looked too spectacular to be anything but imaginary. I couldn't speak; I felt I might cry.

My mother looked from the awe-inspiring spread on the table to me cowering in the corner. She could read me like a book, and probably could tell by my exhausted but elated expression that I wasn't sure how to feel yet. She pulled me out of the corner into her embrace, and it was she who began to cry.

"You've outdone yourself, Fatima," my mother said into my ear. "I've never been so proud of you, Tatu."

We both understood it at the same moment: I'd found my path.

"Well, dig in!" I mustered over her shoulder, through her thick dark hair, and then the first person picked up the big fork to help themselves to slices of turkey, and then someone else took a huge spoonful of mashed potatoes, and the meal began in earnest.

It was both excruciating and exquisite: everything hurt . . . but I felt so satisfied and had the strangest sense of accomplishment. I waited for everyone else to be served, which gave me a chance to watch them taste my dishes, to watch their faces as they registered the flavors, the care that had been put into each one.

"My god, this is delicious!" an auntie exclaimed.

"Better than a restaurant," I heard my second cousin say to his wife.

"Not bad for a sixteen-year-old," Imtiaz joked to a friend.

The words of praise found their way to me as I made my way toward the table to eventually serve myself. Somehow, despite all the tasting I'd done along the way, I discovered that I was hungry, and after piling my plate with little bits of everything and finding a seat with my mom, I found that the meal I'd cooked tasted even better off a plate with a fork than it had in the kitchen as I frantically checked each dish for seasoning off the back of a spoon before sending it out to the serving table.

We took a photo that captured the joy. It wasn't just the achievement of cooking that made me so elated; it was the triumph of feeding people. That was my moment of epiphany: *I'm going to be a chef.*

chapter 16

MY MOTHER'S BLESSING

Fatima

———

AFTER COOKING THAT ENORMOUS CHRISTMAS MEAL for my extended family, not only did I know that I didn't want to participate in the preordained procession of university, job, marriage, children, which to me felt like a charade, but I understood that I could find a way to manifest another reality for myself by doing what I love. Somehow amid mashing the potatoes and straining the gravy, the notion that food could truly be my passport to another life took root in me, and from that day on, everything I did became about realizing that goal.

When I was seventeen, I verbalized to my mother what she must have already sensed.

"Mom, I've been thinking about what I want to do with my life and for a career," I began. My mother looked at me patiently, doing an excellent job of pretending she had no idea what I was about to say.

"Yes, Tatu, what is it that you've come up with?"

"Well, I want to be a professional chef."

I'd said the words before to my closest friends, I'd said them to myself in the mirror, but saying them out loud to my mother, the woman I looked to for guidance and whose own independence helped shape me, was different. Her reaction was the only one that mattered. If she got behind me, I'd be able to pull it off. If she didn't, then I wouldn't have the courage or the capacity.

"Well, that's what you should do, then," she said, simple as that. And then: "But you must get a bachelor's degree."

Of course, the woman who had been denied an education in favor of an arranged marriage at the age of nineteen would not hear of me skipping the opportunity and essential schooling that a degree would provide. This seemed not only fair to me but sensible, but I knew I couldn't wait until after college to start cooking.

I went to my trusty laptop and I put three words into Google: "America." "Culinary." "Bachelors." The first school that popped up was the CIA—the Culinary Institute of America, in Hyde Park, New York. Boom. I would go there.

"Ma, of course they have a bachelor's program! It's like the Harvard of culinary schools!" I told my mom soon thereafter, sliding in details day by day to persuade her. And then there was convincing my father, who would pay for my education, that his money would be well spent.

"See, Baba, when I'm older and you want to retire, we can open up a restaurant together after I've worked in some restaurants in New York City and trained," I coaxed him.

They relented in the end, my mother and my two dads. I think they knew as well as I did that it was my destiny.

I wanted to become a chef because I wanted to feed people. I wanted to re-create that magic feeling I'd had when I cooked for my extended family of sixty on Christmas the year before. I wanted to reproduce that feeling of exhausted satisfaction—of being appreciated and admired—every day of my life. Perhaps I could trace it back to the beginning with my dad: He connected to us through food; it was our language of love. And my mother, who worked hard to provide for us but was never too short on time or funds to take the hungry children of Karachi into a dhaba and buy a meal for them. And my grandmother, Nano, whose culinary genius gave gratification to and impressed every guest who crossed her threshold, I wanted to give the gifts of sustenance and pleasure, the sense of well-being that eating well uniquely provides. I wanted to learn my craft and then harness it and do it on television, like Martin Yan and Nigella Lawson, where the maximum number of people—of little brown girls, especially—could see me do it and understand that they could do it too.

I didn't think I was so special, but actually that was the key: If this ordinary Pakistani girl could pursue the thing she loved most—cooking—and could make it to the tippy-top and do what she loved on TV, then what was to stop all of us little brown girls from carving out new paths, from calling attention to the hungry children, the silenced dreamers, the oddballs and rebels who longed to go against the grain?

Though my best friends knew that cooking was my destiny as much as my mother did, they were astounded by my college application process as well.

"You've only applied to one university?!" my best friend Mariam said, aghast. "Is that really *wise*?"

It was late in the evening and we were clearing our dinner plates at one of our houses. My closest friends—Zainie, Mariam, and Tano—and I often studied after school together and then had dinner before going to our respective homes.

"It's the only place that's right for me," I explained. "Why would I apply somewhere else?"

"But what if you aren't accepted?" Mariam said earnestly. "I mean, I'm sure you will be, but . . . what if you aren't?"

"I'll get in," I told her, and I knew that I would. After all, I had excellent grades in my elite competitive Pakistani high school. I was an avid student and my marks and extracurricular activities proved that I was well rounded. And anyway, I *had to* get in because it was my destiny. So, no, I wasn't nervous. I knew it was going to happen. So as my friends were poring over SAT tutorials and admissions essays, I was cool as a cucumber. The place I needed to go didn't require test scores of that kind.

Though I'd sold my parents on culinary school, the principal at Karachi Grammar would not be so easily convinced. As a prestigious and rigorous school, the best students in each class regularly applied to and attended schools like Oxford, Cambridge, Harvard, Yale, Brown, Columbia, and the like. The notion that a student who got grades like mine and excelled in extracurricular activities would "waste it" on cooking school was horrifying to them. They equated all cooking with being a bawarchi, a low-income domestic staff cook. When they caught wind of my application plan, the principal's office reached out to my mother and summoned her in for a meeting. I met her in their office. The senior faculty were all within, lined up like a firing squad.

"Do you have any idea where Fatima is applying for university?" the principal began, assuming that my mother must be in the dark, as no parent in their right mind would allow this for a student like me.

"Yes," my mother said without missing a beat. "She's applied to the CIA . . . the Culinary Institute of America. She's very excited about—"

"What even is the *SEE-EYE-AY*?" a senior staff member snarled, cutting her off. "We've never even heard of it!"

"Please," my teacher pleaded. "With grades like Fatima's, she could go anywhere. She should be applying to Harvard,

Princeton, and Stanford, if she wants to be in America. She should get a proper degree. I'm sure she could even get a scholarship."

"Does her father know?" one of the committee members asked, pouring salt on an old wound, trying to sow doubt in the independent woman my strong mother had long since become. They were accusing my mother of not being a good parent, of not knowing what was best for her child. I braced myself, my palms sweaty and my fingers clenched at the seat of my chair.

"My daughter wants to be a chef and it's my daughter's choice," my mother said plainly. "It's an excellent culinary school and she has all of our support and endorsement."

There was a brief silence, in which you could almost hear the committee's disdain.

"Cooking is my daughter's calling," my mother continued. "So she's going to the best school for it so that she can learn to be the best at it."

My fingers loosened their grip on the edge of my chair. My mother had come to my defense. She'd shown those musty professors. As my eyes darted up at their sour faces, I wanted to jump up and down, maybe do a little victory dance, but I contained myself apart from a barely perceptible sly smile.

"Thank you all for your concern for my daughter's well-being," my mother continued, while gathering her things. "Fatima, come along," she said as she stood, nodded her head to them, and escorted me out of their offices with her arm over my shoulder.

"Thank you, Mom," I exhaled when we were outside the school walking to the car park and I could breathe again.

"You don't need to thank me, Tatu," she said, her arm still around my shoulders. "I knew from the moment you made us that Christmas feast that this was your calling. Promise me one thing, though."

"Anything, Mom."

"Promise me you will always do your best. There's no room for mediocrity if you are taking this path. Work your hardest and excel."

With tears in my eyes, I shook my head up and down enthusiastically, not sure if I would burst out laughing or crying as the words caught in my throat. "Yes, Mom. Yes, I promise."

PART II

chapter 17

A TASTE OF FREEDOM

———

Fatima

———

I N ORDER TO LEAVE PAKISTAN AS SOON AS POSSIBLE, I was going to have to be the best: top of my class in school, good at sports, a model daughter. At school, our teachers told us about the Global Young Leaders Conference, a ten-day program in New York City and Washington, D.C., that brings students from all over the world together to explore cultural differences, practice international diplomacy skills, and consider how to help shape the future. If I was accepted, it would offer the twofold benefits of looking great on college applications and giving me my first taste of freedom as a teenager in the States. I applied and was accepted and, hoping to make as much out of my adventure as possible, I asked my stepfather, who had lived in the States for many years and had a lot of connections there, to call in a favor to a friend who worked with Marriott hotels, and he managed to get me an internship in the kitchen at the Bethesda, Maryland, Marriott for right after the GYLC trip.

Everything about the trip was eye-opening. I met kids from Ghana, Sudan, Iceland, Australia. We were kept somewhat in check by the team of teachers' assistants who kept an eye on us, discouraging us from straying from the group, but, as always, I found ways to indulge in a little mischief. I was the only one with a fake ID. The friends I'd made on the trip looked like they were twelve, but with my broad shoulders and darker complexion, a little makeup went a long way and I looked like I was twenty-two. I've always known how to present myself depending on the situation, and although I am extremely goofy, I can also be very serious, matter of fact, and direct. This used to make people treat me as if I was older than I was. After we'd spent half an hour on the Empire State Building's observation deck peering down on New York City, I told one of the teachers I had to use the bathroom. But instead, I ran to the nearest deli and bought a couple of six-packs of strawberry wine coolers so that my friends and I could drink them before our final party, which was like a GYLC prom. I was pretty proud of myself for pulling this off and not getting caught. My friends were impressed and so was I!

At the party, Rihanna's "Umbrella" came on and I started showing off my dance moves, which I thought were pretty great at the time, as my friends shrieked and cheered, "Oh my god! There goes Fati!" I was dancing with this really hot guy, who it turned out was a TA and he thought I was one too, though of course I wasn't. I was just a seventeen-year-old Pakistani girl letting loose in New York City for the first time, really feeling myself. Somehow during dancing I learned that he lived in Maryland, right near where I was headed for my internship after the GYLC program, so at the end of the night, we exchanged phone numbers.

My internship in the Bethesda Marriott kitchen consisted of me following my executive chef around and doing whatever he asked me to do. I cleaned scallops and shrimp. I scrubbed carrots and peeled potatoes. It was actually far easier than I'd expected, because unlike in a real kitchen job, the executive chef didn't work me to the bone, so when he couldn't think of something for me to do or he simply didn't feel like teaching me, he sent me out to explore the city.

I was staying with Imtiaz's friend, and I don't know where I got the guts, but I somehow convinced the TA, who lived nearby, that we should hang out and go to dinner—that it was no big deal. A former wrestler at Notre Dame, he had piercing blue eyes and was kind of enormous at six-two. At a quintessential American chain restaurant, he ordered a huge plate of shrimp and I ordered curly fries. I felt myself making note of everything that was occurring, mentally zooming in on details, as if I were a film director controlling an audience's experience of a scene. Small gestures—the waitress nibbling on the end of her pen as she took our order, the wrestler scratching his stubble and reaching for his glass to take a long pull through the thick plastic straw, the sound of a child having a meltdown a few tables away—felt magnified and somehow significant, as if these details were being sewn together into a garment I'd always wear. There we were in this completely American environment—the land of enormous portions and sides; I was with an older guy (my TA!), and we were having a great time. But I couldn't help noticing that he was eating the whole shrimp, including the tip of the tail, which was obviously not meant to be eaten, and for some reason *the shrimp tail eating* was the part I was most incredulous of, watching as the small deep-fried translucent shells disappeared between his straight white teeth.

Afterward, he dropped me off a few doors down from where I was staying so that my stepdad's friend wouldn't see me get out of his car. We stayed in touch. I had only a few days left. I was almost done with the internship and then I was supposed to go meet my family in California. We decided to meet up

again. I told him I'd meet him on this dark corner, inconspicu-
ously, so I could jump in his car, because I was so nervous that
someone would see—that my stepdad's friend would see me get
picked up by a boy and then my mom would find out and forbid
me to come back to America, which was her main threat when
I was caught misbehaving.

We went to his house—a place he shared with a buddy,
which was of course really messy and quite gross because, well,
they're boys. He offered me a beer. We sat outside on his deck.
We talked. Then we started not talking. We were making out.
So far my only sexual experience was making out with a boy
from my class at an ice cream parlor in Karachi, and this felt so
different that it's hard to even use the same term, "making out,"
to describe it. We were alone with no prying eyes to stop or
judge us. He was a few years older than me and it was clear that
he knew what he was doing, which was a relief since I didn't
really. The touching, the kissing in private, the progression of it
all was what I'd sought out. I had absolutely orchestrated this, at
least as much as someone who doesn't have much sexual experience can. Eventually he said, "Are you sure you want to do
this?" And I said, "Yes." And I was sure: I wanted to know what
all the fuss was about. I wanted my first time to be on my terms
and it was, even if I fumbled a little bit. I had wanted this experience on my own terms and I got it.

Sleeping with this person was empowering because it was
something I chose: who, where, when. I told myself, *I am in
control. I am able to do this.* Sex with a man was supposed to make
me feel good. It was also supposed to help me seem less weird:
to show family and friends that I was normal, even though of
course I never planned to tell my mom. My mother certainly
wasn't in a rush to marry me off as my grandmother had been
for her, and probably didn't expect me to remain a virgin until

some eventual marriage to a Pakistani guy she'd approve of, but she didn't need to know that I was having sex with this dude in Maryland (or anyone, frankly). Some things are just better saved for downloading with friends.

I found it all pretty amusing: I lost my virginity to this white American guy in his messy bedroom in Maryland. It wasn't incredible, but it wasn't awful. Mainly I just felt relieved, like it was something I had to get through, like it was something I had to do just to move on to the next phase of my life. I knew my friends were going to freak out when I told them; that they were going to beg me for all the details. It's this thing that the world has put on females: getting our period, waxing, shaving, getting our eyebrows threaded, these rites of passage that girls must get through in order to be a woman. Losing our virginity is supposed to be this scary thing, a painful experience, and my feeling was mostly that I'd gotten through it, that I'd survived it and could move on.

I felt so trapped living in Pakistan, where everything was so conservative and considered taboo. I never felt like I belonged there. When I was offered a more open and accepting society, like in the United States, I wanted to take advantage, to take it in in huge inhalations. I wanted to breathe my liberty in deeply and live a little dangerously. I wanted to have these experiences so that I could take them home with me and keep them in a secret place inside myself to turn over and over again, memorizing their contours, reliving the details whenever I felt imprisoned.

chapter 18

THE BEGINNING OF THE REST OF MY LIFE

———

Fatima

———

I GOT MY WISH. I WAS ACCEPTED INTO THE CULINARY Institute of America for a bachelor's degree in Professional Studies. My mother, Imtiaz, and Bangu had moved to Islamabad for a year, and then Imtiaz wanted to explore real estate opportunities in Dubai, so I spent my senior year living with Nano and Sarah, as Mohammad and Saadia had long since left for university. My mom came back to help me get organized and to see me off from Karachi. A few days before I departed, I was sitting with my mom when she said, "I'm so excited for you and this opportunity that you're getting. I wish somebody had believed in me when I was your age."

It was a stark reminder of how lucky I was to have these options and not just be forced to marry or study something more traditionally acceptable that would funnel me directly into a more predictable and "normal" life.

"You are so lucky, Fatima, to get to go after what you believe in, your passion; you have to make every moment count," my mother said earnestly, somewhat wistfully. I wanted her to believe that I understood how lucky I was.

"Mom, I will never disappoint you," I responded. "I promise I will make you proud. I will not take this for granted and I understand what you're saying."

For weeks my mother helped me prepare, ticking items off the list that school had sent telling us about when to arrive and what to expect. We bought sheets and towels, laundered my favorite comforter, bought a brand-new computer, notepads, stationery, and clothes, and a first-aid kit. We coordinated with my father's nephew, Sibte, who lived in New York City, so that he would meet me when I landed, with an American SIM card for my phone waiting.

Nano has a travel ritual in which she makes you put your hand into a bowl of *aata* (flour) and then swirls some rupees over your head and says a prayer. Then she makes you kiss the Quran and go from under it through the door out to the car. The money and the flour are given away to poor folks who need it as a *sadka* (alms) for good energy to follow the traveler and protect them. I laughed with irrepressible glee as I bent beneath the Quran. Somehow this made it feel real: I was going.

My mother saw me off at the airport, managing to layer a brave smile over the flood of tears she always shed when saying goodbye to her children for an extended period. She handed me an English translation of the Quran.

"Don't forget who you are or where you come from," my mother said as she locked eyes with me—yet another layer of Mom: the serious, strong parent. "Don't get dazzled with American stuff. Have fun and enjoy yourself, but be responsible. Make friends, travel, and see the world. Soak everything in. Savor every moment." And then, her voice faltering, betraying a fragility she was adept at mostly keeping hidden: "Stay in touch, keep me updated. As soon as you land, give me a call."

"I will," I promised, as a response to all of her commands. And I meant it.

Twenty-four hours later, I landed at JFK with two enormous overstuffed purple suitcases. As I came out of customs, I picked out Sibte amid the sea of other brown faces who were holding taxi and town car signs, and he drove me from the airport to Penn Station, where I boarded an Amtrak train to Poughkeepsie. Outside the grand hundred-year-old Poughkeepsie Station, I found a Jamaican taxi driver to take me on the last leg of my journey. My face was pressed up against the window as I stared at this foreign landscape: a dingy, threadbare town obscuring the lush Hudson Valley around it, and then eventually the constellation of brick buildings of CIA's campus. When I paid the driver, I had a momentary impulse to hug him. This Rastafarian stranger had delivered me to the rest of my life. I was chomping at the bit to become the bawarchi my teachers had so disdained—only I was going to redefine what it meant to be a cook in Pakistan. I was going to become the first great and well-known Pakistani chef, a Pakistani Jamie Oliver, and that long-awaited "someday" started now.

All of the international students arrived a day early to get our bearings and begin to acclimate. There were 102 students in my year, and every three weeks, we changed classes from Butchery to Gastronomy, for example, or from Produce Knowledge to Kitchen Safety. The first day, while we were in orientation, the dean walked in and took over for a bit.

"If you're told to peel two pounds of carrots, what are you doing in your head?" he asked us.

"How can you make menial tasks—because you will be doing menial tasks all the time—how do you make them better?"

Everyone just kind of shifted around in their seats. I thought, *Everyone is either really dumb or really nervous.* I raised my hand and said, "All the things you could be cooking with carrots."

"Yes," he said. "Good job."

It was such a silly first question to answer, but somehow it was also completely fundamental, and the fact that the answer was perfectly obvious to me gave me an immediate sense of belonging. Of course then some dude had to raise his hand and say, *How big are the carrots?* And then another chimed in and said, *But what should I do with the carrots?* And then *What do I do with the peel?* And so on. I'd broken the ice and now my classmates weren't afraid to ask their rudimentary questions. The cadences of first days are the same everywhere, in all places for learning: feeling like a fish out of water, making tenuous eye contact with someone who might be your new best friend, wondering where the restroom is.

First, I learned about the classic French chefs of gastronomy. Next was Produce and Knowledge and History of Food. And then finally we got our hands dirty with Meat Butchering. I was always trying to look over Chef's shoulder to better understand their angles and technique. Some of my classmates looked like they might be sick when it came to whole-animal butchery, but perhaps thanks to those childhood market visits with Nano, when she chose which chickens would be slaughtered in front of us for our supper, I wasn't squeamish. I certainly wasn't thinking about the chicken's soul as I fastidiously butchered it in the requisite competition at the end of our butchery session. I was thinking about doing it with the same meticulous precision as my professor, which made the meat and skin and sinews appear to be made out of tissue paper and warm butter, so easily did they fall away from his worn but razor-edged chef's knife. I didn't win the race, as I was too consumed with accuracy, not just speed, but I didn't come in last, either. I was on my path, doing things my way: with exactness and care.

Home felt so far away, which I frankly didn't mind. I often called and messaged Mohammad, who was now in Australia. I'd barely seen him since he'd left Karachi for university there four years before. I'd send him slightly self-righteous recipes and instructions, like how to make the perfect risotto or how one should never season a steak with anything other than salt. I liked the feeling of building my knowledge base around food and wanted to show it off. In school, I learned about food science and Ferran Adría of el Bulli, his molecular gastronomy temple in northern Spain, where he manipulated ingredients into physical and chemical transformations. When I told Mohammad about him over Skype, he was incredulous. I sent him a link to Adría's liquid olive as an example. "That's an olive?!" he said of the spherical liquid pod that jiggled in a shallow spoon on YouTube. "Wait, what *is* that? Is that even food?" he asked, just as I'd hoped he would, sharing my awe and delight. We began keeping lists of restaurants all over the world that we wanted to eat at together.

During my first year at the CIA, I was mindlessly looking at a bulletin board between classes in the main building when I saw something that made me shriek with delight: A paper was posted on the board announcing that Martin Yan, Mohammad's and my childhood idol, would be coming to the CIA to give a lecture. I tried to explain the significance to my friends, how during my childhood, Pakistan only had four or five TV channels (one of which was fuzzy), and that Mo and I stopped whatever we were doing on Sunday mornings to watch when our dad called to us to say that Yan was on. Later, we had a black-and-white TV in our room and even with no color the food he would cook was incredibly eye-catching, and he cooked it with finesse and fire. It was seminal for me. He was my first culinary hero, and he was coming to the CIA! My American friends didn't know who Martin Yan was, but my Asian friends were, like me, ecstatic. After his seminar, my Japanese friend Aya and I got in line to meet him. We wanted more than a photo with him. At the end of every episode, he said, "If Yan can cook, SO CAN YOU!" which Mo, my dad, and I shouted in unison along with him. When it was our turn to meet him, we asked if he'd let us take a video, and sure enough, he said it: "If Yan can cook"—and we chimed in gleefully—"SO CAN WE!" It had the sublime feeling of a dream come to life and it gave me the audacious feeling that if I could meet Chef Martin Yan, what other childhood dreams could I manifest? It was intoxicating, the gutsy sense that dreams just may come true.

chapter 19

BLACK RICE, SPANISH MOON

Fatima

ONE OF THE MAIN REASONS I PICKED CIA FOR MY culinary education was because it offered students the chance to travel as part of their learning experience. I could select the wine country of Northern California, or a region in Italy, the epicenter of streamlined ingredient-driven cooking, or I could visit Spain, with its promise of endless tapas. I decided to go to Spain, in part because one of my favorite teachers was Spanish, and I'd become entranced with his stories of tapas and pintxos, Albarino and Sherry. Those YouTube clips of molecular gastronomy at El Bulli had stayed with me. I wanted to go to this culinary wonderland. My two closest friends from CIA, Aya and Sandra, were in agreement.

The three of us landed in Barcelona and hurled ourselves immediately into the bounty of the city, first visiting Antonío Gaudí's Sagrada Familia, which reminded me a bit of a drip sandcastle I'd made as a child on the beach in Karachi; we wandered through Parc Güell and rambled down Las Ramblas. We were out with faculty, one of whom was our favorite teacher, a

Spanish chef, and he guided us toward all the things we had to do and see, leaving our evenings free for us to eat. We went to Cuatro Gatos, the famous café that had been a home to Modernism thanks to regular creative patrons like Gaudí and Pablo Picasso, who had his first show there when he was seventeen years old. There was an energy to the room, a buzz and banter as if the air itself were alive—with the sounds of laughter, a story told in lisping Spanish, a fork crashing to the tiled floor, and the smells of jamón and fried croquetas and sherry that it carried. I'd always wanted to experience Europe; I'd tried to imagine the romance of its streets, the café society, energy, the people, and there I was, actually in it for the first time. There were a lot of tourists in Cuatro Gatos, of course, but no matter, we were all there for the history. We kept our ears cocked for the secrets the walls might share.

We ate pan con tomate, or pa amb tomàquet, as the Catalans call it in their indecipherable tongue. How could just four ingredients—tomato, olive oil, bread, and garlic, all so familiar and basic, be suddenly so exceptional, so bright yet rich? The secret, I learned, was the dash of sherry vinegar and salt, which turns up the volume on any flavor combination, but especially the sweet acid trip of tomato pulp. Fat sardines that tasted clean and fresh and briney and oily all at once sent me into a split-second reverie of my favorite books of childhood: I imagined one called *Fatima and the Sardine Factory,* where instead of chocolate the protagonist gets high on canned and cured Spanish delights that come in pretty little tin boxes. My brain was whirring, my eyes were watering, my gut was shaking with laughter, and I was signaling for another drink. Next, we tucked in to a whole John Dory, one of my favorite fish, seasoned perfectly, but so simple, with pristine grill marks that carried a message to me from the chef that said, *I've done this 20,000 times, and I welcome you, now stop staring and eat!* Cider, verdejo, and an espresso with a churro that left granules of sugar on my lips and chin as I ate it ended the meal.

It was late after dinner and we were full but invigorated. Aya was chomping at the bit, dying to explore, get out and adventure. Sandra had plans with a local and though the other students we were with were baffled, the three of us left the group. Who could resist being taken out by a local! That night we drank gin and tonics at a gin and tonic bar and martinis at a martini bar and did shots at a packed little place in Barrio Gótico. We rode our jet lag into the wee hours and then our friend's friend, the local, asked if we wanted to come back to her house for a snack. We all looked at each other and drunkenly screamed: "YESSSSSS!"

The house was fairly far up the hill to Gràcia and we walked, rambunctiously, weaving in the streets, drunk on our freedom as much as on the cocktails, so that by the time we arrived, we were even more famished than we'd been outside the cocktail bar. Within minutes of arriving home, she had the water simmering on the stove and sofrito, the Spanish equivalent of mirepoix, the flavor building blocks, warming in a pan, releasing its enticing scent of onions and garlic and peppers and tomatoes . . . punchy flavors united and tamed into dulcet ones by heat. I watched transfixed as she pulled a plastic sleeve of squid ink from the refrigerator, an ingredient so essential and commonly used there that it had been optimized into an accessible, easily purchased pouch, no squid or ink pod dissection required. We ate fideos negro, the palate-coating, unctuous take on paella with tiny noodles subbing for rice, sprawled out between the kitchen table, kitchen counter, and floor, smiling at each other through silky blackened teeth, gloating about what we'd accomplished: We were eating Spanish food in a Spaniard's kitchen in Barcelona! We'd won.

As I traversed Barcelona and we made our way northwest toward San Sebastián, I allowed myself to consider existential questions I'd been pushing aside in favor of the daily tasks of school and learning my craft. Long train rides and travels in foreign lands have a way of making you meet parts of yourself that have been hiding or ignored for long periods of time. Believe it or not, there was a part of me that had wondered if I wanted to remain front of house in restaurants, to be a restaurateur rather than a chef. I had begun to wrestle with whether the grueling physical labor while making crap money was really what I wanted for myself. Although I'd always known that I wanted to be a chef, it was on this trip that I challenged myself to know how firm my commitment was: Was I willing to accept all the hardships and the pitfalls in order to work toward my dream?

In San Sebastián, our group visited a cider house with a huge orchard. The proprietor was a short, squat woman with enormous glasses; she herself looked like an apple. She told us, through a translator, what it really meant to take something from seed and bring it to bloom, and as she spoke of the many phases of planting and pruning and harvest and fermentation, I realized that I wanted to be a part of that evolution too, that I wanted that satisfaction of having someone taste the process and appreciate the work.

At the end of every meal in Spain, we all laughed and told each other that we'd never be able to eat again, and yet after our stroll through the orchards, when it came time for lunch, we were starving, her stories having whetted our palates. We sat down to lunch at a long table in the cider house. She greeted us and then told us to fill our glasses, which we did, one by one, at a little tap attached to a barrel. The cider shot out with the conviction of a baby wanting to be born. We filled our cups and then got out of the way for the next person and the next until every last one of us had a glass of cider.

As she'd led us through the orchard, she kept repeating that it was very rude to hold a full glass of cider, that you only ever wanted half a glass. I suppose that having a full glass indicated to your host that you didn't like what was in your glass, so the idea was to always appear to be enjoying it. I could get down with this. On my way back to the table, I took a few gulps, just to be sure my glass was not at an offensive level of fullness.

The cider maker told us to toast by shouting the word "Txotx!" She said it means: *You can't drink alone—you must have family and friends to taste what you've created.*

"Txotx!" she shouted.

"Txotx!" we echoed back.

Finally, I had a chance to properly savor the slightly effervescent aerated amber liquid in my glass. It was sour, but not citrusy sour; sour like something sweet had decayed . . . like a cute little baby with fat cheeks who turns into a total bitch, but there's still something sweet about her—she still has rosy cheeks and a glow in the evening. The first course came: It was huge platters of walnuts that we had to crack for ourselves. These were walnuts from a paradise where not one could be bitter; you knew that the man who picked them knew the difference from their exterior shell. They tasted like cake and wood and endives and radicchio tops.

We followed our patron into the kitchen to see the next course being finished. I'm not sure what I was expecting, but I suppose after a couple of years in cooking school and lots of cooking-show-watching on TV, I had some expectations of what all professional kitchens looked like. I was so wrong. There was not one inch of stainless steel, no scrubbed shiny surfaces or fancy equipment. Here the walls and floor were concrete and, in the corner, a woman who looked like a nonna, a nano—a grandmother in any language—a comforting presence who will insist you eat more and more of the nourishing dishes she's been making, flawlessly, without a recipe, for years and years and years. This chef grandma wearing a dirty apron was working a charcoal rotisserie grill with two tiers of T-bone steaks. She glanced at us, noting our presence fairly ambivalently, focused instead on her T-bones. It's clear she'd been doing this her whole life.

This woman was not some tattooed, backward-hat-wearing douchebag from the south side of Brooklyn who is aching to make a point. This was a nonna who knows the temperature just by looking at a T-bone steak, perhaps touching it with one finger. She knew its readiness by its scent; she'd felt its sinews as she seasoned it. She knew the meat's contours and anatomy the way we know our lover's hands. Preparing meat this way was a daily practice. My mouth became like Niagara Falls. I ached to stay, but I had to return to my seat, from where I stared at the kitchen door, waiting to be reunited with my steak. And then it was in front of me, only salted because pepper would mask the flavor of the fat, of the meatiness, of what the red is supposed to taste like. There were no utensils, so we devoured it with our hands: tearing, munching, licking, you name it.

If cooking the holiday feast at sixteen for my extended family of sixty in Karachi had been the moment I could see and believe in a future in the kitchen, this private realization while surrounded by people at a cidery near San Sebastián vindicated my unusual choice. It made me want to work those awful hours, become a part-time scrubber, be the person who organizes a freezing walk-in when everyone else is long gone for the night. It just made me want to cook.

I'd been thinking about food that whole trip so far. Hell, I'd been thinking about food my whole life! But that old woman stripped away all the artifice for me and reminded me that what I loved was the craft. I knew that you could put that steak in front of any critic, any Michelin-starred chef (which is to say, the best chefs in the world), and their reaction would have been as ecstatic as mine. It didn't matter who was seasoning it or slicing it; it was just a plate of food that brought joy.

We'd been going to a lot of white tablecloth restaurants, temples to molecular gastronomy, and tapas bars, and of course I'd been living and breathing the tradition-based culinary classes back home at CIA. It was as if someone had been writing "food" over and over in minuscule precious cursive handwriting on thick embossed stationery, and then someone just scrawled FOOD across a tabletop with a Sharpie. It was pure and simple. This was how I wanted my food to be.

We weren't really supposed to hang out with the patrons, the chefs, but after our visit to the cidery, we went back to our hotel and cleaned up and then met up with our Spanish chef-teacher. Because he was a local he knew all of the pintxos places. You could walk from end to end of San Sebastián in an hour. The Atlantic Ocean waved to us the whole time. In the old city, there were these folkloric houses, unimaginable to live in. We went into a bar and discovered platters on display covered with pintxos—the little savory bites of bread and meat or marinated peppers or cured tuna all held together by a toothpick. No sneeze guards kept our suddenly salivating mouths from them— the health inspectors of America would have lost their minds. It was half restaurant, half bar . . . Why doesn't everyone make restaurants like this? It's what everyone wants!

The owner seemed to know our chef. Aya and I took two

plates and filled them with padron peppers, sea urchin toasts, tiny open-faced sandwiches of cheeses and meats. Everyone smiled at us, but not awkward smiles, not stiff or judgmental; their smiles were embraces, inviting us to eat their food. As I walked around with our Spanish chef and my friends, I noticed people staring at me. I guess it was a bit unusual to see a brown person wandering the streets of San Sebastián. Somehow the staring never felt objectifying or unsettling. Everyone's eyes seemed to smile at me, and several people even said, "Que guapo," which means not *How pretty* but *How handsome*. I loved that they found me attractive but used the masculine for me.

We tasted morsels of perfectly cooked octopus, tortillas, to-stadas with cured tuna and pickled peppers and cheese cro-quettes. We carefully took out the toothpicks and the bartender gave me a little pour of delicious Txakoli wine from a carafe with a spout. I choked a little of course, but I laughed more than I choked, and was so satisfied. Just the act of her pouring this slightly sparkling acidic nectar down my throat was so sen-sual, so indicative of intimacy and friendship, because who would do this for a stranger? That's how every gesture felt: fa-miliar and affectionate. That entire day made me feel like I be-longed.

The night went on at this delicious pace: Sip txakoli to wash down the pintxos. Nibble pintxos to stave off the tipsiness. I followed our chef-teacher, who had grown up in San Sebastián, around town to the next place and then the next. I was bone tired from a day of learning and tasting and drinking and then doing the whole thing all over again at nighttime, and I knew that we had a full day of more edible exploration tomorrow. The logical side of me said to go home and get some sleep, but the wild side of me told me that this was a once-in-a-lifetime chance—to follow a local chef through the San Sebastián night—and that the night was going to end up in some epic adventure, and it did.

Very late, we found ourselves in a new bar with lots of beers on tap that catered to tourists. A lot of these places that we went were "vertical not horizontal," with everyone standing side by side, pressing close and speaking into each other's necks and ears; the closeness meant you had to interact, though the local men only spoke Basque, not even Spanish, so I couldn't understand a word. But I knew, as one always does, that they were telling me how beautiful I was, talking with their hands and gesturing toward my face all night. The unmistakable look of appetite for beauty in men's eyes.

We hung out for a while with a few Basque guys, trying to chat with them through gestures and nods over the music and drunken conversations around us, before my girlfriends decided it was time to go home and left. I decided to stay out with the guys. Believe it or not they took me to another bar or two, though at this stage I was too full to eat or drink more; then we made our way back to their place. I can't even call it an apartment or house. It was a hovel, the grimiest, grossest version of a Basque guys' house imaginable.

I probably should have split, but I was so taken with the way they had been looking at me all night. I couldn't understand their words, but they kept communicating with their hands about my eyes . . . and my eyebrows. We got to their living room and one of the guys opened up the doors to a tiny balcony, over which hung this beautiful Spanish moon. They were musicians—I'd sort of caught that from some gesturing they'd done back at the bar, strumming imaginary guitars and such, and sure enough they pulled out instruments and started to play and sing. One played his txistu (similar to a flute) while the other strummed a guitar and sang glorious indiscernible words in a gravelly voice. We smoked a joint of Spanish hash and they serenaded me and their city under the yellow moon.

As they sang and strummed, I knew I was too tired to make my way back to my hotel and that I'd stay in this filthy den of the sweet young Spaniards. I'd miss the bus and our field trip the next day, but it didn't matter. I was having an adventure of my own. I felt blissfully alive.

chapter 20

A PERFECTLY
RIPE PLUM

——

Fatima

——

I'D HAD A BOYFRIEND DURING MY LAST YEAR OF HIGH school in Karachi. He was the type of boy who was perfect on paper: handsome, rich, from a great Pakistani family. If I'd wanted to stay put and have a predictable future set up for me like some of my peers, then he was a great bet, but that wasn't what I'd wanted at all. I'd known that I wanted out and that food was my ticket, and dating felt like doing something that was expected of me, like my O Level exams, checking an item off a list—like losing my virginity, getting it out of the way because it was looming. Losing it to that American jock in Maryland made me feel wanted and desired, but afterward a bit indifferent. But most important, it made me feel free.

While at CIA, I'd started dating a thirty-two-year-old man, Cesar, whom I met in our local bar. He was a former marine from the Dominican Republic who worked in Poughkeepsie as a security guard. Initially, I thought he was incredible, and I talked him up to my friends and family.

"He's so amazing," I told my mother of Cesar. "He's just so

special, so strong." (He was extremely buff, which I found novel and fun.)

"Okay," my mother said. "But what makes him *so* amazing, Tatu? Can you explain what he's like?"

That was a fair question, and I'm sure at the time I had an answer for it, but looking back, I cannot fathom what I saw in him. Perhaps it was how he looked at me, my reflection in his eyes. I enjoyed seeing myself through men's gazes as this young, exotic, ambitious force, but I can't say that I was truly engaged in my feelings. I was what we call a "dil pheyk" in Urdu: Romantic to a fault, I willingly tossed my heart irresponsibly into the grasp of others. Cesar was one of the many examples of my "heart-strong" tendencies, but everything felt different when it came to Laura.

Laura also went to CIA, but was a couple of years older and was finishing up her bachelor's degree in pastry just as I was starting mine in culinary science. Though nearing the end of her program, Laura planned to stay on with a job at the school and so would be on campus even after she graduated. Once I laid eyes on her impossibly attractive face, I seemed to see her everywhere. One day, I sat down with my friend Rob and described her, asking if he knew who she was.

"Yes," he said. "That's Laura. She's a lesbian."

"But not *really*?" I said, aghast.

"Yes, *really*," he said, laughing at me.

I couldn't stop thinking about her.

In Pakistan, sex—heterosexual sex—is taboo enough, something we are taught to do only with one's spouse. Homosexual sex is just not an option, so I was confused by my undeniable crush on her. I couldn't stop thinking about her. I had several sleepless nights trying to grapple with why I would be feeling this way.

Laura and I started hanging out among a group of mutual friends. At first, I tried to get to know her as a new friend would. She had been a model in Puerto Rico; she was very tall and androgynous with short hair and big green eyes. Just gorgeous. She was a baker. We walked together from one side of campus to the other; I asked her about herself, her family, her life before CIA. I didn't *think* I was flirting with her, and since I had never been with a woman, I figured she would know I was straight and see me as friend material. But as I began to get to know her as a whole person, with ups and downs and family baggage like the rest of us, my allegiance to her grew. Instead of making her less attractive, getting to know her made me long for her presence even more. My crush on her permeated all my thoughts, and I was losing my mind. One night at a party and after a few drinks, I danced flirtatiously with Binda, my best friend from childhood who had come to CIA a year after me to study pastry. I was hoping that it would get Laura's attention and make her jealous. I felt like a lunatic, but I couldn't keep her out of my mind. I sent Laura a cupcake necklace for her twenty-first birthday, which she evidently thought was the sweetest thing ever, and she asked me out on a date.

The first time we kissed, we were sitting in her car. It smelled like her, like terrible Juicy Couture perfume. I was talking incessantly about something silly, and she said, *Come here.* Like an idiot, I asked if she meant *me* . . . Who else could it be? I was the only one there. *Come here,* she said again. My heart was pounding and I leaned forward and we kissed. She had by far the softest lips I'd ever kissed, plump and smooth and made for kissing, like biting into a perfectly ripe plum. I felt my face flush and I had this feeling that I was supposed to be doing this, that I had been missing out on this for so long. If kissing her was what kissing was supposed to feel like, I should have tried this years ago.

The contrast of being with Cesar and then being with Laura was like night and day. Laura simply felt so right in a way that no one had before her. At first, I played it down to my friends and said that I was just bored, that men were assholes, that this chick was hot, but that was not the full story: I was in love with her.

While I was experiencing feelings like none I'd known before, Laura was going through a particularly difficult time with her family. I tried to be her rock, even though I myself felt completely blindsided by my emotions. We only dated for eight or nine months, but it was the most intense, heated, irrational, crazy, spontaneous love that I ever had. My first girlfriend. My first love. It felt like I was being dissected, like I was a foie gras being sliced and deveined with a paring knife. I couldn't stop crying, even when it was good. That first experience of love was so potent and intense that my senses and emotions could barely process what I was feeling. And underneath the excruciating ecstasy was the knowledge that I was engaged in something unacceptable to my culture and family. I knew there was no future in which I could share my love of Laura with the people I loved most, simply because she was a she. Eventually, I confided in a couple of very close old friends, including Binda and her sister Fatimah. Initially they reminded me of my own early excuses:

"You said this was 'just a phase,'" Binda echoed back to me. "That you were 'experimenting' . . ."

Being confronted by the white lies I'd told them made the truth all the more unmistakable to me: I thought, *I prefer women.* Hearing my own excuses made me angry and regretful, and the intensity of telling the truth made tears of love and relief stream from my eyes.

"No, I *loved* Laura!" I shouted at a bewildered Binda. "I was completely in love with her and everything else was a lie; it was me trying to convince myself that I was not a lesbian."

Binda was in tears too. They were also tears of love, but for me. I must have been quite a sight, impassioned by my first lesbian lover and the realization of myself to the point of crying.

"We're happy for you, Choti," my friends comforted me. "It's good you're being honest with yourself and that you feel clear."

They weren't surprised that it was a woman who had won over my heart. I suppose they felt it before I did. The friends who had loved me longest, without judgment, had known who I was maybe even before I understood it myself. And it hadn't fazed them one bit.

There was one caveat, though.

"Don't tell Fari Khala," they advised in unison, referring to my mother with the affectionate *auntie*. "Get comfortable with yourself before you tell your family."

My best friends reminded me of what I already knew: that I was my mother's pride and joy, the vessel into which she poured her dreams, by which she measured her own success, as a mother and as a person. My mother wanted what was best for me and for me to be the best, and instinctively I knew, as my friends did, that this did not include dating women. While she might not object to my being with a woman per se, her greatest fear was that I should be the subject of gossip and scorn, as she had been after her divorce from my dad, and what could be better fodder for gossip and judgment in a country where homosexuality is taboo than my preferring women? I knew my family would never approve of this part of me.

I desperately wanted to, but I avoided telling my mother and brother about this newly discovered facet of myself. It bothered me to not be entirely honest with them, but I tried to take my friends' advice, at least for the time being. I was exclusively with women for five or six years after that, and this freedom became linked to my staying in America.

chapter 21

YES, CHEF

———

Fatima

———

I MADE THE MOST OUT OF MY TIME AT THE CIA BY TAKING the initiative. I arrived early to class and left late, attended as many seminars as possible, focused on traditional techniques that, while seemingly outdated, helped to inform my skills. I was completely clear and committed to my future as a chef, and I loved learning and striving to be the best, just as I always had. But just as it had been at Karachi Grammar, being the best— winning—wasn't about beating others; it was about beating myself, transcending my own victories and accomplishments. Working hard and doing well came naturally to me, and it seemed like a waste of time to not do my best, especially since my goals were lofty ones.

While deciding to become a professional chef made me an outlier at Karachi Grammar, I was also a somewhat unusual case at the CIA. Many cooks find their way into kitchens after struggling with other professional paths. It's a select few of us for whom it's the first choice and therefore who invest in the education to the extent that I did, for a bachelor's degree. Additionally, there were relatively few who were privy to the quality of the education that I'd had at Karachi Grammar, and on top of that, I'd been a strong student who loved the challenges of school and homework. My peers from home were using the same education I'd had to do pre-med, to become lawyers, so I was set up for success in whatever I could have chosen to study, which in my case was culinary. With my ingrained study habits and genuine passion for the subject matter and where knowledge of it could take me, I was able to fully dedicate myself to school and to the work.

In order to graduate, all CIA bachelor's degree students must complete a mandatory externship semester. I'd lined up mine at Café Centro, the bustling French eatery in the MetLife building just north of Grand Central Station in Manhattan. The first day, as I walked through Grand Central Station, my palms damp, my mouth dry, I thought of what I might be walking into. I'd heard stories about male-dominated New York City kitchens. What role would my brown skin play in how I was treated? Would there be immediate disdain for me because I was Muslim?

My call time was one p.m., so when I arrived, everyone was already deep into dinner prep. I assumed I'd be peeling potatoes or chopping onions, typical first-day drudgery, but no: my executive sous chef handed me a hotel pan full of short ribs to sear for the evening's pot au feu special. With the hotel pan in my hands, Chef quickly introduced me to the team of cooks whose heads were down, focused on their tasks, communicating with their own language of grunts and tired inside jokes. By way of introduction to me, he shouted their names one by one, but the joke was on me: Each one was identified by a name that correlated to a barnyard animal . . . or maybe he just called them out by what they were prepping: chicken, piggies, moo cows, etc. It would have been funny if I weren't so nervous and already thinking about the short ribs I didn't want to screw up.

He gestured toward a station and I fell in line to begin my work, seasoning the short ribs as professionally as possible, trying to transport myself to the low-pressure zone of a classroom in Poughkeepsie. I knew how to do this. I knew I was ready. There was a part of me that felt fearless. Internally, I repeated a mantra: *I am not going to fuck up, I am not going to fuck up.*

After I finished searing the short ribs, I checked in with my sous chef to ask what I should do next. He gave me a look of barely veiled skepticism and walked over to examine my work. Using a pair of tongs, he turned over the ribs in the hotel pan, pressing them with a finger to feel how springy the meat was and hence how cooked they were; he sort of nodded to himself. Then he grabbed two bottles of wine and a half hotel pan of mirepoix (carrots, onions, and celery all cut to the same size) to which he added thyme, garlic, bay leaves, and salt and pepper. I remember wishing that I had enough time to pull out the little Moleskine notebook that I'd bought for myself as a symbol of preparedness for my externship. It was wedged into my knife kit, all fresh and clean and ready for notes on my new life, but in a real kitchen, there's no time for scribbling musings or even notes on how Chef navigates a simple task; there's only time for observing, memorizing, and staying alert. After he finished seasoning the mirepoix, he asked me to go get some beef stock from the walk-in and pour in just enough to submerge the ribs.

Alone in the strange cold cell, surrounded by containers marked with names and dates scrawled in Sharpie on blue tape, I allowed myself an instant to consider where I was. *This was happening: I was in chef whites in a walk-in refrigerator in a restaurant in New York City.* Then I grabbed two quart containers of beef stock, returned to the warm hive of action, and watched him cover the ribs with foil.

"Get someone to help you with this," the executive sous

chef told me. He was right: The hotel pan with the ribs, the two bottles of wine, and the beef stock was heavy and unwieldy, but who was I going to ask? I didn't know any of the crew's real names and I wasn't about to refer to anyone by a barnyard moniker. I chose the person who looked the nicest and had the sweetest face. He turned out to be pretty shitty and selfish once I got to know him, but on that first day, he helped me get the short ribs into the oven.

The rest of the day was a blur of people screaming and French onion soup. Finally, at the end of service, I sat down in Chef's office at the back of the kitchen with my quart of Coke that someone had handed me, like a lifeline, mid-service. At restaurants like that, ones that do an average of three hundred covers during a typical day, you don't have time to drink between the order fires, but if you don't hydrate you will literally collapse or cut yourself or, worse, screw up an order. A quart container of soda on ice will save you. Chef flipped through my externship book, a bit incredulously because there was so much paperwork that both he and I needed to fill out.

"Well, Fatima," he said, pronouncing my name with a thick French accent, "welcome to Café Centro. I'll see you tomorrow at one p.m."

Over the next three months I worked my way through the various kitchen stations. I began, of course, with garde manger, where I assembled cheese plates, shucked oysters, and organized seafood towers quickly to hit tables as the first course, as well as salads from my mise en place (prepped ingredients, such as chopped chervil, sliced shallots, brunoised pears), tossing and garnishing them à la minute (when each order was fired). Then I moved on to the hotline, supporting other cooks by working the fry station, finishing roast chicken simmering in jus and plating it with piped mashed potato.

Finally it was time for me to work the fish station, the apex of responsibility in a professional kitchen because the product is expensive and the easiest to screw up. Timing is everything with fish, and thirty seconds can make all the difference between just right or overcooked, crisp seared skin or gummy, tepid flesh. With fifteen minutes before service, I checked my mise en place: mushrooms for the trout, peas and tomatoes for the char, Jerusalem artichokes, capers, and leeks for the halibut. I looked up the reserve twenty times. I wiped down my station like a nurse sterilizing a patient so that the doctor could make that first irrevocable cut. My fingers were shaking, which I tried to hide by keeping them busy.

The cook with whom I was paired, Sam, came over and jovially, like a senior captain about to run a track relay with a freshman first-timer, asked, "Are you ready, buddy?"

I nodded my capped head.

"So you do sides, I'll do fish," Sam said.

I nodded again. My throat was dry. I felt as though I'd forgotten how to make a sound.

There was a shifting of energy, and for an instant it was as if the entire restaurant held its breath. Then on the exhale, the first ticket sputtered out of the printer. Dinner service began and we braced to begin the race.

"Order fire: chateaubriand for two!" Chef shouted out, and "Order fire: chateaubriand for two!" echoed back from the meat station beside me.

I mentally sighed: *It's not me.* Like a game of tag, I had to stay one step ahead.

The next ticket buzzed into our world like a prophecy, one that included the poached halibut with Jerusalem artichokes, leeks, capers, and jus. The cook coached me through it and we successfully put out a hot and beautiful plate, timed just right with the other entrées on that ticket. I felt elated, like I could walk on water, like I could fly, but only for a second. As the rhythm and speed of service increased, tickets began to fill the rail. Our entire plancha overflowed with orders and I started to lose count.

"Chef called for three halibuts. *What the fuck: I don't have three halibuts!*" Sam swung the lowboy (the undercounter refrigerators by our knees) open frantically looking for more raw fish. "Go to the back and check for more halibut!" he shouted.

On my way to the walk-in, I grumbled to myself, *It wasn't my job to count the damn fish. I was in charge of mise en place, not the protein.* When I got to the fish rack in the walk-in, there was no halibut to be found. I rushed back and informed the sous chef, who had stopped expediting and taken my place while I stepped off the line. Chef turned around and looked at me with a stare that could melt Medusa, pointing to the back prep kitchen. "Get the fuck out of here," he said to me. I blinked. I trembled. I did all the things you do when something bad happens so suddenly that you're tempted not to believe it's real. As I made my way out of the kitchen, I heard chef shout "Eighty-six halibut!" and the echoing back of "Eighty-six halibut" from the kitchen team and from the manager standing in the pass, and I swear I could even hear it reverberate throughout the dining room from server to server, my dirty secret that everyone knew in an instant.

There is no longer, more brutal service than one spent sitting on the sidelines. I waited out the next hour and a half of service, shaking, leaning on the railing outside Chef's office, where all the linen and checkered chef pants were piled up. My mind went into panic mode. *Am I about to get fired?* My externship was nearing completion, but I stupidly thought Chef and I had forged some kind of relationship, something slightly more substantial than just an executive chef and a stagière. Had I imagined approval in his eyes when I'd shucked those oysters so quickly and cleanly and trussed the game hens so tidily? Perhaps it would be worse if he *had* begun to see potential in me: the further I had to fall when I let him down, which surely tonight I had.

Finally, service was over. I hung my head, shamefully, sneaking furtive glances as the kitchen wound down for the night. Chef walked past me, entered his office and sat at his desk, lighting up his usual post-service smoke, and poured himself a glass of Pernod, which he cut with water. He faced me but stared at his computer, completely ignoring me. Then, when his cigarette was nearly burnt to the filter, he acknowledged me. I took the three small steps necessary to cross the threshold into his office and waited to be admonished.

"I should tell you to leave now," he said in a dangerously quiet voice. "I had to tell three tables"—he held up three fingers, as if I didn't know what three was—"that we didn't have their food tonight."

Silently he put out the cigarette and lit another one. I trembled, but in my head, I just repeated the words, *Don't cry, don't cry.*

I stared at a map of France that was posted on the wall behind him. Bordeaux was just above his left ear, so perhaps I would appear to be making eye contact if I kept my gaze trained on that word with a cluster of grapes beside it. Imagining a purple growth growing out of his left earlobe distracted me enough from my mortification that it kept me from crying.

"I'll see you tomorrow," he said. "These things happen. You've just got to learn from it."

He flipped his cigarette in his hand to motion that it was time for my exit before it got any worse. I left quickly, grabbed my things, and scrambled upstairs to the locker room. I felt relief. I felt like I was thawing out after being outside for too long on a cold Hudson Valley February day. But instead of warmth spreading through my fingertips and feet, what I felt was a sense of belonging. He didn't want me to leave this meticulous kitchen run by smelly middle-aged men, his kitchen family, of which I had become a part. I felt like a little girl—small, young, and foolish, but a little girl whom they had made space for, a little girl they wanted to keep.

When I got back to Poughkeepsie from my externship, I knew how to do way more than my friends, because I'd learned by doing while my friends kept to their knife cuts. I had heard that in most externships you're only allowed to peel and cut, but that wasn't what happened for me. Sure, I crumbled on the fish station—but I had learned a great lesson from that shitty service: It's not enough to just do what I am told. There's always more to be done.

From then on, I remembered to check and overcheck. I made sure the cook I was working alongside had enough product. Sometimes I sort of hid it, stashing extra portions for us as a buffer to make sure we had enough no matter what. What's wrong with protecting us a little? I made sure that even if someone else made a mistake, I could swing out another sheet tray, to always know before we ran out so that I could tell Chef, *Okay, Chef, we have five more halibuts all day before we are eighty-six,* or filet mignon, or whatever it was. I just made sure there was a contingency plan.

Culinary school gave me more confidence in my cooking skills and knowledge as well as a strong foundation, built upon by my externship at Café Centro. I knew how to make remoulade, hollandaise, bechamel; I learned how to truss and roast chickens. But there's no question that the best way to learn is to get in a working kitchen. Nothing prepares you for that rush of pressure. Once you get the rhythm of it, it can be almost fun, like in a Mad Hatter kind of way. When people are smiling, snickering a little bit, you feel like you're in sync. Everybody knows their part and is playing it. That said, a single kink in the chain can throw the whole thing off. But the days when things run smoothly are magical, and are often celebrated by the team with a good drink or two after service. Those are the days when you really feel supported, like you've got a kitchen family. And the comfort that comes with this sense of belonging trumps any aching shoulders, sore feet, chafed hands, and burned forearms.

On the day I graduated, as valedictorian, I sat among my peers in the sea of black gowns and awkward hats and I promised myself that I would never stop pushing until I could undo some of the wrongs I had felt plugged inside of my heart. I was born simply by luck, by the chance that God was feeling generous that day, to a Pakistani family of means and progression. I could have been one of those boys with bloated bellies and empty eyes on the road outside Ami's Paan Shop in Karachi. I could have been a girl without any ambition because it was simply not allowed to her.

I'd spent the last three years focused on learning—the foundation for my craft and future—and as I prepared to give my valedictorian speech, it struck me what a luxury that was. As a child, I'd sworn to myself that I'd find a way to help the hungry children of Pakistan. I'd promised myself that I would be their voice someday, and on that June graduation day, it was clear to me that I'd gotten closer to fulfilling my oath. With my education as armor, I needed to make my way into the world and figure out how to make it better through food. No more excuses.

chapter 22

THE UNPALATABLE TRUTH

Fatima

I'D VOWED TO MY MOTHER TO DO MY BEST AND TO BE the best, so graduating at the top of my class was fulfilling my promise. I feared that her reaction to my personal choices would be far more complicated.

My mother found out about me and Laura after we broke up. I was twenty-two. I was so emotional after having gone through that breakup—my first and with someone I loved. My heart ached unceasingly and I needed to talk to my mom; I sought her comfort specifically. I'd just returned to New York from being in Lahore for Binda's wedding, and I was Skyping with my mother who was in Dubai.

"I saw your Facebook post," she said to me, referring to something I'd posted about heartache. "Are you seeing anyone?" she asked gently.

I was nervous and knew that I was crossing a line that I might never be able to turn back from, but my feelings had been percolating for so long, my heart was raw from the loss of the relationship with Laura, and mothers are our original source of comfort and soothing. I wanted that from mine. I rationalized that my mother had been my greatest champion in terms of my career choice and my goals and ideas with my school. She'd not only allowed me to choose a professional path completely off the straight and narrow, but she'd advocated on my behalf to my teachers and for my father to support my culinary endeavors financially. Though I knew I was taking a great risk, I desperately wanted to share my truth with her.

"Actually, yes, I have been seeing someone," I began. "A woman. I like women. Mom, I'm gay."

I couldn't believe I'd said it. The instants that followed were loaded with fear and hope, in equal measure.

"Oh," she started. "Well, it's all right, these things happen. A lot of women go through this."

Was this really happening? I'd told my mother the thing I'd most feared sharing with her and she wasn't angry; rather, she was trying to understand. She *was* comforting me. She gave me examples of people she knew who had experimented with women.

"This feeling will pass," she told me gently.

"The thing is, Mom, I don't think that it will," I said.

At that moment, my sisters entered the room that my mother was calling me from in Dubai. My mother looked momentarily alarmed that they might catch wind of our discussion, so I explained:

"Don't worry, Mom," I said. "They already kind of know."

My mother's expression fell and her energy changed completely.

"What are you talking about? You told your sisters?" she said, suddenly flustered. "You shouldn't tell *anyone* about this."

My sisters, who had once excluded me, had long since become confidants, but apparently I shouldn't trust anyone with this information. From there the conversation spiraled uncontrollably.

"I never should have let you go to the States. Letting you go to school in America was a mistake."

I listened as if she was talking about someone else. At first I felt conviction, that I knew myself, that I knew my heart, but as she became upset and wagered the highest stakes over me—pulling me from my budding American life and taking me back to Pakistan—I began to question all that I'd felt certain of only moments before. I was heartbroken, this much was true. I felt a great sense of loss from the breakup and bewildered by my predicament—by even having had a girlfriend. As my mother's momentary support morphed into the threat of being pulled from my life in New York, I began to reprioritize things incrementally.

"I'm coming for graduation and then you are coming back home to Pakistan with me. We will find you a nice husband and you will forget this entire episode." She was resolute.

Internally, so was I: There was no way I was going to abandon the opportunities that I was only just beginning to carve out for myself by going back to Pakistan. My survival instinct kicked in and my recent heartache took a back seat to my eventual inevitable misery if I was forced to turn my back on the potential future that awaited me here in the States. The career I'd dreamt of and was moving toward, the independence I enjoyed in New York, the opportunity to succeed on the world's stage—these chances did not exist for me if I immediately moved back to Pakistan. To buy myself time, I promised to reframe how I thought about my relationship with Laura and got off the Skype call as quickly as I could.

My plan was simple: I decided to channel my energy toward

working hard for the rest of the school year, only a couple of months, and then find myself a good first job in New York City. Hard work was what I'd promised my mother, hard work was what had gotten me this far, and I hoped that if I made hard work my complete focus, the crux of that painful conversation and her threat to take me back to Pakistan would evaporate. I applied for an Optional Practical Training visa and for a job as a line cook at a restaurant called Vermilion, where a graduate of the CIA, Maneet Chauhan, was the executive chef. Maneet is also a brown woman, one who left the familiar cultural traditions of India to follow her passion for culinary to the United States. I got the job. I hoped that if I could create enough professional momentum that showed my commitment to my career and climbing the ranks, my mother would let me remain in New York.

My admission to preferring girls, however, would not be swept under the rug. My mother saw my relationship with Laura and my broken heart as proof that my childhood and teenage traumas—my parents' divorce and remarriages, my molestation and feelings of abandonment—were the sources of my low self-esteem and ongoing quest to be loved by the wrong people. She wanted me to heal the primal wound, to learn to build myself up and work on those damaged foundations, so that I wouldn't make choices that were sure to cause me more harm and continue the cycle.

My mother insisted that I start seeing a therapist to help me adjust my view of myself and to foster healthy decision-making going forward. Navigating one's sexuality can be complicated even in the most normative situations, but in my case it was tangled up in past traumas, our cultural norms, and my mother's and my intense relationship. My mother longed to shield me from the negativity and judgment that she'd experienced so harshly as a divorcée, and I was a headstrong twenty-one-year-old who knew her own heart . . . or felt she did, even when its whims sometimes changed with the seasons.

"You are not a lesbian!!!" my mother wrote to me. "Neither are you confused about your sexual orientation!! You are lost and confused as a person because of the baggage you are carrying, which has stunted your emotional maturity to grow up and understand your inner self . . . you suffer from extremely low self esteem . . . you actually have very little self worth and hence the need to seek constant attention and love, regardless, whether it is positive or negative, healthy or unhealthy."

There was some truth to what she said: Certainly my father's lack of consistency as a parent, Zaman's abuse, and Imtiaz's failure to acknowledge the abuse or apologize for it occurring at the hand of his trusted henchman contributed to my distrust and in some instances actual disgust toward men. But that didn't seem like the full story of my sexuality. There was a rightness that I'd felt being with Laura that was completely separate to any prior experiences. The curiosity about women had always been in me. It manifested in crushes on girls in grade school and my (utterly naïve) description of sex between girls in the slam book I got suspended for in seventh grade. It felt innate. But I was furious and I was determined to assert myself:

I know you're holding on to the fact that I was with men, but I did it because I so desperately wanted to be normal.

I am willing to do whatever you would like, simply because you have asked it of me. But you WANT me to want to "get better." If getting better means letting go of my low esteem and emerging a happy, independent person then yes I want to get better. But if you think that getting better means that I won't feel deep inside my gut

what I know to be true . . . then I don't think there is any
cure.

Part of me just wanted to be the daughter she hoped for—
the daughter that she needed—because that daughter would be
accepted and also allowed to continue on her path, her career, to
continue on with her dreams. Yet there was also a stubborn
voice in my head, a voice that I'd tried for years to ignore and
drown out. It was a voice that predated Zaman. It was a voice
that spoke in the accepting, affable tone that my oldest friends
had used when I'd told them that I was in love with a girl.

Mohammad and I spoke at length and he reminded me of
some truths I'd been avoiding in my response to my mother,
including that I was angry and lashing out, longing to prove a
point. I left the conversation willing to go to therapy, conceding that I had traumas to work through, but clear that I didn't
think it was going to straighten me out.

That's the thing about identity, isn't it? My preference for
girls felt like only a part of who I was, not the sum total of it . . .
yet, when I was told I could not be that slice of myself, that that
part of me was lost or broken or wrong, then that fraction became the whole. It became as essential and undeniable as my
brown skin, as my being Muslim, as my passion for cooking, as
my femininity, as my family. I am the sum of these things, but
if you try to take from me one tenet, I will fight as though that
piece of me is all that I am.

I think the reasons my mother listed for my "disorientation"
were ways she subconsciously felt she'd fallen short as a mother,
the traumas were things she felt responsible for. All the guilt
and failure she carried with her as a parent were manifested by
my preference for women, as if it was her punishment.

"I believed in you," she said. "You talk about how broken

you are because you have hurt some girl who you just met for a few months. How little you understand of what you have actually done to hurt your mother. This has to be the worst ever in my life. I trusted you and gave you every opportunity that was possible so you could pursue your dreams and passion because you convinced me to allow you this opportunity and that you will never let me down. You betrayed my trust."

My sexuality, or rather me being judged for it, was her badge of shame.

Saadia, Sarah, and Mohammad were expected to bear some responsibility in sorting me out too, but apart from checking in on me every once in a while, what were they supposed to do? They certainly weren't going to convince me of anything, or even try to. It eventually dawned on my mother that no modern-day New York City therapist worth their weight was going to try to "fix" my sexuality—help me work through childhood trauma, sure, but straighten me out? Not so much. While America is far from perfect and has more than its fair share of bigots, New York City is a mecca of acceptance and individuality, a melting pot of identities who fly their freak flags proud and high.

When my mother came to the CIA for graduation—and, theoretically, to take me home to Pakistan—I broke the news that I'd already lined up a job and an apartment in New York City. *What was the point of CIA if not to use that knowledge in the real world?* I pleaded. I begged her to let me have one year in the city getting experience working in restaurants and I made it a fight for my professional dreams rather than an issue focused on my sexuality or freedom. I also promised to do everything I could to "fix myself," as if I was flawed or broken, a chipped porcelain cup, in order not to let this opportunity go to waste. It was an act of self-preservation.

My mother had a tendency to react badly to situations that triggered her, and then swing back to being the more open-minded, modern woman I saw her as, and I prayed this situation might be like that. Indeed, she eventually acquiesced and allowed me to stay in New York, but with an enormous qualification: She was moving to New York to be with me.

chapter 23

THE WOMAN I MADE

———

Farezeh

———

ON THE CUSP OF HER GRADUATION FROM CIA, I LOOKED at Fatima, who despite being the portrait of a strong, focused, persistent, and tough young woman, was emotionally very vulnerable. I knew how trusting she was and how she assumed the best of everyone around her. It was easy for her to fall in love, and I believed it came from insecurity, and a hunger to be loved and embraced.

There were so many traumatic events in Fatima's life that would leave an impact on anyone in her position. There were times during her childhood when I was unavailable to her—whether it was because I was tending to my sick brother, or because she was at CIA, or because I was in Dubai with my husband. So much had changed, so many new people had joined each of our lives, and somehow the distance between us grew as she let go of my hand. I decided I was going to make her my sole focus. I was again peering at her through the ICU window as a baby. I was going to hold on to her. I was not going to abandon her—a pattern that too many people in Fatima's life had repeated, whether it was her father, my own diverted attention onto Saadia and Sarah, then later onto my brother and mother, and even Mohammad's adolescent aloofness, which must have sucked so much confidence out of her.

Fatima was always so sure that every person she was with was The One. From what I could tell, she dove headfirst into these relationships and turned them into mythological mountains and miracles. There was a predictability to how she built up these characters she was seeing, these model humans who ticked all the right boxes, and after a few flops, we had started greeting her sweeping descriptions with some polite skepticism. The important thing, I rationalized, was to bring her to a point where she was sure and uncompromising about how she deserved to be treated, so she didn't feel like she needed to fill the space occupied by various people she loved and trusted but who eventually abandoned her, leaving a void. She was worthy, she was brilliant, she was a superstar, and she didn't need to seek this out from anyone.

When Fatima told me she was in love with a woman, all I saw was a gaping void she was trying to fill. And I felt like anyone who would say and do the right things to and for Fatima would be welcomed into her life and positioned as a permanent fixture, no matter how ill-suited they were for her. As she tearfully told me over Skype, all her trauma came to the fore and the uncomfortable realization dawned on me—how could anyone experience the things that Fatima had and remain emotionally healthy?

Maternal guilt set in strong, and began to ravage my insides. I felt wholly responsible for allowing her to get to this point. My choices, neglect, and distracted gaze had led Fatima to a place that was unhealthy for her, and any relationship springing from those roots would surely be doomed to fail and cause her more harm. The pain I saw in her eyes from this relationship breaking down made me flash back to all of the times she must have felt this, felt abandoned, or rejected, or some sort of failure she may have internalized. I would not have that for my daughter and Fatima was going to get the help she needed to fortify herself. She was going to set her broken emotional bones right.

But until she was in a healthier place emotionally, I did not want people to know—loose lips might cause further damage, unwanted attention and judgment that would threaten what I believed to be her vulnerable state even more. Unfortunately, I couldn't prevent this, and when the knowledge fell into the hands of those who did not have Fatima's or my best interests at heart, it was weaponized and used against us. That Fatima failed to see this inevitability only frustrated me more: She lacked perspective, maturity, and good judgment. And I needed to intervene and get her to where she needed to be instead of where she was.

Perhaps I was projecting, but Fatima becoming the subject of gossip and ridicule triggered every protective instinct I had. I had been intimately undone by gossip, from the moment my father died through to the time I left my husband. I have seen what it can do, the decisions it can drive us to make. And while I knew Fatima thought she had skin thick enough to survive it, I was not going to let her unclothe herself like this.

My plan was to bring her back to Pakistan after her graduation from CIA. I sensed that she'd not been ready to leave the nest in the first place, and was at risk of getting lost in the jungle of New York City life. Fatima, on the other hand, had already set up a life for herself: a job and an apartment.

And then, through my fog of concern and anger, I remembered my time in Austin. If Fatima had to work on her self-esteem, there was no better opportunity than to become her own person in a city where it was only possible to make it if you had the tenacity and drive. I would not deprive her of that, knowing what it did for me.

So I changed course: I came for her graduation and brought her eleven-year-old brother Bangu with me, and stayed on with her in New York City for six months, helping her set up her own little place and find her rhythm in this bustling, mad metropolis. We three lived in a small one-bedroom in a four-story walk-up on the Upper East Side.

It was my first experience of my daughter as an adult, of witnessing firsthand her commitment to her craft and professionalism, her deep love for what she did. She got up to go to work before dawn. Every night at midnight I called her to see when she would be home and she said, "Mom, go to bed. I have to close up." She'd get home at one in the morning, then leave again at seven a.m. I'd visit her in the afternoons sometimes when I knew the restaurant wasn't busy with lunch or dinner service, and Fatima was so serious, so intent on what she was doing, she'd give me a quick hug and then shoo me away.

It was so clearly Fatima's destiny to become a professional chef, and I encouraged her and supported her culinary education, but it dawned on me as I waited up for her at night or heard her tiptoe out while I was still sleeping that I'd had no idea what that really meant—what the life of a professional chef looked like. The hours on her feet, the backbreaking work in scorching kitchens, the machismo and hierarchy she had to climb through on her way up from the bottom. I had understood none of it. Perplexed, assuming she was working that hard for the income, I offered her money, but she refused. It was autonomy she wanted: freedom and respect.

Although I arrived in New York intending to bring my daughter back with me to Pakistan, I saw that Fatima was thriving despite the long hours and physical exhaustion and the daily challenges of beginning a career. And the city was seducing me as well. New York is a heady drug. Bangu and I would walk every day for blocks and blocks, finding snacks to eat at hole-in-the-wall restaurants. Every time I took its energy in, I understood why Fatima wanted to be in New York. I completely got why she was smitten with her life here. It was positively riveting in comparison to what she would be able to do in Pakistan.

I told my husband that I thought the best thing he could do for Fatima's sisters was to send them to New York for graduate school. I wanted this sense of opportunity and accomplishment for them, too. We didn't have a lot of money, but Fatima had her apartment and that meant the girls could all live together. I knew that if they stayed in Karachi that they'd soon be married off, in keeping with the indelible pattern of things. In New York they could all hustle and find their respective ways; it would be good for them to feel independence, to learn more about themselves and this world. To be the women I knew they were meant to be.

chapter 24

CHICKEN INTESTINES
AND PROCLAMATIONS

—

Fatima

—

AFTER MY GRADUATION FROM THE CIA IN 2011, MY mom and I signed a short-term lease on the Upper East Side for the summer. Then, in the fall after Bangu left, Saadia joined us in New York and the three of us lived in a 475-square-foot one-bedroom on Thirtieth and Second Avenue in the Kips Bay neighborhood of Manhattan. It was a quintessential New York first apartment—fourth-floor walk-up with a mice infestation—but less typical was that as a young college grad, I was living in my tiny New York apartment with my mom.

My mother and I slept on cheap futons in the living room, the type that folded down the middle like tacos and became sofas during the day—and Saadia slept in the tiny bedroom. It was intense living in such close quarters with my sister *and* my mother and also when my mother returned to Pakistan and Sarah took her place. Our proximity echoed the early years of my mother's second marriage, when Saadia, Sarah, and I all shared a room. Thankfully we three sisters had grown up quite a bit since then. The days of mean taunts and exclusionary conversations between them were long since past. I was happy to help Saadia get a part-time hostessing job at Vermilion, where I worked, which kept her busy along with her studies, and show her the ropes of the city that I already felt at home in.

For my part, I dove into my line cook job. Chef Maneet Chauhan had opened Vermilion two years before in Midtown and the CIA had flagged the opportunity for me, because Maneet was also a graduate. I'd done my research: Maneet, an Indian-American from Punjab, was twenty-seven when she landed her first executive chef gig at Vermilion in Chicago; that was only five years older than I was when I walked into the kitchen of Vermilion's New York location for the first time, straight out of school, ready to take on the world. At this point, Maneet was about thirty-five, enough older than me to inspire awe and idolatry from afar, but the moment I walked into her kitchen, I felt supported in my learning and safe to ask her anything. Chef often walked around with a smile, but she led her kitchen team like a heroic general and cussed like a sailor, a particularly appealing combination in someone who was six months pregnant. I adored her immediately. Whenever I went to her with questions or curiosity about a process or an ingredient, she made the time and space to answer every one of them and to teach me. I think she saw something familiar in me: I, too, was a brown girl who had chosen a less-traveled path into the kitchen. We had both opted for culinary school over traditional degrees. I think she saw my determination and ambition, which made me the first one in before service and the last one out, departing with exhausted satisfaction. The first three months were exhilarating—glorious, mind-bending days when my legs shook from fatigue as I climbed the stairs home and I fell asleep writing notes to myself in my Moleskine notebook, trying to safeguard the day's lessons before, after a few hours sleep, it all began again.

I actually saw more of Saadia at work than I did at home, since it was at work where I spent most of my time. I'd been hired as both a sous chef *and* the floor manager, so I spent three days up front and four days in the kitchen. I was doing seven-day weeks, fourteen-hour days. While I was theoretically happy to learn more about both "front of house" (the restaurant positions that interact with guests, such as servers, bartenders, and managers) and "back of house" (the kitchen positions, like sous chefs, line cooks, and dishwashers), there was a problem: The general manager seemed to have a vendetta against me from day one. He followed me from station to station, from the prep kitchen into the walk-in, from the host stand where I checked the reservation books back into the kitchen, badgering me and bullying me, trying to get inside my head.

During culinary school, when Binda had been doing her externship and had struggled with a superior at work who gave her a hard time about everything, she'd come to me.

"I don't know why the head chef hates me so much," she'd said through tears.

"It's not personal, Binda. You can't let it get to you or get you down. Instead, just try harder. Prove to the chef that you are more committed, more passionate, more hard-working. Force her to teach you," I told her.

I recalled this conversation with Binda when things were bad at Vermilion and truly tried to take my own advice, but to no avail.

Three months into my time there, when Maneet left for maternity leave, the GM's harassment became unbearable. I reported him and he was immediately fired, but the environment was tainted for me and I wanted to move on and start fresh. I wasn't going to let that experience break me, but I also wasn't going to wallow in a place that had become sullied. I wish I could say that my five months at Vermilion was the last time I saw aggression or men in positions of power abusing subordinates, but in our industry, of course it wasn't.

Maybe it was some leftover rebellion from having been bullied as a kid in Texas, or perhaps it was the whiff of similarity to the subjugation of women in Pakistani society, but I simply wouldn't take it in my new life. From that point, if things got ugly, I just quit.

I found out they were hiring at Café Centro, the restaurant where I'd done my externship during culinary school. I jumped on the opportunity to work under Chef Jan Hoffmann, who ended up not only hiring me as a junior sous chef, but encouraged Patina Restaurant Group to sponsor my visa, which they did.

About a month into my new job at Centro, the chef de cuisine quit suddenly, so as a twenty-two-year-old sous chef, I quickly found myself in charge of the whole place. I worked breakfast, lunch, and dinner, and catered VIP holiday parties. I would get home from dinner service at one a.m. and then wake up at four for a private breakfast event. I worked sixteen-hour days, wedging in a drink with friends after a shift, coming home after my family was already asleep and leaving for work before they were awake. I was very casually seeing someone, which was tricky while I was living with my mother—but my total focus was on my career. The priority was strictly to gain more real-world kitchen experience and confidence, to climb the ranks. But I also tried not to lose sight of my wider goals.

In Pakistan, I'd spent all those afternoons watching cooking shows, dreaming of someday having one of my own and creating a platform where I could make an impact. It was obvious:

The more famous one was, the more money one made, the more good one could do, and there was so much work that needed to be done, so many hungry bellies to feed.

But no one was going to "discover" me in the sub-basement of a restaurant kitchen, so I knew I needed to be proactive, to "get myself out there," and creating an on-camera experience felt like a logical first step. A chef I was working with at the time encouraged me to apply for the Food Network competition series *Chopped,* and I pored over the application with my mother's help. It was a good thing she was a pusher too, or else perhaps I would not have had the courage to go for the interview.

They immediately accepted my application and invited me to participate. My mother was almost as excited as I was, and on my day off took me shopping for new clothes and makeup to wear to the shoot. In each episode, four contestants are given a box of ingredients they must use to create a dish under intense time constraints, and then the dish is judged by a panel of well-known chefs. At twenty-two, I was the youngest competitor of the four. I had graduated from the CIA just eight months before we shot it in the winter of 2012.

When I found out that I was selected to compete, I felt such pressure to win, not because of the $10,000 cash prize, but because of the validation. Winning would be tangible proof that I wasn't crazy to pursue my culinary dreams. It would show my friends and family and all the folks who had encouraged me outwardly but inwardly thought, *She'll never make it big as a chef,* that I was on my way. The day of the filming for the show, my stomach felt like lead and my fingers shook. After the show aired, people often told me, "Fatima, you looked so confident and beautiful! You were made for television."

Little did anyone know that I retched in the bathroom for fifteen minutes before the first round, hoping I would somehow regurgitate the brick I felt in my gut. I didn't want to win simply for the sake of winning, or the money, or the recognition. The stakes were far bigger. I knew that countless Pakistani girls were questioning their futures or inwardly railing against what was expected of them, and I wanted them to know that a little revolution is possible, that we girls, too, can find our own way. The more accolades I could achieve, the likelier it was that I'd be able to stay my course and continue my career in America, where everything was possible: the restaurant dream, the TV show dream, all of it.

There were moments of serenity during the chaos where I did what I do best: I cooked like a Pakistani, reaching for that cardamom, the chilies and cloves and ginger. That's who I am. And that is what saved me. Despite my determination, I gave far from a flawless showing when it came time to compete. For the first course, forced to create a dish using chicken intestines, I made a spiced chicken intestine purée with miso-clementine braised cabbage. It was innovative and tasty, but it was, well, gray. We eat with our eyes, so the ideal color for food is *not* gray. Gray is *not* good. For the entrée we had to use duck breasts, Malabar spinach, cherry cola, and olive loaf. Olive loaf is somewhere between bologna and meatloaf. It's cured pork and beef with pimento peppers floating around in its gelatinous jiggly pink matter. As a Muslim, I can't eat pork, so I couldn't even taste the product and had to use my sense of smell and take a leap of faith: *What's unanimously delicious?* I asked myself, using my instincts and common sense in a tricky moment. *Fresh fried croutons are!* I decided to turn the olive loaf into pan-fried croutons, which the judges unanimously loved, but my sous vide duck breast was flawed, with a thick layer of fat that I didn't have time to sear off, and I thought for sure this would be my downfall.

When the judges asked me why I wanted to win, I surprised myself by tearing up. "I've traveled so far," I began. "It would just be a huge stamp of approval. It would mean so much."

My meal was far from perfect, but because we were all flying by the seats of our pants, I managed to pull ahead of my cocky competitor to a first-place win!

After filming was complete, the first thing I wanted was to call my mother, who had returned to Pakistan and was waiting up on the other side of the world to hear how it went.

"Hello? Tatu?" I could tell she was trying not to sound too anxious.

"Hi, Mom," I began, wickedly making my voice crack as if I was on the verge of tears.

"Oh my Tatu, did it not go well?" my poor mother began without missing a beat. "Don't worry, Fatima, it's okay, it's all right . . . All that matters is that you tried your best, you should feel proud about that . . . These things happen, it's no big deal."

I couldn't contain myself any longer. I began to laugh. "No, no, no, I *won*, Mom, *I won*! I did it, I was the winner!"

My mother screamed—at having been pranked, with joy at my having won.

"Oh my god, Fatima! I knew you'd win. I knew it!"

She was so proud that she called everyone she knew to tell them, starting with my siblings, and one by one I got congratulatory texts from them.

Over the following days and weeks, I reflected on the intensity of that day. Competing for myself was a strange notion after being in a kitchen environment where I was trained to be part of a team, rooting for everyone around me to succeed.

Suddenly I'd been in an each-chef-for-themselves environment. With my imperfect performance, the only way I could have won was if my competitors stumbled, and I'd so longed to win that I'd found myself hoping they'd screw up. I was not proud of this.

I cannot say if it was mere luck or my ambitions that allowed me to win *Chopped*. Perhaps a bit of both? As a winner, I was automatically invited back for *Chopped Masters*. I was the youngest person to have ever won the show, but I was also the first Pakistani chef—non-American, brown, and Muslim. These are layers of myself that I didn't necessarily lead with in the kitchen, particularly not at twenty-two, but even on a short show, these facets of me were undeniable. I was reminded anew about how food can tell a story and how I wanted to be the best storyteller I could be, how I wanted my "story" to reach the most possible people so that Pakistani cuisine and culture could begin to be reframed. I believed that I could get people's attention through my food, use their taste buds as a way in—because who can be fearful or judgmental when they are eating fragrant biryani or mutton korma?—and make them connect to an unfamiliar culture they'd been taught to fear. Then I could change Western minds about Pakistan. I itched to be a part of that process and instinctually, I felt this was why I had gravitated to becoming a chef. It was never *just* about the food for me. I thought the food was the tip of the spear and that it could lead to immeasurable change. I also found my suspicions had been correct: I loved being on camera.

There was a swell of national pride based on my winning *Chopped,* and I got some press back home. A lot of Pakistanis started to follow my career a bit more closely, and the *Lahore Sunday Times* invited me to write an essay for them. Titled "The Belly of the Beast," it was about how the hunger and poverty of my nation inspired me to try to help people through food, to feed those in need, to inspire young girls to push past their societal limits. It ended with this:

> In the next few years, I hope to take Pakistani cuisine to a level of sophistication it has never been exposed to before. By introducing myself and my country to the world in another light is all I hope to achieve. We are, as a nation, known for a great many things—some good and some bad, but never extraordinary. One day that will change, and I'm not silly enough to believe I can achieve that single-handedly. I'll need a little help from my friends . . .

I forwarded the pieces in the *Times* and the recent segment of Voice of America in which I was interviewed to my family. One by one they congratulated me, and then, one by one, they reminded me to stay humble. The *Chopped* victory hadn't been easy, but I still wanted them to see proof that all the sacrifices they'd made on my behalf had been worth it. I wanted so much for them to be proud of me, to validate my choices and hard work, but, as usual, it seemed that there was more I had to do to win their confidence. When Mohammad and I next spoke I could hear the pride in his voice when he told me how happy he was for me.

"Thank you," I began, but unable to keep anything from my brother, I continued: "I feel like everyone reminded me to stay humble," referring to the family emails that he'd been copied on.

"We all just want you to be happy and stay focused on what's important, which is your craft," my wise big brother explained. "Don't let the media attention go to your head."

I wanted to argue and say, *I'm not! I would never!* But I knew there wasn't any point. Mohammad knew me better than I knew myself, and he was right that I relished the attention. I craved the validation—even from the faceless masses—telling me how talented and interesting I was. A predictable reaction to having a detached dad? Probably. Unsurprising from the daughter of a distracted mom? Possibly. These thoughts ran through my head in the silent beats on my end of the phone as I absorbed what he said from my apartment in New York.

"You're doing so great, Fati," he encouraged me from the other side of the world. "Just stay focused on your craft and the rest will fall into place."

chapter 25

THE PECKING ORDER

———

Fatima

———

BACK AT WORK AT CENTRO, I GOT ATTENTION BOTH positive and negative thanks to my *Chopped* win.

From my subordinates, it mostly meant I commanded even more respect. Chef Jan was supportive and participated in the interview for Voice of America. The HR department sent me a congratulatory note from the executives of the company. It felt good to be noticed and told that "the team was proud of me," though unfortunately the sentiment was not universal. One sous chef in particular treated me differently after *Chopped*.

"Chef Fati, can I have a quick word after service?" the new chef de cuisine asked me one day.

"Of course," I said, as an ominous feeling lurked.

"Marisa told me the walk-in was a mess when she arrived for dinner service after your shift last night," the CDC began in his office a few hours later. "And that the buvette steaks were not properly prepped out. I've never got a complaint before about how you've left things after your shift, so wanted to check in."

I was stunned, speechless for a moment. I would never leave

the walk-in in a disorganized state. It was one of the last things I checked before I clocked out. I was religious about it.

"I'm not sure what to say," I stammered. "I checked the walk-in and the freezer about four forty-five, before I left, like I always do, and everything was super tidy, labels out, first in, first out, as it's meant to be. Are you certain Marisa was talking about yesterday after *my* shift?"

Chef paused, shuffling some papers on his desk. "Maybe I misunderstood," he then said.

Our eyes met. His gaze was steady without an ounce of doubt or disapproval.

"Forget I said anything, Fati," he continued. "You know, you've just had a great moment in the sun, and sometimes the shade can feel even cooler after that moment passes. Let's assume this issue won't come up again, and leave it at that."

"It definitely won't happen again," I started, "because it didn't even happen this time. I know I double-checked the walk-in and I did the buvette steaks myself—"

"Seriously, let's forget it. I have a hunch that this is a misunderstanding."

That's one way of putting it. I'd later learn that Marisa, another sous chef who was a few years my senior and had been at the company for a long time, had been talking smack about me to anyone who would listen. Being given a hard time by a man is one thing. It's a bore, it's pathetic, it's frustrating. But being put down by a woman hurts in a whole different place. There's no more awful feeling than when women make it seem like there's only enough room for a few—that fierce competition among women to be "The Woman," or "The Best Woman." Thank god I only experienced that occasionally. Usually it was *We are going to do this thing together, work together, rise together.* Then when *We* helped each other out during service, *We* went out to celebrate after, and it was all love and support. There's nothing like that feeling of women holding you up, knowing that they will catch you if you falter.

After a monster of a service, sometimes we would go out together to blow off steam, to drink beers and eat french fries and laugh. When I swapped my kitchen whites for street clothes, I encountered another strange dynamic. Without my minimizer sports bra, with a little bit of lip gloss, in tight jeans and with my hair down, I suppose I appeared to be a different person entirely, one that surprised my colleagues. Released from my uniform, my male colleagues sometimes uttered in disbelief that I was beautiful, something they admitted they'd never realized in the kitchen. Suddenly I was noticed as an *attractive* woman, perhaps even a romantic or sexual prospect, which could change how I was treated at work.

I squashed my femininity because I felt like if I could be one of the guys—that if they didn't think that I was sexually available—then I could just be present and do the work. Cooking culture has long been associated with masculine energy: being a little bit tough, highly confident. Being short with someone when you speak to them and being assertive are widely considered to be male traits. Traditionally, to be feminine is to be quiet, introverted, softer, empathetic, and understanding. My question is, just because someone has these characteristics, why does it make them automatically more masculine or feminine? It shouldn't. It doesn't. The classification is what I disagree with. Just because I'm assertive, I'm not any less female or any less a woman.

These are all social constructs—wearing dresses and makeup, having a certain career path mapped out for you, behaving in a way that aligns with your gender—and you have to fit into a bubble in order to make sense; otherwise people won't be able to justify you, to understand you, to put you safely in your box. I can't pretend that they don't exist here in America too, but they are even more unyielding in Pakistan. There have been so few who really challenge the "norm." I think it's completely ridiculous, because more and more people are blurring those lines, breaking down social constructs and throwing them away, so that individuals are beyond definitions, so that they are just themselves, but that's not happening as much in Pakistan as it is in the West. There's still such enormous pressure there to live within the lines.

I've felt this way ever since I was born, which is why I felt I could no longer live in Pakistan. I love my country. I love my family, our traditions, and the generosity that pervades our culture—of feeding, of family, of caring for each other—but I don't belong there because I want to live outside the lines, outside the easily defined. And this push-pull, this vacillation lives in me constantly, as I try to be true to myself and loyal to those I love and the country from which I came.

So although I knew that I could have a much easier life, one with a lot more socializing and pedicures and blow-outs, if I returned to my homeland, I wanted the messier life that I was cultivating in New York City. I wanted to haul my grocery bags up the stairs to my shitty little apartment in Kips Bay that I shared with my two sisters. I wanted to be cleaning my own bathroom and taking out my own garbage. All of that felt amazing, because it felt like freedom and I loved every delicious and terrifying second of it. Delicious because it was hard won and terrifying because untethering myself from the confines of my culture also meant there was no safety net, that I had to take responsibility for everything I did, and that if I failed, I could only blame myself. I had to take the reins and ride that bull every day.

chapter 26

CHEF LIFE

———

Fatima

———

I SPENT A YEAR AND A HALF AS SOUS CHEF AT CAFÉ CEN-
tro and then Patina tapped me to help open Stella 34 Trattoria,
their new Italian restaurant at Macy's Herald Square. It was my
first restaurant opening, an experience more exhausting, exhilarating, maddening, and satisfying than I could have ever an-
ticipated. There are two types of cooks: those who like openings
and those who don't, and I found that I was the former. Despite
the insane hours and drudgery, it was a step up, as I was now
executive sous chef. With this title came more responsibility: I
was expected to do the ordering, a daily task often performed at
the end of service to replenish ingredient stocks for the following day. It was my job to align purchasing and inventory and to
maintain food costs below 26 percent. I oversaw our staff of
over thirty people. I was in charge of all hiring and training new
employees. I developed dishes and managed the staff schedule. I
had a lot of responsibility, but I could handle it. It was the practical application of what I had learned at CIA combined with
the skills I'd learned on the fly when being thrown into the deep
end at Centro when the executive chef quit. The only differ-

ence was that it was an opening, which meant that it was like starting from scratch.

The menu featured homemade pastas and wood-fired Neapolitan-style pizzas all made fresh from the sixth floor of one of New York City's biggest department stores. Mohammad's reaction to my new job in a Facebook message was hilarious, if slightly snarky: "So sis, you're cooking in a *mall*?" Eventually, I convinced him that Macy's was possibly the most renowned and storied department store in America, but his annoying question struck a nerve with me: *Could I be doing better?* Patina's restaurants were well regarded and busy, and most significant, they were sponsoring my visa, but they weren't challenging in terms of the caliber of the food or the menu. My mother and Mo were always encouraging me to take risks and look for jobs in kitchens outside of New York City. The visa was important, but if I wanted to take bigger risks, where would I go? Who would I work for and learn from? Perhaps like many young cooks I imagined myself eventually working for world-famous chefs like Thomas Keller, Daniel Boulud, and Jean-Georges Vongerichten, or at one of Danny Meyer's New York City favorites, like Gramercy Tavern or The Modern, learning from the likes of the great Michael Anthony, who'd worked everywhere from Blue Hill to Daniel. And if I was really honest with myself, I would have loved to skip a big restaurant group in favor of a scrappy brilliant chef with one shop, like Missy Robbins. But I also knew these coveted positions were less likely to come with visa sponsorship. Being able to stay in America was my top priority.

Those frenetic years of school abroad and the beginning of my career were chock-full of new experiences, but they were missing one essential and irreplaceable element: my brother. Mohammad had left Karachi for university in Australia in 2004.

I'd seen him a couple of times since then, but not since I'd come to the States for school. Somehow, between an immigration quagmire in Australia and issues getting a visa to come to the States to see me (the American embassy in Sydney held his passport for six months), five years had passed without Mohammad and me being together in person. I always sensed his presence, a Facebook message or an email away, ready to listen, usually to lend support, often to challenge me to do my best, but we hadn't spoken as much as we should have. The time difference and my insane work schedule were easy excuses, but it was also hard to imagine him understanding my new life, and maybe also hard for me to imagine his. So when he finally was able to secure a visa to the States to visit me in New York, I was at once elated and nervous. There's no one I look up to more than my brother, and I wanted to prove to him that I was succeeding. I planned our eating adventures carefully, wanting him to be impressed by my knowledge of the city as much as my culinary know-how.

The rest of the family came to visit me in New York at the same time. I took a day off work and arranged for us all—Mom, Imtiaz, Saadia, Sarah, Bangu, Mo, and me—to all go to the Sea Grill at Rockefeller Center, another Patina property, for lunch. I wanted my family's experience to be perfect, but instead it had an awkward start. The Sea Grill specialized in seafood and raw bar items, so Mohammad and I of course wanted to indulge in oysters, crab, clams, prawns, you name it, but every time we requested something from the raw bar menu, we were told that unfortunately it was unavailable. I was beyond disappointed. While we tried to figure out what else to order, Mohammad and I chose a bottle of Spanish Albarino, knowing the salinic white wine would go well with fish. But then my mom chimed in that no, she wanted her usual pinot grigio, and I shifted in my seat, embarrassed by her unsophisticated choice.

But then the tides turned. Suddenly the sommelier and our server reappeared tableside each with a bottle in their hands— a bottle of the Albarino and a bottle of pinot grigio for my mother. Just as we were taking our first sips, a procession of waiters began to deliver impressive seafood towers of raw and grilled and steamed shellfish . . . all the things they'd said they were out of! The hopeful sound of a Champagne cork popping sealed the deal: We were not just in good hands; we were in the process of being spoiled rotten. If I'd had any doubt that Patina valued me, it was washed away by the effervescence of the Champagne, the lobster, the octopus, accompanied by mountains of french fries and all the sauces that landed on our giddy table. There was another awkward moment as the chef came out of the kitchen to greet us and addressed Mohammad by saying, "So I hear you are the sous chef at Stella 34?" Mohammad, gracious as ever, explained that actually it was me who was executive sous at Stella. *Typical,* I thought, my ears burning with annoyance. *Of course they think the young man at the table has the important job, rather than the young woman.*

When the check came, I tensed inwardly, fearing for a second that they'd charged us for all the extras, but I should have had faith, because whatever was on that check was so minimal that Imtiaz laughed when he saw it and stuck his credit card in the billfold. They'd comped practically our entire meal. It was such a success that we'd luxuriated at the table for hours and had completely missed our time slot to visit the Top of the Rock. It didn't seem like anyone had any regrets, so full and happy were my family, and for my part, I was at once full of gratitude and pride: My family had seen how valued I was by my employer.

In August 2014, a year after launching Stella 34, Patina transferred me again, and I became the executive sous chef at La Fonda del Sol, their Spanish reinvention of a famous midcentury "Pan-Latin" restaurant of the same name in the MetLife Building. It was a welcome change to incorporate Spanish flavors and techniques into my arsenal. Naturally, making paellas and tortillas and patatas bravas made me think of my first taste of Spain and my seminal CIA trip to San Sebastián years before, which had refocused me on staying in the kitchen.

Mariam, one of my best friends since grammar school, came to visit me in New York from London, where she'd been living since university. She visited me at Fonda and sat solo at the bar to hang with me while I was working. I played with the ingredients we had on hand, riffing on the restaurant's classic Spanish fare and sneaking in hints of our shared Pakistani taste profile. Patatas bravas (fried potatoes) with a chili garlic sauce in lieu of the traditional tomato cream Spanish hot sauce. Tuna tacos that were usually served with avocado and cilantro, but to which I added chili and ginger. I put up taste after taste for her and while she was eating, a group of young-ish businessmen gathered at the bar next to her. They kept looking over her shoulder at the plates landing in front of her.

"What's that you're having?" they asked her. "We want that too!"

"The chef is my best friend," Mariam explained. "These items aren't exactly what's on the menu."

"You must be a VIP!" they replied, impressed.

Meanwhile in the kitchen, members of my team came up to me with questions and addressed me as "Chef Fati," and Mariam thought this was hysterical. "Yes, Chef Fati," they'd say, and she would give me a look and then laugh.

"Do they know who you are?" Mariam said through a smile.

"You're just my gross best friend—don't they know that? Look at you, commanding so much respect!"

I loved it: being seen in my element . . . not just at work in my chef whites, but also in New York City. I took Mariam around Brooklyn, where I was living at the time. We walked and walked from Red Hook to Brooklyn Heights to Dumbo, where we collapsed in Brooklyn Bridge Park with double-scoop kulfi ice cream cones in our hands. It was one of those New York September days that feel like July: balmy and lush.

"You're doing so well here, Fati," Mariam said sincerely.

"Am I?" I asked her. I wasn't sure if I wanted my friends from home to believe I was flourishing or, like Mo, to challenge me to do better.

"Yes, just look at you: You're a boss lady at work. Everyone knows that you won *Chopped*. It's all happening."

We were both depleted from two nights in a row of going out. I'd taken Mariam to dance to Panjabi MC until the wee hours of the morning, and the last night's late escapades were at a gay bar in Williamsburg. In the afternoon light, we were drunk on the sweetness of New York in summer; a day off spent with a visiting best friend, walking the streets and people watching, experiencing the city as if I was a tourist because I was with one.

Mariam had been unequivocal in her love for me when I'd told her about my sexuality a few years before, when she visited me at CIA. I'd explained how angry my mother was about my preference for girls, how painful her reaction felt, and Mariam had listened and tried to help me understand my mother's perspective, but she'd never condemned or judged me, though she was one of my most religious friends.

"Pray to God," Mariam had said, when things were particularly difficult with my family and my mother was threatening to pull me back to Pakistan. "Cry to God. He knows what's in your heart."

I liked this notion of God being able to see into my heart. It gave me comfort, because everything that was in my heart was pure. Imperfect, certainly, but also utterly pure . . . I care deeply about being a good person. I strive to be one and think that I am one.

"What are you thinking about?" Mariam asked, interrupting my reverie.

"There's still so much I have to get done," I said, looking at the Brooklyn Bridge, briefly imagining what it took to build it.

"Where do you think you'll be five years from now?" Mariam asked.

"That's easy: I'll have my own restaurant."

"What's it going to look like?"

"I'm going to cover it with framed Lollywood posters," I told her. "You know I've always loved those. And truck art. I want it to be a little bit retro, like you are going into an old person's basement in Karachi and discovering treasures from another time. The feeling I got when we moved into the Tanzeem house and found relics and clues from before. I want people to be surprised when they walk in and encounter these rich, colorful, absurd, sexy images and funny things. I want them to be a bit enchanted. Like when you walk into Uncle Boons and there's so much to look at."

"What's Uncle Boons?" she asked.

"It's this Thai restaurant in Nolita that's so good. Everything about it. The food is amazing—it's got a Michelin star—authentic Thai, not sweetened or dumbed down for American palates, but somehow using ingredients that would probably never show up on a menu in Thailand, like sweetbreads and snails . . . and the music is all Thai versions of classic songs from the seventies and eighties. And there's so much to look at—all these tchotchkes and Thai kitsch. I want to do that, but for Pakistani food and with Pakistani stuff. I want the culture to be embedded in the ambiance, so people are discovering not just what it tastes like, but what it *feels* like to be there. What it feels like to sit on a charpai in a little dhaba by the side of the road in the countryside, eating halwa puri with aloo curry and chole and dahi."

"It seems like that doesn't exist here," Mariam observed correctly.

"It doesn't. No one knows about our food here and people barely know about our culture . . . except for the fact that Osama bin Laden was discovered hiding out in our hillsides. It's time for some new information. I want to use our food to disarm them."

"You're going to do it," she said. "You're so nearly there. By the time you're thirty, for sure you will make it happen. And I'll come sit at the bar there and tell all the people freaking out about how good the food is that I know the chef. That she's my best friend since grade school. That she's a total idiot."

"Deal."

The ice cream disappeared, and then so did the daylight. Mariam left soon after, but our conversation stayed with me. I'd better get busy if I wanted my own place by the time I was thirty. *I have to be strategic,* I often thought while I was changing into my chef whites and putting on my clogs in the locker room at work. Have you ever noticed how we make our biggest plans when we lie in bed at night right before we fall asleep? We say, *Someday, I'll do this* . . . or you have an idea for a great original dish, and then all of it, the big plans, the brilliant recipe, they dissolve into the deep breaths of sleep, forgotten for the time being. The walk and train ride to work and the changing room there had similar effects on me: I felt motivated and determined to dream big, to work hard on manifesting and to be brave, but by the time a long shift was over, all I wanted was a beer, a burger, and my bed. My big plans could wait one more day.

At Fonda, I was given enough leeway to create specials depending on what was in season, but I also knew my place: It was my responsibility to make sure we had the essentials that upped check averages and kept American—a.k.a. *Give me whatever I want whenever I want it!*—palates happy. As I ordered bags and bags of avocados for ubiquitous and popular guacamole and our best-selling tuna tacos, I inwardly cringed: There's nothing authentically Spanish about guacamole! Things like this were starting to grate on me disproportionately. My memory often flashed to my mini epiphany at the cidery north of San Sebastián, when I bit into the simple bisteca cooked by that unassuming old Basque woman, the furthest thing from a New York restaurant chef, and I had thought, *I want to cook like this woman: I want my food to touch people . . . to wake them up.*

Sure, I felt confident in my ability to poach octopus in wine and aromatics and finish it on the plancha, to make a mean aioli that would make my Nano proud, but was my food actually touching people? Was anyone enjoying my parrilla-grilled chicken so much that they put down their cellphones and lost their train of thought? Was that even possible at a midtown Manhattan restaurant that was part of a constellation of respectable but safe eateries that catered to local businessmen and women dining out on expense accounts? I was still taking the train every day to the same subway stop—hell, Fonda and Centro were in the same building! My paychecks still had the Patina logo on them, and the part of me that longed to go out on a limb, to learn from an executive chef with a bigger name, and to travel to a new destination and dive into another cuisine, begin another food life altogether, was growing hungrier and more restless.

For years, Mohammad had been quietly pressuring me to leave Patina and stretch my wings, and I heard his urging whenever I got wind of something that seemed impossibly exciting, a dream too grand to contemplate for long. Stories of Chef Gaggan Anand had come up in conversations with other young cooks here as we prepped croquetas before service or sat around eating late-night burgers after closing. The Indian chef from Kolkata had talked his way into an internship with the molecular gastronomy god Ferran Adría at El Bulli and was now making waves at his own eponymous restaurant in Bangkok. Gaggan's highly technical, conceptual, yet playful tasting menu was unique enough to be discussed in a burger joint on the other side of the globe at 1:57 in the morning, and the idea of working for someone like him made my pulse quicken. Would opportunities like that ever be open to me? Would I be able to take advantage of them if somehow they were?

One day, I received a call from a headhunter who told me that she'd seen me win *Chopped* and wanted me to compete on *Top Chef.* I almost couldn't process what she was saying. I'd dreamt about a moment like this, an opportunity like this, a phone call like this. *Top Chef* could be my "big break." *Top Chef* could change everything for me.

During a lull in service, I did something I'd never done before: I asked a colleague to cover for me and I stepped off the line and left the building through the back corridor, where our daily shipments of eggs and vegetables and fish came in from various purveyors. Before I crossed the threshold from the service entrance onto the street, I dialed my mother's cell in Dubai and waited, fidgeting, staring at my clogs, then up at the skyscrapers, as it rang.

"Hello, Tatu," my mother's voice said in my ear.

"Mom! Mom! I just have a few minutes," I told her. "I am in the middle of service, but guess what—guess what, Mom! Someone called me from *Top Chef*!"

"What is *Top Chef*?" my mother asked.

"It's a cooking show! It's where they call all these chefs and ask them to come and compete! It's a big one. What should I do, Mom?"

"Well, what do you think? How do you feel about it, Tatu?" my mother asked.

"I don't know, Mom," I started. "I want to do it. I mean, it's my dream to do it . . . I just don't know if I'm ready yet."

There was an almost imperceivable pause as my mother took in the information I'd just provided and made her calculation.

"Well then, trust your gut, Fati. If you don't feel ready, then tell them to give you time."

In a way, her advice was music to my ears, but nonetheless, I rolled my eyes slightly. How could my mother understand how high the stakes were? To be invited to participate in *Top Chef* was my dream, but it also was a dream shared by many ambitious cooks who wanted their chance to shine and supercharge their careers. Only a mother could be so biased in their love and admiration for their child that they'd think their daughter deserved a second chance.

"But, Mom, what if they don't call me again?"

"Don't worry, Tatu. If they are interested in you enough to call you once, they will be interested enough to call you twice."

Hearing her say this with such conviction gave me the confidence to follow my gut.

"Well then, I think I am going to let them know that I'd love to but am not yet ready," I told her before saying I loved her and rushing back onto the line.

"I need more time to work and hone my craft," I told the recruiter over the phone after service, probably the first person in history to say such a thing to her when offered a chance to compete on *Top Chef.*

I recounted the call to my friends over dinner, and they were horrified that I told the headhunter I wasn't available because of my job, but it was true. I didn't even have to ask my bosses or HR, because I knew their answer.

I tried to console myself: *There will be other opportunities. There will be other calls like this. And besides, the most important thing is to be able to stay in America—the land of opportunities, where opportunities like this happen!—and Patina underwrites my visa. Plus,* I persuaded myself, *Patina Group holds me in high regard; Patina is there for me.* When I reported bad behavior, HR listened; they tried to keep me happy. I worked hard for them and they recognized it. I felt that I was of value, of service, and that I was safe. I recommitted to working hard where I was and worrying about how to make my dreams come true later.

chapter 27

GUILTY GOOSE (MUST SPREAD HER WINGS)

—

Fatima

—

OR FOUR YEARS, I'D STAYED IN THE MOMENT, FOCUSED on the daily grind, keeping my head down and working hard for Patina, studiously ignoring the nagging sense that I should reexamine my trajectory and consider other paths forward. After a year making Spanish-inspired fare at La Fonda del Sol in the MetLife building, I was transferred to 8½, Patina's brasserie on Fifty-seventh Street, and I found myself once again making French food and working with my former head chef Jan Hoffmann. I went along with the transfer, almost like an automaton, but the patterns were becoming too recurrent and glaring to ignore. Four years earlier, Chef's lessons had been invaluable to me. He'd taken me under his wing—I'd been his pet project, a source of fascination, I suppose: a young Pakistani woman in a kitchen who could hold her own. It felt like eons ago. At 8½, I was experienced and adept enough at my job that many of the duties I performed each day—from prepping to cooking to managing staff—were now robotic. The work was no longer challenging or interesting.

My mind began to wander while I performed the same repetitive tasks. Checking the walk-in and dry storage and making lists of what needed ordering took some focus, but a monotonous task, like brunoise-ing carrots or shelling beans, made me lose any sense of time and place. Prepping the meat and poultry for service: Trimming, peeling, dicing a product until it barely resembled what it came to us as. No heads, no tails, no bones, no souls—we cooks are like magicians conjuring an illusion of what our guests would like to see. Reformatting a life until it's delectable. The gory parts, the slaughter, the detritus, the rest of the being, out of sight, out of mind.

Bent over an obese goose liver, I ran my fingers over the engorged lobes, as I had hundreds of times before, removing the tiny nervous veins from what I would turn into silken, decadent, desired foie gras. A dash of brandy, a sprinkle of white pepper, a smattering of pink salt . . . I whipped it all together then rolled it into a long log, enveloped it inside a white napkin, tied it tight at either end. I simmered it in a water bath at precisely 132 degrees for no less than twelve minutes and no more than sixteen. I did this all without thinking.

I thought back to when I was eighteen and first made foie gras at culinary school. I'd been so eager, so curious. I was so ardent and passionate then. Yet at $8\frac{1}{2}$, I felt almost nothing as I prepped this nameless, numberless duck liver. It's a numbing process: the repetition of a task from when it's a challenge through to when it becomes second nature; the superfluity of working with pricy, extravagant ingredients. It used to bother me that the food considered such a treat costs more in the United States than vaccines do in my own country—for the price of a lavish night out in New York, lives could literally be saved in Pakistan, yet somehow over the last four years, I'd managed to put aside my principles in the name of doing my job well, of climbing the ranks at Patina.

Four years before, it took me an hour to clean and marinate my first foie gras and, in the middle of it, I left the kitchen for fifteen minutes to cry in the ladies' room. Four years before, while my fingers slid and my knife trembled over the pale slippery organ, my mind had returned to the impoverished plains of Pakistan and I'd rushed to the toilet to retch. My childhood was comparatively sheltered and lavish, but I wasn't oblivious to the cruel poverty around me: The prevalence of and proximity to so much hardship was impossible to ignore, and my mother had made sure that I acknowledged it when she rounded up the hungry, homeless kids and filled their bellies with fresh hot plates. I saw those needy faces scattered around my car as my chauffeur drove me to and from school. They scampered around me, begging for a penny—begging to be saved. As a child and many times since, I'd promised myself that I would indeed find a way to feed them, that I would make a difference for my country doing what I loved, but as I took in the underground kitchen of 8½, it dawned on me: Was I getting any closer to doing so by prepping countless logs of foie gras?

During service, once the foie was finished being poached and chilled, I sliced a blush coral disk from the cylinder, placed it on a pristine white plate, and garnished it with two triangles of buttery toast dusted in pretty icing sugar, dots of crimson port wine reduction, three cubes of poached pear, and a sprinkle of soft sea salt. A predictable setup for an upscale Midtown restaurant. I mindlessly ran a folded kitchen towel around the periphery of the plate, removing any drips or grains of sugar, and pushed the finished plate onto the pass.

Foie gras—we neophyte cooks and New Yorker newcomers with expense accounts are taught—is divine. It's heavenly. It's the apex. It's how you show others that you've *arrived*. Order after order, plate after plate, fork after fork, mouth after mouth, it disappeared. My glossy eyes followed the plate of foie gras as it hit its table and the group of investment banker bros grabbed their toast wedges like they were nachos and dug into the foie as if it were cheese dip. I confronted it finally: It's deplorable. Not only is the foie itself made with the most inhumane practices—force-feeding farmed geese—but it's disgraceful how easy it is to forget our true motivations. Over the preceding four years, I'd blithely abandoned mine.

I was having some sort of crisis. I was waking back up, thawing, and I admitted it, finally: I'd lost track of the big plan, lost sight of the reason I'd wanted to become a chef in the first place. What I wanted for myself and what I wanted for my country had once been intertwined: My career as a chef was meant to serve my country. But these notions had somehow become detached from each other, and I wasn't even sure if I was still being true to myself.

What if I was squandering the sacrifices my mother had made for me, the personal sacrifices I had made in the name of "my career"? I'd told myself so many times that I was on the right path, that I was doing what was necessary to stay in the States, to progress in my field, but I realized at that moment at $8\frac{1}{2}$ that I was not doing enough.

I lay down my knife.

I'd once been so earnest and fervent because I loved what I did and I wanted to be the best at it. *If I am a great chef,* I'd thought, *I will be seen. If I am seen, then I can make a difference: I can shine a light on those hollow-cheeked children with hunger-dulled eyes. I can help the forgotten children* . . . I had lost sight of the children in the name of supposedly advancing my career, of staying in the States.

I pulled off my chef cap.

"Cover for me for a sec," I said over my shoulder to the line cook on garde manger, and I left the pass for the ladies' room. I splashed water on my face in the sink and dried it with a rough paper towel. In the mirror, I looked myself in the eye and I made a decision, or rather I said out loud to my reflection what I'd already realized was true and essential in my own mind: I quit.

Yes, my perpetual rationale that I relied on Patina for my visa was true, but there had to be another way, and if I used a fraction of the energy that I applied to doing my Patina jobs well to find that other way, then I was bound to discover it. There had to be another way, one in which I could be true to my original motivations and inspirations. There had to be a path that would challenge me again, from which I could begin to learn again.

My burnout was real, but Patina Group was loath to let me go. In four years I'd taken barely one sick day. Now, I wanted to challenge myself, and, most important, I wanted to make food that was more reflective of who I am. For the first time in four years of my professional life, I was free.

Freedom was a bizarre sensation after the incessant hamster wheel of years of kitchen work. I woke up unsure of what to do with my days and took to the streets, walking from one neighborhood to the next, over the Brooklyn Bridge, through Chinatown and Nolita, through the East Village. Walking helped me burn off the energy that would normally be spent prepping for service and then getting through service. Walking helped clear the cobwebs from my head and helped me get comfortable with the change I had made, which had happened in a day and yet felt like a cosmic shift, from which there was no going back.

My feet took me up Lafayette onto Fourth Avenue and into

the bustle of the Union Square Farmers Market, where I watched New Yorkers pick their perfect produce and watched chefs pick up preorders of tardivo and the late-season bulbous golden and red and green tomatoes that looked like they'd been tie-dyed. Off Union Square, there was a place I'd eaten at a few times and loved called DesiShack, a Pakistani paratha fast-casual concept with two locations by Union Square and in Murray Hill, and I decided to try to connect with the owners, who turned out to be a lovely couple, the Ibrahims. They were welcoming and receptive to a conversation with me, and speaking with them and seeing how they'd executed their vision was comforting and inspiring. We liked each other so much that even though theirs was a fast-casual concept, which was not really my thing, I wanted to find a way to work with them. On the one hand, I felt out of my comfort zone, but on the other, it was a return to the flavors and techniques of my roots. Crossing the threshold into their Union Square shop and entering a scented cloud of anise, cardamom, and ginger with fresh mint, coriander, and raw onion underneath it, felt like an embrace from an old friend.

We discussed trying a more elevated concept together, with me as head chef. The Ibrahims told me that they would sponsor my visa regardless of whether or not I worked with them, which was incredibly generous and validating, and they introduced me to a wonderful immigration lawyer, Seth. We went back and forth about it for months, but eventually pressed pause on collaborating. As much as we admired each other, we had such different culinary identities, and it would be a huge departure for each of us. But their support was essential to my getting the real-life version of *Charlie and the Chocolate Factory*'s golden ticket: Thanks to them—and Seth—I got my green card, which meant I no longer needed to be tethered to a restaurant for sponsorship in order to stay in the States. If America had been my coloring book, a place where I had to stay within the lines, now it felt like my blank canvas: I could create what would truly suit me.

chapter 28

INTRODUCING MY CRAFT
TO MY CULTURE

—

Fatima

—

NOT WORKING FOR THE FIRST TIME IN FIVE YEARS, I succumbed to my mother's pleas and decided to return to Pakistan for a stint to check in on life there, spend time with my family and old friends, and consider my next professional move. It was surprisingly easy to fall back into the routine of Lahore life. I had a bit of local notoriety thanks to winning *Chopped,* and opportunities lined up easily for me. My mother's best friend, my Yasmin Khala, had a successful Italian restaurant called Cosa Nostra in Gulberg District and was planning to open another more casual concept place, Delicatessen, and hired me as a consultant to oversee the opening. Though both restaurants served Italian food, opening Delicatessen couldn't have been more different than opening Stella 34 in New York. The local staff I oversaw didn't know what to make of me. Years of cooking professionally in the West had left their mark. Physically, I was strong as an ox; I butchered quickly and with precision, and I trusted my instincts enough to command an entirely male cooking squad who had never been bossed around by a woman or seen a female chef like me before. If at first they had doubts about me, they were quickly dispelled by my skill and replaced by awe and interest. One evening, a few nights before we opened to the public, Yasmin Khala took me aside.

"Fati, I think you should know what the other cooks are saying about you." Yasmin Khala tried to keep her lovely, half-Italian, half-Pakistani face from emoting, difficult given her naturally joyful eyes. I took a deep breath and prepared myself for what my khala was about to say.

"Oh, god. Okay, out with it, Yasmin Khala."

"I asked them how you were doing and they said, 'Madame, she cooks like a man.'"

Together we erupted into laughter. This was the highest compliment that a Pakistani male chef could give! After a couple of weeks, they seemed to mostly forget that I was a woman and were entirely focused on what they could learn from me. None of these guys had gone to culinary school; they'd learned to cook by doing and by following the owners' instructions. Our kitchen prep sessions were a window into an entirely novel exercise in learning about food, and I enjoyed teaching as much as they seemed to enjoy learning. I taught them butchery skills and tricks that they'd never had occasion to learn in the context of cooking in Pakistan. Among cooks of any level, it's often the subtleties that make our pulses quicken: plating a routine dish differently, thickening a sauce by using the pasta water, finishing with fresh herbs or citrus—these little flourishes, as much as the by-the-book techniques I'd acquired, were a source of constant curiosity and thrilled my brigade.

It felt good to command the respect of Pakistani men and also validating that Yasmin Khala—who'd known me since birth and ran the business with her siblings and her daughter, my dear friend Zahra—trusted me enough to hire me to help launch their new endeavor. Once we opened, Yasmin Khala used to summon me from the kitchen to meet an important guest, perhaps someone who she thought might be able to help my career in Pakistan, perhaps even an eligible young man, and I always laughed internally at the subtle change of her expression as she took in my unkempt hair, knotted at the top of my head in a messy bun, and my workout pants beneath my apron. I was trying this on—cooking in Pakistan—but I wasn't going to try too hard with my appearance . . . and the last thing I wanted was to be set up with a "suitable" Pakistani man.

With Cosa Nostra's successful opening behind me, I decided the next logical step while I was in Pakistan was to organize a pop-up, to see what it would feel like to cook *my* food for the community from which I came. Mohammad and I were at our dad's house talking about food, of course, the language we spoke most fluently with Dad, and without giving it tremendous thought, I suggested dishes like lobster bisque and stuffed veal for my Lahore pop-up menu. Dad smiled and encouraged me immediately, as upscale dining in Pakistan is synonymous with Western cuisine. But Mohammad looked at me as if I were nuts.

"Is that *really* the food that you want to make, Fatima?" he asked me incredulously. "The same old shit?" There it was again: Mohammad, forever challenging me to do better.

"It's not, actually," I admitted a little sheepishly. He had jarred me to consciousness like a bucket of cold water to the face, waking me up to my shortsightedness.

"What if there's another way to show off not just your skills, but your *perspective*," Mo offered, prodding me gently, leading me toward the answer, as he had when we were children.

I felt a momentary prickle of fear on my back, like in a dream where you have a test for which you haven't studied. I took a deep breath. *Fatima, you've studied,* I told myself. *You know this.* I closed my eyes and let the information rise to the surface.

"What if we asked our friends with farms and properties outside the city if we could source from their land and gardens?" I suggested tentatively.

"I love that idea," Mo encouraged.

"What if we only use local fish and meat, like more of a farm-to-table concept?" I felt a pang of pleasure behind my diaphragm, where a minute before there had been a pocket of self-doubt. "No upscale or fine dining restaurant in Pakistan has that kind of sourcing perspective," I continued.

"That would be so cool," Mo said, with genuine pride in his voice. And then to our father: "Dad, you must have some friends with big vegetable gardens at their farmhouses outside the city. Can you call in some favors for Fati?"

And so began a mini workshop in which we brainstormed who grew vegetables and had fruit trees, who kept goats and lamb and chickens on their hobby farms.

Once, when I was about six and a half and we were newly back in Pakistan from Texas, Mo and I were on one of our typical escapades out in an undeveloped area not far from the Shamshir house. I was Mohammad's shadow then, and he occasionally teased me, gently, or wrestled me onto his shoulders or catapulted me onto a tree branch so that I could climb it. On this particular day, Mohammad was using me as a guinea pig for a trick he must have picked up from his classmates at school: He'd grab ahold of my overalls where they tapered on my back, about midway between my shoulder blades and my bottom, and he used the knuckles of his fabric-clenching fist to push me, gently launching me forward. An instant later, the safety cord of taut fabric in his fist caught me before I fell on my face. Naturally this made me laugh, that fleeting sensation of falling, each millisecond stretched out as if it was too late to be tugged back, and then each time finding myself saved at the last instant by my brother. It reminded me of dozing off, nearly dreaming, then tugging myself back to wakefulness. That day on our adventures, we came to an enormous hole—an unfinished well—at the bottom of which was a large metal pump and a few pathetic puddles of spoiled brown water. We stood at the hole's lip and looked into the wide mouth of it, and suddenly I felt that familiar tug and thrust—of falling, of flying. Mohammad had grabbed my overalls and had pushed me forward, but this time something was different, something had gone awry. He'd lost his grip or he'd misjudged the lip, and he couldn't yank me back. For a few heady seconds, I could have sworn I was flying. The hardness of the metal pump was jolting after the rush of air, and for a moment I could only blink into the shadowed, rust-smelling damp.

I was too stunned to scream or move, and when gradually my wits returned, I heard my brother frantic above me, crying, screaming my name, reaching for me through dusty red air to drag me out. I was winded and sniffling significantly by the time Mo got me back up onto the lip, where we lay holding hands and panting, as if he'd just pulled me out of the sea. I was astounded that he'd dropped me, but even then, I couldn't hold it against Mo: He hadn't meant for me to fall. I saw that clear as the bright day that I'd returned to. Shocked, but miraculously unhurt, I forgave Mo instantly. I had never actually been angry, only surprised by the rush of air lasting too long and then the hard slap. I never told a soul. I knew he would never drop me again, and he hadn't.

Mohammad had always known me, in some ways perhaps better than I knew myself. He knew I crumbled under criticism.

He knew my standards for myself were so high that I felt perpetually on the verge of toppling over, of tripping myself up with my own insecurities. Mo and I had lightly tossed around restaurant concepts for years, but this conversation about native sourcing in Pakistan marked the beginning of a new chapter in our creative collaboration and dream weaving. I realized then how much I'd missed my brother's guidance all those years in New York: a steady hand on my back, steering me, tugging me, launching me, supporting me if I fumbled, the gentle pressure of which made me feel I *could* fly.

Chef Fati's Pop-Up

MENU

mooli (radish flatbread), raw cow cheese, tomato,
   olive oil

pine nut, paprika rusk, preserved lemon, coriander

beet, blood orange, raw buffalo cheese, greens,
   kumquat

basmati, baby spinach, desi egg, truffle

sole, shakarkandi (sweet potato), red chili,
   cauliflower, moongre (Punjabi radish pods)

lamb, shaljam (turnip), pistachio, chard, kale

carrot, kaju (cashew), rose, black tea, milk

Lahoris were flabbergasted by my pop-up, and I don't necessarily mean in a good way, at least not at first. A few of Yasmin Khala's friends came through and offered us homegrown items. Someone gifted us some extraordinary unfiltered homemade olive oil in a label-less bottle that tasted of the hillsides of Sargodha, a lush region north of Lahore where orange trees and olive orchards proliferated. A few days before the pop-up was scheduled to start, several crates of game birds, pheasant and chukar partridge that were freshly shot, showed up on the door-step of our dad's office, like an offering from another era.

I followed the paradigm that Mo had helped me identify as actually original and truly a reflection of my identity, and used local, seasonal ingredients—meats and fish but especially veg, but combined them in ways that would never occur to someone who hadn't cooked in the West. Thanks to chefs like Dan Barber of Blue Hill Stone Barns, it's not inconceivable to have a vegetable as humble as a turnip as the star ingredient in a fine dining restaurant in New York. But in Lahore, a tasting menu starring radishes and sweet potatoes was unimaginable. Guests were literally scratching their heads and kicking each other under the table, unsure of how to mentally digest what they were eating.

I'd trained the staff to host and serve in a way that had become familiar to me in the West but had never been done in Pakistan. As servers carefully placed each dish from the guest's left side, they quietly explained it, as they would in a temple of gastronomy. Servers precisely poured sauces and broths with their left hands over elements, with their right hands tucked neatly behind their backs. I choreographed these meals to be aligned with what we were taught about old-school service at the CIA, but in Lahore it was a strange and wonderful revelation.

Yasmin Khala and Zahra told me after service that the room got very, very quiet, but as the meal progressed, guests must've gotten caught up in the pleasure of the table, of gathering, of gossip with old friends—maybe they even began to enjoy something actually novel—and by the next day, everyone was talking emphatically about my food and seemed truly enthusiastic. At the end of the meal, when Zahra came and got me from the kitchen and brought me out to the diners, the room erupted in applause. People stood up. I got a standing ovation for my utterly untraditional feast. We sold out all three nights.

It was impossible not to notice the support for my presence in Pakistan. My four parents together have large networks of friends and acquaintances who championed me, spreading the word about my pop-up; even strangers had a bit of interest and pride in me because I'd represented Pakistan on TV and done well. "Fatima Ali, the young Pakistani chef" was something of a curiosity: a female in a male-dominated profession who was making good on her dreams in the West. So on the one hand, there was an effortlessness to being in Lahore and it was easy to get comfortable and enjoy the feeling of the road rising up to meet me. Yet a part of me kept wondering: *Is this the right road?* New York City, with its inherent challenges—the chaos, the expense, the competition, the red tape of health inspections and permits—called to me still.

The Lahore pop-up gave me confidence and the clarity to return to my adopted home of New York with new conviction. I applied to be a part of Smorgasburg, the weekend food market in Williamsburg, Brooklyn, where a hundred vendors sell their offerings. It was a strategic choice: Smorgasburg was a steppingstone that would bring me that much closer to having my own food truck or even a brick-and-mortar restaurant. I could finesse recipes and test the receptivity of New York's culinary waters, where I most longed to establish myself. I named my stall Van Pakistan, thinking ahead to its future mobile iteration. My logo was a peacock, my favorite bird—alluring, grandiose, a little absurd, pretending to see all and lure in the finest mate with its illusion of many eyes. On my Instagram, I called myself Bawarchi, a word used by the small-minded to refer to domestic cooks. I wore it as a badge of pride. I would *not* let myself be pigeonholed. I was on my way, independent of a restaurant at last.

I remembered how I relished those first years of cooking professionally in New York City. I actually enjoyed the crazed hours that any non-industry person would balk at. I loved the camaraderie of restaurants and the silly banter that sprang up as we stood shoulder to shoulder, scrubbing carrots beneath gushing icy water. I loved the familiar slap-slap of fillets as we easily, tidily unfastened them from bones and lay them on parchment-covered sheet trays, preparing for service. I loved the symphony of service: the "Order fire . . . !" by the expeditor (sometimes my own voice) followed beats later by the opening of lowboys, the popping of quart containers being opened and sealed, the sizzle of the fry station, the sound of a stainless-steel spoon gathering jus in the gut of a tilted pan and basting a skirt steak. But Smorgasburg, I quickly realized, was a beast unlike any I'd before encountered. With Van Pakistan, I was flying completely solo, a team of one.

I left my apartment in Carroll Gardens at six each morning and headed to the commissary kitchen uptown, where I leased time and space, to prep my ingredients. Then I took the prepped food (all in awkward-to-maneuver vessels, like hotel pans and dozens of quart containers stacked in milk crates) to my storage locker in South Brooklyn, where I picked up the equipment— the hotplates, the rice maker—that I needed for my booth, and went to the Smorgasburg site on the Brooklyn waterfront, where I negotiated my way to my stall and got set up for the day. We opened on Saturday, June 20, and ran every Saturday and Sunday, rain or shine, through November. Those were frantic, maniacal prep and service days. With my halal hat, I served thousands of portions with a smile, even though every part of me ached. Though it hadn't worked out to partner with the DesiShack team, there I was making my own fast-casual concept work, 100 percent on my own.

Meanwhile, I'd long since stopped trying to define my sexuality as either gay or straight: I liked who I liked and it was not about their gender, and I'd begun dating a guy named Josh, who graduated from Brown and was a food entrepreneur starting a paleo brand. He was helping me tremendously with the Smorgasburg hauling, and, in turn, I was helping him with research and development for the health food line he was planning. I'd told my family all about how smart and capable he was and introduced them when they visited New York City. Unfortunately, it didn't go over well. My extended friends and family came to visit me at my Van Pakistan stall at Smorgasburg, and of course they ordered my food, trying to be supportive and enthusiastic of my every endeavor. But the nuances of the situation went over my boyfriend's head, and he tried to charge them all for what they'd ordered, which I had no intention of doing (this was my family, after all, and charging them would go against every aspect of the Pakistani hospitality ingrained in all of us and is one of the tenets of my being). It wasn't a great introduction to the guy I'd been talking up to them, to say the least.

A night or two later, we all met for dinner and, perhaps sensing that he was being scrutinized, Josh behaved weirdly and sat himself between me and my family members, giving off a sort of protectiveness, which put them off again.

Mohammad made an extra effort to get to know him, to try to see in him the things I had described, but to no avail. Mo and I took a walk one evening soon thereafter and sat on a stoop near my place in Brooklyn and talked about it all.

"Fati, why are you giving him twenty-five percent equity of

Van Pakistan when he's only giving you one percent of his paleo project?" Mo asked me with disdain.

"Well, he's doing physical labor, helping me move stuff, helping me set up," I explained lamely. "The stuff I am helping him with is so easy and his thing won't be profitable until down the line."

Mohammad looked incredulous.

"Sis, you could do so much better," he said. "We've all really tried to get to know him, to bring him into the fold of the family, but he's made no effort with us."

"He's really been a help to me," I argued to Mo. "And he lets me have my freedom," I added. I'd found that openness in a relationship suited me.

Josh and I had a tacit understanding and both saw other people, though we didn't really discuss it with each other, and this was part of what made our relationship work. This exchange was central to our being together, even if it might seem strange to outsiders. And anyway, our relationship only lasted as long as Van Pakistan did.

Coming up with Pakistani street food that utterly embraced the flavors of my youth, my heritage, my essence, but also had playful nuances that told my twisting story with a foot in both America and Pakistan, made me feel that I was stepping into my true path. My menu featured dishes like Buttermilk-Fried Chicken Biryani, with kachumber salad (tomato, cucumber, onions, lemon juice, and chili) and cucumber yogurt; Lamb & Lentil BunKabob with egg, a dirty chutney, tamarind plum sauce, and pickled cabbage. I even incorporated one of my favorite all-American dishes to make a Cheeseburger Chaat, which was crazy delicious and a huge hit. But lugging ingredients, gallons of prepped food, equipment, dry goods, and sundries from borough to borough four times a weekend, let alone standing solo at my stall for eight hours serving a couple thousand portions, was backbreaking. The perks of a youthful body combined with years on the line meant I had both strength and stamina, but the physicality and repetition of Smorgasburg almost undid me. Oddly enough, Smorgasburg was the hardest thing I'd ever done professionally. I got through my seasonal commitment and let the organizers know that I wouldn't be coming back. I had another trick up my sleeve.

In anticipation of achieving my long-term goals, a few months into Smorgasburg, I'd applied for a competition called Center Stage via Chef's Roll, an international online community for cooks, that would help me find a mentor, and, if I won, offer me a monthlong internship at the Michelin-starred kitchen of my choosing. Imagine spending a month learning from the likes of Dominique Crenn of the Michelin three-starred Atelier Crenn in San Francisco, or Daniel Humm of the Michelin three-starred Eleven Madison Park in New York City, or David Kinch of the Michelin three-starred Manresa in Los Gatos. These are some of the finest chefs and restaurants in the world, and if I won, I'd be able to learn directly from them.

I'd be able to watch Chef Crenn put final garnishes on a dish, each one of which was symbolized by a line of poetry rather than as a menu item. Or, if I picked Manresa, then I might get to observe Chef Kinch as a crate of newly foraged chanterelles arrived from the NoCal woodlands. These were the kinds of opportunities that aligned with my brother's vision of me, of my vision for myself: taking risks, traveling, learning from the very best. The first several rounds of the competition were done via photo submissions with dish descriptions and Skype interviews. I made it through those, and then the final round was done in person in Los Angeles, where I competed as a Center

Stage finalist against three typically tattooed male chefs. Well, I won! I got to choose where I wanted to go—the opportunity of a lifetime—and I decided to be a stagière at Meadowood, the idyllic Michelin three-star restaurant run by Christopher Kostow in the Napa Valley. In addition to Chef Kostow's reputation for mentoring, the revered Meadowood had its own farm and grew a good portion of its own produce. Plus there was something about California, beyond the coveted NoCal food and wine scene, that called to me. I hoped Meadowood might offer me a taste of a fresh experience of America.

chapter 29

PATTA TIKKA

———

Farezeh

———

CHRISTMASTIME IN THE REST OF THE WORLD IS wedding season for us in Pakistan. Weddings stretch from days into nights of celebrations that go on for weeks. In December 2015, Fatima came back to Lahore for one of my best friend's son's wedding, a grand affair with lots of friends and family.

Fatima and I were catching up with friends during one of the many evenings of dance practices. One second she was beside me sipping a glass of wine and the next she had vanished. I looked for her ivory and plum dress in the rainbow of silk shalwars and gowns that spread across the room around me.

She was nowhere to be seen. I searched the crowd and finally spotted her talking to this old man, the head cook and meat expert who had spent a lifetime mastering the art of barbecue particular to the northern region of Pakistan. He and his team were called specially from Peshawar by Afi, the groom's father, on special occasions and were there to make their renowned patta tikka for the celebration. Afi, Erum's husband and an adored paternal figure to Fatima, understood that the quality of their craft was more important than the dish's humble-ness.

Patta tikka is a very rustic and basic food made from sheep particular to northern Pakistan, its fresh liver being the most prized, simply cooked with a bit of salt in its own fat, no masala, no froufrou. There was Fatima, in her unconventional gown with pretty makeup and jewelry, holding her glass of red wine, talking to people who everyone else hadn't even taken a second look at, even as they chomped down on their wares. In fact, it is expected for the low-ranking cooks to be relegated to the back of events, like an eyesore that must be camouflaged. There is no reverence for their craft for most. They are there to cook and make sure the food is good for whenever guests are hungry enough, not really be seen or be part of the scene. I suppose in some ways the presence of the cooks may be a little confront-ing and inappropriate given the massive class divide between them and the revelers. It feels a little flagrant to indulge in luxu-ries in plain sight of many who may never be able to experience them in such abundance and with such abandon. So typically, these folks are sectioned off and relegated to some noisy corner of the property to get on with their job and cook. Just as we don't want to see the slaughter of the animal, simply the crispy little nugget we dunk into our sauce, these cooks, too, are a part of the process that we are happy not to witness.

Half an hour later, dinner was announced. Fatima and I stood together near where the food was being laid out and along came the patta tikka master. In a sea of dark, silk-wrapped, and bejeweled silhouettes, he had found her and offered her a plate he had made just for her.

"*Bibi,*" he said, meaning madam. "*Yeh khaas aap ke liye banaya hai. Kha ke batao!* I've made this especially for you. Just take a bite, tell me what you think." From the way he looked at her, confident, but curious about her opinion, it became clear that he held what she thought in high esteem. The way expertise respects expertise.

Fatima introduced him to me like you would introduce a friend, and he asked her to give it to me to taste too. That he approached her in this setting, where classes were so obviously divided, was evidence of the respect she'd shown him in their earlier conversation, the reverence she must have expressed for his honed technique.

Under the gentle pressure of his gaze, we both tasted the meat, which melted succulently in our mouths, and as I let the flavors reveal themselves to me, I realized how wrong I'd been to ferry her away from this humble master of his craft. I saw the anticipation and pride in his eyes, and I saw that my daughter had touched him with her interest and thoughtful questions about his process and technique. I saw that he felt honored to be acknowledged by a woman like Fatima, and that she appreciated his artistry. How many times had he been summoned from Peshawar to cook and serve his patta tikka in this affluent home, but apart from our hosts, Eram and Afi, and perhaps some of their children, no one else had ever meaningfully engaged with him. People came, ate, drank, socialized, and left. But no one acknowledged the labor and care behind the delicious meal before my daughter did. Fatima connected with him instantly and wanted to learn and appreciate and celebrate his simple and sublime craft.

Just a half an hour before, I had felt it urgent to pull my daughter away from this man to greet my friends, but as I chewed and swallowed and told him how excellent his patta tikka was, I realized that the two were exchanging a gift. She was more comfortable talking with him about his food than she was chatting with Lahore society, catching up on gossip. Fatima probably would say that it was *he* who had given *her* a gift.

Fatima used to say, "Mom, *you* taught me to be this way, to be this person." But it's the things she taught me, much more than what I taught her. Fatima could always see past a person's class, their dress, the color of their skin. She always only saw the person.

chapter 30

AN INTERVIEW
WITH FATE

———

Fatima

———

AFTER SMORGASBURG WAS FINISHED, I RETURNED TO Lahore for the holidays to see my family, knowing that in the new year, I'd make my way to the Napa Valley to train under one of America's finest chefs. I had the distinct feeling that an important new chapter was commencing.

As usual, Lahore in winter swallowed me easily into its delicious swarm of old friends and weddings and parties. The holidays have a familiar cadence everywhere, but ours was the rhythm of nightly celebrations and stopping by friends' houses daily for gossip sessions and the embrace of Pakistani hospitality: more food offered than any guest can consume; fresh fruit and gifts pressed into our hands as we departed. But despite the familiar beacons—the impermeable fog, the chai-scented street stalls, the imploring eyes of the homeless at stoplights, and the terrifying lawless driving—being back this time felt somehow different from other visits: I knew that I had a hard out with my stage at Meadowood organized for March.

Something else unexpected and monumental happened while

I was back in Pakistan: a recruiter from *Top Chef* contacted me again about competing in the upcoming season. This was the second time that *Top Chef* had approached me, and I knew that I couldn't put them off again, as I had three years before, and expect to ever get another chance. The pang I experienced upon reading their message was complicated. I knew that if they invited me to participate in the next season, that I had to go for it. But, as with all things that we most desire, I was simultaneously terrified of it not working out and making up excuses for it *not* to happen: *What if they don't pick me? What if I don't win? What if I screw up something stupid? What if . . . ?*

This time I didn't have the excuse of being employed full-time by Patina Group, or my bosses not letting me disappear for two months to shoot a season of the show. And with my green card, neither did I have the excuse of needing Patina for a visa. I'd begun to define my cooking identity through my Lahore pop-up and Van Pakistan. Was I going to wait until I had my own restaurant to compete? No! Competing would help me establish my own restaurant, I was sure of that. Apart from nerves, I didn't have any excuses left to say no if I was offered the chance to compete. It was time to go for it.

The talent scout and I set up a Skype interview from opposite ends of the world, so very late at night, with my top half made up and cute and my bottom half in pajamas, I recounted early food memories to her from my grandmother's rock-hard bed in Lahore. Over the roar of a neighbor's generator, I told her about visiting the Itwaar Bazaar with Nano, learning from her to choose fruit and haggle. I told her about making an American-style holiday feast in Karachi for sixty visiting relatives, the moment I first thought, *I want to be a chef.* I told her about how my brother and I religiously watched *Yan Can Cook* every Sunday in Pakistan. I revealed enough to make her want more, while adeptly evading certain questions, bobbing and weaving like a practiced boxer eluding punches.

"So what makes you a winner?" the talent scout asked me.

"Uh . . . I was very competitive in high school," I chirped lamely.

I watched myself as if disembodied, regurgitating the same story I'd rehearsed many times before. In a way, I'd been preparing for this moment since I was a small child in Pakistan watching Yan and Nigella and Gordon on BBC Food Network. For years I'd told myself that cooking would be my ticket out of Pakistan, and I had made it so: Culinary school was what got me to America. Cooking in New York City kitchens kept me there. But I knew I was at a crossroads: I had kicked off the comfort that came with my Patina Restaurant Group tenure. It was time to up the ante. I had to forge ahead on my own. I was ready for the next big step in my career: I wanted my own cooking show. I felt ready for my own restaurant. And to open my own restaurant in the States, I needed serious capital, investors, and to convince my family once and for all that I belonged in America. There are many ways from A to B, but it seemed to me that the most direct route to my dreams could be achieved by competing on (and *winning*) a show like *Top Chef*.

Yet, when opportunity knocked, I felt oddly distant from my dream, as if the interview was happening to someone else. If I could convince them of my worthiness and pique their interest, competing on the show could catapult my career. Yet the fading whiffs of our traditional Pakistani supper and my grandmother's signature scent of arthritis cream mixed with mothballs and Chanel No. 5 reminded me where I was and the place to which I always seemed to return: the place carved out for the matriarchs of my family, of my culture, which has never felt comfortable to me. Even so, a future in Pakistan, even if I was never able to fold myself into the shape I was meant to assume here, felt more inevitable than this longshot, this girlish fantasy that suddenly was manifesting right in front of me. *After all, who am I to have my dreams come true?* I wondered.

Fatima, focus!

We went through the motions of a classic interview: the headhunter fishing, me embellishing, dodging when necessary. Sometimes holding so much back makes me feel like a phony . . . undeserving of success or happiness. Again the ever-nagging question: *Who am I to have my dreams come true?* And then the tiny voice—the same one that always came muffled from deep inside my heart and made me sprint the last fifty meters when I had no more energy to run the race: *Why not?* the voice of the believer whispered. *Why not me?*

"Well, thank you, Fatima. It's been a pleasure getting to know you better. You'll be hearing from me soon, either way," she said.

And then it was over. I was just me again, alone, half in pajamas on Nano's ornately carved bed in the middle of the dusty Lahore night. But inside me my dream was simmering, changing form, solidifying, whether I realized it or not.

chapter 31

THE NOCAL
DREAM

———

Fatima

———

I FLEW TO SAN FRANCISCO AND MADE MY WAY TO ST. Helena, where I was staying in an Airbnb that Chef's Roll had arranged for me near Meadowood. The splendor of Northern California—the wide, unbridled skies, the thick green hills and valleys striped with vines, the tiny quaint town that felt like a movie set in an old Western—would be mine for a month: my views, my stomping ground, my canvas. I don't drive, so I rode a bike between my accommodations, Meadowood, and Meadowood's farm, where much of the produce used at the restaurant is grown.

I'd never worked anywhere like Meadowood, a place where everything feels brand-new and is kept utterly pristine. It was as if *everything* was made of crystal. I'd go through a big bag of micro-chrysanthemum and pick out the best; the rest was tossed into the compost. The same went for mushrooms. For beans, you cooked three times what you needed so you could pick out the best, the most pristine and pretty, so that the dish could be perfect. Perfection was what guests were paying a premium for. I was floored by the waste. Particularly coming there directly from Pakistan, where children's bellies are swollen with hunger, it was a painfully stark contrast. But aside from this one aspect that rattled me, it was a phenomenal experience.

Each week, I worked two days in the farm-garden, picking things like dainty little baby carrots and turnips, laying down mulch, and clipping edible flowers. Then three days a week I was in the kitchen, at times only a few feet from Chef Christopher Kostow, who was completely different from the executive chefs under whom I'd worked in New York. Chef Kostow was so young, so passionate and inspiring in a different sort of way. My time at Meadowood frankly felt too good to be true: I'd been transported to the land of opportunity, a fairy-tale castle I could actually inhabit.

I suppose there was something a bit backward about me going to Meadowood at this point—reverting to the peeling, cleaning, chopping, and mixing that I had done in the earliest days of my career, but it didn't feel like a step back. For five years I'd worked in a large restaurant group and I'd climbed the ranks from a junior sous chef to an executive sous. I'd managed a staff of thirty. I'd done banquets, off-site catering, prepped and run service for breakfast, lunch, and dinner. I'd seen it all. Being a stagière at Meadowood meant that I didn't have any real responsibility; I simply had to do the tasks I was assigned to the best of my ability. Cleaning peas just so. Slicing surreally perfect radishes particularly. There's beauty in this meditative exacting work, and it's a beauty that I missed out on experiencing when I was younger. Meticulous tasks with flawless ingredients allowed me the invaluable opportunity to observe and to reflect on what kind of chef I wanted to be and what sort of career I wanted to build for myself. Staging there made me realize just how corporate my professional experiences had been, and clarified anew that there were so many other paths to explore, so many new styles. Finally I felt a part of a much bigger, yet simultaneously more personal, picture: someone's dining experience that they would never forget—a tiny part, but a part nonetheless. In my many blissful moments of working in the Meadowood kitchen garden, I thought about how I would interweave what I was learning into what I hoped to someday create. *Something transporting,* I thought. *But intimate.* I wanted the restaurant that I was dreaming up to run like the well-oiled machine of a Patina business, but with the immediacy and magic of dining at Meadowood . . . but without formality . . . with the simple pleasure of dining in a dhaba in Pakistan. These were the musings that ran through my head as I turned the soil.

Chef Kostow would open his second restaurant in a couple of months, and my days were consumed with repetitive tasks that contributed to the well-being of their whole culinary universe: slicing and picking out the seeds of kumquats for marmalade; pulling winter plants to make space for the summer crop; weeding, shoveling, raking, which was exhausting and rewarding.

My mother joined me in NoCal for ten days and together we ate at some of the legendary local restaurants, sipped wine in tasting rooms, snuck wine into movie theaters to enjoy with our popcorn, and basked in each other's company in a way we hadn't in a long time. Some evenings, a song would come on the radio in my Airbnb, and she and I danced around the kitchen together as we cooked dinner. In a way, it reminded me of the connection we'd had long before in Austin, when I was child. We were rediscovering each other in a way that had eluded us when she'd descended into my life in New York. It was as if those middle years of her trying to control me and me trying to evade her had fallen away, and we were back to our core of acceptance and respect that had been there, dormant, all along.

Having my mother stay with me in Napa felt so different from her New York visits, where she understandably was a bit horrified by my shabby apartments. In California, we had our own little house! This was when it began to sink in that there was a world beyond New York, the city I'd clung to so persistently for the last six years. These days were full of prosecco and rosé, sunshine and laughter. We sat on the porch together talking for hours, both feeling our closeness just as we felt the mist on our skin as it rolled down the hill in the evenings and onto the valley vines.

Mom was her usual combination of immeasurably proud and predictably pressuring me to sort out what was next. My stint in Pakistan had convinced her that the road would rise up to meet me there (which she may have been right about), and that I should grow roots there and open a restaurant in Lahore.

"Come back to Pakistan," my mother said between sips at a local vineyard. "You have so many options there. What about that cooking school that wants to hire you? And didn't that hotelier ask you to design his new restaurant?"

"Mum, I want to *be* someone," I told her. "I want to open *my own* restaurant . . . but not there."

I knew that while she entertained the idea of me returning to build a career in Pakistan, she also was laying the groundwork for something else.

"Come back and figure it out," she'd say. "Maybe you'll surprise yourself by meeting a nice boy and *wanting* to settle down."

Depending on my mood or my exhaustion level, I either played along or I argued with her, but in my heart I didn't want to return to Pakistan yet. I wasn't done with the States and I wanted an excuse to stay, maybe even a job that would allow me to stay in California. One thing I was certain of was that I did not want a nice Pakistani husband.

And then, a week before my stage at Meadowood was to come to an end, I got the email: I'd been chosen to compete on *Top Chef,* season fifteen.

"Mom!" I screamed from my bedroom where my laptop was set up.

"What is it?" she responded as she appeared in my doorway on high alert, fearful I'd gotten bad news of some kind.

"They chose me for *Top Chef.* It's happening. I got on the show."

We jumped up and down holding each other's forearms and screaming like two schoolgirls.

"I knew you would get it," my mother said gleefully. "My Tatu, when does it start?"

"Filming is in three weeks, in Denver," I told her. I had a week left of my stage before we planned to visit Nano, who was staying with Saby Khala in Palm Springs, and then I'd head home to New York before flying to Colorado for the shoot. I had so much prep to do.

A little while later, as we were getting ready to go to dinner, my mother interrupted my racing thoughts.

"Fatima."

"Yeah, Mom?"

"Just do your best. Your best will be good enough," she said.

She always had an uncanny ability to read my mind. I'd just been thinking to myself that I hadn't won *Chopped Champions* when I'd been on it, that I hadn't been cast on *The Next Food Network Star,* which I'd auditioned for the year before. I used these perceived failures to make a case in my own head as to why I wasn't good enough.

"Thank you, Mom," I told her. And indeed, I was thankful for her being there, her encouragement, her belief in me . . .

especially in moments like this one when I was doubting myself.

On my last night in St. Helena, my mom and I dined together at Meadowood and it was the most exceptional restaurant meal of my life to date, all the more so because I understood what went into making most of it. Like any daughter who enjoyed feeling like an expert around her mother, I peacocked a bit and explained the dishes to my mom as we went.

"We're starting with little amuses bouches—that's the French term that literally means amusements for your mouth. First, sweet grassy field peas that I actually picked myself. Chef recognizes how perfect they are and so he leaves them whole and sautés them quickly and serves them in a chickpea crèpe and split pea puree."

I watched my mother with the kind of anticipation that I imagine parents must feel when they watch kids open birthday presents. They want their kids to like the gifts as much as they do, to recognize the effort that went into selecting them.

Next, little nutty sunchoke beignets were earthy one-bite delights, perfectly puffed with a dusting of morel mushroom powder; then local Miyagi oysters, briny and creamy at once, with fermented kohlrabi granita. Like the very land Meadowood sits on, these two dishes straddled the woody hills and the cold Pacific.

"Mom, don't you think that these two bites back to back are just like how you come around a corner on the highway here and go from the forest onto a sea cliff? Just with these three little bites, Chef Kostow has begun to tell the story of this place at this moment for the diners, do you see what I mean?"

"I think I do," my mother said.

"Oh, this next dish is just sublime," I said as two plates

floated toward our table. "It's sea eel that's been hot smoked, wrapped in beef tongue and grape leaf nori and pan-seared until the nori is puffed up and crispy. It's like the fanciest, most thoughtful surf 'n' turf in the world."

"I've never tasted anything like it," my mother said with a look of genuine surprise on her face. She was nearly speechless.

I relished the opportunity to teach her my language, one that at Meadowood I frankly felt I was only beginning to learn myself. Asparagus that I'd helped harvest from the Meadowood farm, wrapped in wakame seaweed and steamed slowly in ashes. Dungeness crab served with its roe, almond, and salsify. Whelk with onions, horseradish, and nasturtium. Chicken thighs baked in bread, seared in chicken fat, and served as a sandwich with roasted radicchio and black trumpet mushrooms. Cooking at Meadowood felt like finishing school: It made me reexamine flavor combinations, techniques, but above all, the ingredients that were possible. It underscored how big the world was, how much of it I longed to see and be a part of, and I understood the urgency finally: that it was time to get out there and explore, which is what my brother and mother had been pushing me to do for years.

I explained it to her as two captains were preparing hawayej-spiced lamb neck shawarma with black lime jus and sheep's whey sauce tableside, and when my mother tasted it—a shawarma unlike any other she'd ever experienced—she looked up at me with a peculiar sort of smile, as if we were in on a secret together. When the meal concluded and we asked for the check, we were told that there wasn't one, that we were guests of Chef. My mother and I were flabbergasted, bowled over. I was just a stagière! A nobody! How could they have bought us our meal? My mother interpreted it differently.

"I am so proud of you, Tatu," she said, eyes misty.

"But I didn't do this, Mom. I didn't make this. I've been sitting here with you getting spoiled rotten."

"But you've done something, Tatu," she said. "You've done your job well—whatever your job was here, you've done it so well that they realize what a gift you are to them."

She looked at me as though I was an object of wonder—familiar, of course, but also still a mystery. I loved being the subject of her gaze then.

"You're keeping your promise to me, Tatu. You're doing the best you can."

"I'm trying, Mom," I replied. And then: "I think I understand what you and Mo have been wanting for me now. You've been wanting me to do things like this: to be among the best, right?"

"Yes, Fatima. That's exactly right. You belong in places like this, in restaurants like this. You should be learning from chefs who have this level of creativity, who make up their own language, their own rules."

"I feel it, Mom. I've been missing something, but I hadn't really been able to put my finger on what, and now I think I see what I have to do."

"All that matters is that you see it now. And we will always support you in your journey. Just make sure you are always striving for the top."

Chef Kostow came out to say hello and to meet my mother, and he embarrassed me a little by telling her that someday I was going to be famous. I blushed visibly hearing these words from someone I so admired, but I was only a little bit embarrassed, because mostly I hoped that he was right.

chapter 32

THE CONTEST
IN COLORADO

———

Fatima

———

I RETURNED TO NEW YORK AND TRIED TO PREPARE MYSELF for the competition ahead. I did Bikram yoga twice a day. I read cookbooks like novels, studying techniques as if they were sonnets I'd have to recite, and memorizing key ratios for pastry dough, bread, pasta, and ice cream, that I could lean on in moments of turmoil during the taping. I spent time with my closest friends who lived in the city, like Zainie, whipping up classic Pakistani dishes—whatever she was most craving—for us to eat for dinner. I wasn't practicing cooking "my food," exactly; it was more like staying fit, working a muscle, keeping my hands busy. I showed off a little bit for fun, chopping an onion for the biryani that Zainie had requested at lighting speed while she cheered me on.

I was allowed to bring a small array of my key ingredients with me, and Mohammad and I discussed what these should be at length over text and on the phone. What should I bring that they might not have stocked in the *Top Chef* pantry? What should I bring that the other chefs—and judges—might not be familiar with, as my arsenal of signature secret weapons? *Spices?*

Black cardamom? Kashmiri chili? What about Rooh Afza? What about Pakola? Oh, I know: What's that super-fragrant kewra paani (screwpine flower extract) thing for biryani? What about dried plums? Rose!! Yes, yes, rosewater . . . Or maybe dried rose petals—my favorite. Do you think they will have besan (chickpea flour)? I went to Kalustyan's, the Curry Hill Middle Eastern and Indian grocery mecca, to pick up cardamom, saffron, and rosewater, which reminded me of home as I inhaled their deep scents.

I packed two suitcases with outfits that I imagined would look good on camera and got on a plane to Colorado. A driver picked me up from the Denver airport and took me to a hotel, where I was told to not speak to anyone. A couple of hours later, two producers knocked on my hotel room door and proceeded to go through my things, removing any recipes, cookbooks, novels, magazines, cellphones, and computers so that we couldn't look things up. We had to rely only on the intrinsic knowledge and experience we'd brought with us. Goodbye to all of it for the next eight weeks of shooting. When they were done sorting through my bags, they told me to be ready to go to the set at six the next morning.

I slept restlessly that night, imagining the moment, only a few hours away, when I'd be cooking for Padma Lakshmi, Tom Colicchio, and Gail Simmons, plus an impossible-to-guess cast of guest judges, all food world stars.

At six a.m., tired and nervous, I got into the car that had been sent for me and another chef. We weren't supposed to speak to each other, so I studied him from the side of my eye, allowing myself to make snap judgments because they distracted me from the tight knots in my stomach. *Of course,* I thought to myself, *another typical chef dude: big, tattooed, hair gel.* But before I could make more assumptions about him, we arrived at the studio and there was Padma—the living goddess I'd watched on

TV for so many years—looking stunning, even at that hour. And there we were—the fifteen of us competitors—in the room together for the first time. We didn't even have a chance to check each other out, because immediately after welcoming us, Padma announced it was our first Quickfire challenge of the season (we would have one in every episode along with an elimination challenge): We needed to make a family-style dish—one meant to be shared—that would be good for a potluck. I made rice with tomato and yogurt dipping sauce, a straightforward dish that tasted of home, and we were off to the proverbial races.

After the Quickfire challenge, we had our first elimination challenge: putting our own spin on "meat and potatoes," which we were serving for local chefs and restaurateurs on the restaurant row of Denver. I decided to make my take on a samosa: classic potato and pea component, but deconstructed and served with braised chicken, a tamarind beet and plum sauce, mint chili yogurt, pickled chilis, and chicken skin. Padma aptly dubbed my dish a "Pakistani nacho," which felt just right, especially when she said I got "that chat-patay feeling," which is like Indian umami. Though I tried to handle this compliment with grace, internally I was screaming with joy: *Padma Lakshmi, who I watched on BBC Food for my entire childhood, liked my dish and recognized a bit of herself in it!* This meant that by leaning in to my Pakistani identity, I was doing something right.

As I was packing up, I caught one of the other competitors looking at me. I couldn't tell if she was sizing me up, admiring my turquoise snakeskin knife bag, or giving me the hairy eyeball, so I kept my gaze down, wiping my knives down with unfailing focus.

"Hi," she said, suddenly a foot away from me on the other side of the counter I'd been working on. "I'm Adrienne."

"Hi, I'm Fatima," I said, because what else was I supposed to say?

"I think we have a friend in common," she said, while most definitely staring at my hands, which were busy with my knife kit, then raising her gaze up to my face. "Brian? You two worked at Fonda together—"

"Oh my god, you know Brian?" I said, smiling, a reference from home, putting me immediately at ease.

"Yes, I met him when he was staging at Le Bernardin," Adrienne said, referring to one of New York City's most extraordinary restaurants, Chef Eric Ripert's three-star Michelin French temple to seafood in Midtown Manhattan.

"Of course you know Brian . . . you Michelin folks all know each other," I joked. Indeed, the cooks who had Michelin aspirations for themselves all worked at restaurants with Michelin stars. They are their own tribe.

Adrienne told me later that Brian had described me as a total badass in the kitchen, and that he'd said we would get along great because Adrienne's a beast too. He was right. Adrienne knew her way around just about every aspect of kitchen work and cooking, particularly fish; she kept her head down, kept her cool, and executed like the pro she was. Adrienne eventually admitted to me that in fact she *had* been staring at my hands that first day, my nails in particular, because I'd gotten a gel manicure before flying to Denver and she was trying to understand how someone that Brian had described as "a beast" in the kitchen could also have red gelled nails and sport a blue snakeskin knife roll. I loved hearing this. "Don't assume anything, Adrienne," I'd teased her. "You must never judge a book by its cover. I like to keep people guessing." She was my first *Top Chef* friend.

The next eight weeks were like being in a cyclone, like the

tornado scene in *The Wizard of Oz* when familiar images are floating past Dorothy but untethered from normal life. After the initial challenge, we were taken to our new home, a mansion in the middle of Denver. In it there was a "stew room," with lots of booze and beer, where we waited before a judgment. The whole idea of course is that we would get loosened up by drinking and then say something outrageous. I was very careful not to get carried away or say something stupid. I tried to bring my A-game from the start, to be a serious competitor.

We were all together most days and living together, of course, but for whatever reason, there were certain people that I never seemed to interact with.

"Have you had a chance to hang out with Joe Flamm at all?" Carrie Baird, one of my competitors, asked me one day.

"Not really," I answered, "but he seems great."

"He is," she said. "And I think you two would really get along."

Carrie wasn't the only person to mention this to me, but Joe and I never seemed to cross paths on set or in the house. Finally, several weeks into shooting, we found ourselves in the same car after a long day. We began to trade battle scars, laughing about memories from years in the business and the more recent battle wounds of the prior few weeks of filming. We stayed up late, shooting the shit.

"We have to cook together," Joe said as he made his way toward his room at the end of our long getting-to-know-you session.

"We have to," I echoed back.

Joe Flamm would be my rock for the rest of filming.

Mo and I spoke on the phone a little, but the cameras were always rolling in case they could catch us talking smack about competitors or admitting we missed someone back home, particularly after emotional soundbites from the chefs who'd left kids or spouses behind. Mo and I sometimes cussed unnecessarily to ensure they couldn't use our chats as fodder. It was such a different experience than I'd ever had, being cut off from friends and family and then when we were allowed to speak to them, the whole thing on camera. It was so curated. The cameras wanted to capture every human emotion, but it's not a natural environment. Is one's reaction to what happens in a Quickfire challenge or with another competitor genuine if the whole environment is being manipulated? Our performances definitely dictated how we did, but was there also a plan in place from the get-go from the producers? There's no question that they were after drama—it's reality TV, after all. I, however, felt relatively prepared for the spin and am so used to the world's preconceptions about Pakistan and Pakistanis, so I instinctively knew how to steer around the drama by never losing my cool. Though I tried to stay above the fray, I found myself opening up a lot to my new friends on the show; actually, with people like Joe Sasto and Joe Flamm, Adrienne, and Carrie, whom I was immediately drawn to, I couldn't help but share my dreams and be my usual goofy self.

"I want to be in *Maxim,*" I told Sasto one afternoon when we were talking about someday-goals.

He laughed.

"No, really," I explained. "I want to be in *Maxim,* looking hot, to make men scratch their heads and realize just because a woman is sexy doesn't mean she's not tough as nails, ambitious, and great at her craft."

"Well, that sounds about right coming from you, Fati," Sasto said, smiling.

The only time we were freed from the prying lens of the camera and our perennially eavesdropping microphones was when we were going to sleep, so some nights, when Adrienne and I were roommates, we'd say we were tired and lie in bed talking, not restricted by our mics, until we dozed off. More talk of the future, of course:

"So, Fati, what are you going to do next?" Adrienne asked me.

"I'm going to open my own restaurant," I explained matter-of-factly. "I want to open something that serves everything from traditional Pakistani street food, done with great ingredients, to fine dining . . . and everything in between."

"That sounds amazing," Adrienne said. "But what's your plan until you get it open?"

I had to admit that I didn't really have a plan. The last spell, since I'd left 8½, I'd managed to swing from one opportunity to another: from Smorgasburg, to consulting in Lahore, to my pop-up there, to Meadowood, and then straight into *Top Chef*. With so much at stake depending on how I did on the show, I hadn't really allowed myself to get more specific about how I'd survive in the interim between the show and somehow launching my own place. Although I felt like an underdog (several of my competitors, like Bruce Kalman, Tyler Anderson, and Tanya Holland, already had their own restaurants), I'd come to *Top Chef* to win and I thought winning, or at least doing well on the show, would help set up whatever was next. Listening to Adrienne's strategic, mature line of questioning, I realized I must seem extremely naïve, but instead of making me feel dumb, she told me that she'd be private cheffing after the show wrapped and that she'd be happy to share my contact info with the headhunter who helped her get gigs. It felt like having a big sister: total encouragement and looking out for me without judgment.

Nothing could have prepared me for sleeping in tents at high altitude then cooking in the snow; or for Padma waking us up at six thirty for a Quickfire challenge to make her breakfast. It really felt like an alternate universe; one in which you make friends—whom you are around twenty-four hours a day, whom you are competing against—for life. I'd fallen easily into my usual role with friends whom I adore: the class clown. I cooked for everyone, trying to cheat traditional dishes that in Pakistan would simmer for days and that I had to throw together in an exhausted evening. I always felt sheepish and that my food could be better.

My competitors were winning tens of thousands of dollars and Super Bowl tickets; we were meeting some of the best chefs in the world, from Wylie Dufresne to Paul Liebrandt. It was like a wild dream. But also, it was such an inspiring and humbling reminder that there are so many of us dreamers, so many fighters out there, people who maybe haven't had the best luck but have pushed toward their ambitions every day. If you're someone like me, who has their routine, who likes their morning coffee in peace and a little bit of space, then you have to be prepared to be annoyed a lot. We were exhausted all the time; we were being told what to do all the time, in a way, like preschoolers at the mercy of our teachers. Sharing a space with sixteen other grownups for two months is not something any of us was used to, but it's what we all wanted—to compete on *Top Chef* . . . to *win Top Chef*! Whether I won or not, being a part of it would change everything for me, I was certain of that.

Perhaps the most dizzying experience was cooking for Chef David Kinch of Manresa, his Michelin three-star in Northern California. I'd idolized him from afar for years and had seriously considered staging with him when I won Chef's Roll. He'd traveled the world, working in some of the most interesting kitchens in Japan, France, and Germany before opening Manresa in Los Gatos. He was a host on *Mind of a Chef* and is just a culinary badass, exactly the kind that I dreamt of someday being and longed to impress. I wanted him to taste my personality, my identity through my food . . . I was harboring this as my constant goal. With only thirty minutes for a Quickfire challenge cooking with edible flowers at high altitude, I made a mustard flower–rubbed lamb chop with cumin, mustard seeds, and garam masala and served it with charred broccoli florets, tahini, mint, cilantro, and an orange blossom chili oil with rose salt. I wanted to continue to separate myself from the pack by leaning in to my Pakistani heritage, and it worked. Kinch loved it and the dish put me in the number two spot.

Once again, I was the youngest of the season and sometimes felt more at home with members of the crew than I did with members of the cast. All I had in terms of experience was five years at a restaurant group and Van Pakistan. I knew I should try my best, but also that I was absolutely an underdog. The judges' approval was intoxicating, and when it landed on me, it made me feel like I really could win, but their critiques were equally powerful. I kept telling myself to enjoy the process, the pleasure of cooking for people, which was what inspired me to become a chef to begin with. We all said that we had come to win, but the truth is that a huge part of me didn't dare hope I'd make it as far as I did.

Still, it was gutting to be eliminated. I'd channeled great momentum on a collaborative dish with Laura—our cheese rind cracker—and Van Pakistan had prepared me well for our food truck challenge and my "yum-yum" waffles. But my confidence faltered when Flamm, my best buddy on the show and clearly one of the best chefs of our season, was eliminated in a sudden death round. On some level I felt like if Flamm could get knocked out, then I didn't belong there either. I was rattled and didn't make the best decisions with my Broncos-themed nachos.

Though it didn't happen consecutively when the program was edited and aired, Joe and I were actually eliminated on the same day of filming. We found ourselves reunited in the kicked-off house and immediately began to commiserate. We decided to go for a walk and get coffee, chatting the whole way to Starbucks about the surrealness of our reality TV experiences, and once we got there, we grabbed a table and spent the next three hours talking.

"Soon we'll both have our own restaurants—" Joe said positively.

"And we can meet up and cook together at each of them," I finished his thought for him. "I'm so ready for the big leagues."

"You're so confident," Joe said, teasing me a little bit, but without an ounce of doubt.

"You think that's confident?" I volleyed back. "I want to lead people around the world and into unknown cultures through food, through their palates. Food is always the best way in. It's the best way to understand my culture. All it takes is tasting our naan, our chaat, our sajji. I'm going to take all you guys there. Actually, I'm going to take the world there," I explained.

One of the defining moments for me as a chef and as a person was when Padma challenged me to cook my food, Pakistani food, with the same confidence and creativity that I put toward Western cuisine. And I heard an echo of that again in Last Chance Kitchen, when those of us who were eliminated competed for a chance to get ourselves back on the show. Tom loved my Pakistani taco bar: chana masala, poached quail egg, seven-spice-rubbed strip steak, tamarind chili sauce, and ranch–preserved lemon crème fraîche. He said he wished I'd brought that kind of heat all along . . . and so did I. Though it was painful to be cut, I'd made it to the top six and I'd learned that there was a taste for my food, my way, and that the key to my success would be to lean in to being me. I'd always known I wanted to bring attention to my culture and country through my food, but I began to realize that the mission was much deeper and more specific: I could tell the story of my country, express its complicated beauty and my Pakistani pride, through cooking. More than ever, I understood that the food I made going forward after this experience needed to be a true reflection of me, of the complexities and personal history that make me who I am.

chapter 33

THE LIFE I
ALWAYS WANTED

———

Fatima

———

IN MAY 2017, AFTER *TOP CHEF* FINISHED FILMING, I
returned to New York City, only to get a call from my Saby
Khala, telling me that my beloved grandmother, who had been
visiting her in Palm Springs for several months, wasn't doing
well. My mother was stuck in Pakistan for work, so without
thinking twice, I unpacked my suitcases from *Top Chef* and re-
packed them for a summer in the Southern California desert. I'd
care for Nano for as long as I could.

It felt good to be back with family after the strange suspended reality of filming *Top Chef*. Nano had an abscess in her
neck that had to be surgically drained, and then she needed to
recuperate for six weeks in a home, where I stayed with her day
and night. Weekdays were simple, quiet days, tending to Nano,
reading to her, watching shows, listening to her stories, and
sleeping on a reclining chair by her bedside. How different this
time was to my last visit, right after Meadowood, when Nano
had been in great form. Only a couple of months earlier, my
mother, my grandmother, and I had painted the town. Nano
had been lively, playing cards, gambling in a casino . . . she'd

even delighted me by coming with me to a famous bar for a drag show that everyone wanted to see. But on this visit, though her stories were still vivacious, she was physically frail. On the weekends, Saby Khala took over and I took the bus northwest up to Los Angeles to see a friend I'd met on set in Denver. Eden was an actor and producer who had been moonlighting on the production side of *Top Chef* as a PA, and we'd felt an instant connection. I'd kept a note she'd passed me with a private joke about a lamb shank and her phone number in my wallet, and we'd been texting and speaking often since her last night in Colorado.

I didn't mind the lengthy bus ride. Once again I found the gentle sway of public transportation soothing, cradling me into daydreams about the future, meditating on the fun that awaited me in L.A. Beyond the instant initial attraction, Eden and I were both very professionally driven, albeit in different arenas, and both found creativity essential to survival. I read her scripts and let her sing me showtunes while she drove us around town— happy, absurd, hilarious drives in L.A. traffic and in the green hills that snake up from the flat basin of the city.

I wanted to share my love of food with her, and we went to a couple of special meals out, but mostly we just spent weekends at home in her tiny apartment. I cooked for her, teaching her little tricks that made her more confident and curious in the kitchen. She lived on the edge of Los Feliz and Thai Town, so there were endless som tum papaya salads and fragrant curries, khao soi and boat noodle soups to slurp, between kissing and laughing. I told Eden I'd make her anything she wanted, and she requested stuffed cabbage that reminded her of a childhood meal by a Russian-Jewish relative, so I made it for her, not quite traditional because I laced it with some extra herbs and chilis for heat, as is my way, and served it with bona-fide French-style mashed potatoes with enough butter to take a bath in. For my birthday in August, I took her to Patina, the namesake restaurant of my former restaurant group employer, and treated her to a nine-course tasting menu. The only pleasure greater than cooking for someone you care for while they eat your food is getting to sit next to them, watching them throughout the journey of a meal from right beside them, using the corner of your napkin to remove a crumb from their lip.

It was the best summer. Splitting my time between Nano, swathed in her Chanel No. 5 even in the nursing home, making that sterile room feel homey to me, and listening to her tales of Pakistan in the old days, before Partition, before there even *was* a Pakistan, and then Eden in Los Angeles, our time full of heat and laughter and making the most out of every day and night and weekend. It had a looming end date, as all summers do. I was hungry to get back to work, to feel the rhythm of a professional kitchen again, and I'd committed to managing Chef Tony Mantuano's annual pop-up at the U.S. Open back in New York after Labor Day, so I'd return to the city when my mother was able to take my place at Nano's bedside. But that summer was all about beginnings, not endings. With shooting *Top Chef* behind me, I felt on the cusp and carried a sense of excitement and clarity that I hadn't felt for years, perhaps not since culinary school. I knew where I wanted to go and what I wanted to do; my vision for the future had returned and was bright and clear. It was just about doing the work to manifest it, and in a way, the work is the easy part. It's the precision of goals and the guts to begin that can be so hard to summon. Mo and I were Skyping regularly from opposite sides of the world, preparing at long last to write a business plan for opening our dream restaurant concept. It was time.

The long-standing plan, a conversation that we dropped for

months—years even—and then picked up again seamlessly, like knitting a long unfinished scarf, was that Mohammad and I would do this together, with him running front of house and me overseeing the kitchen. Though not a chef, flavor worship and devotion to his palate grew strong in Mo, too, and he's good with business and numbers, which I'm not. Mo doesn't lose his temper when people frustrate him, whereas I, a born chef, am more prone to lose my patience, wear my emotions on my sleeve, and can be snarky. We've always been able to communicate almost wordlessly, an energetic shorthand transmitted through glances, sounds, years of shared experience, and profound mutual understanding. Mo would quit his job in Sydney and we'd convene and make our dream a reality.

But if we pulled the trigger, the lingering question was whether it would be in New York—the most competitive place in the world to have a restaurant, where we'd be competing with the very best—or Pakistan, where profit margins are far wider, where we'd have a built-in network of patrons, and where we'd get a great deal on a space (we already knew we could take over a space that my dad owned). The concepts were different, naturally. In Pakistan, I'd play with Pakistani staples, inverting them to make my people view their own food in a new way, with an emphasis on valorizing local produce, as I had in my pop-up, maybe introducing some of my weird (and wonderful!) Pakistani-American hybrids, like Cheeseburger Chaat. If I opened a restaurant in New York, I wanted to make impeccable but unpretentious and plentiful Pakistani food—from street food to fine dining—in a cheerful, welcoming environment, raising the bar on ingredient quality and making it approachable and tremendously fun. That nexus of my years of technique and the abundance and accessible food of my youth is what I'd cook. In either place, I would make food that spoke of

my varied life, with a foot proudly in each place: Pakistan and
America.

While considering where to plant roots, my mind often
went to the market stalls and street food vendors of Karachi and
Lahore and their sense of generosity. These were uniformly
working-class people who toiled tirelessly to feed their families,
but when they sensed a kindred spirit at their street stall, they
almost always added a little something extra. As I'd perused the
markets for supplies and inspiration for my Lahore pop-up, I'd
been struck by this again: the pride that the farmers and purveyors put into their products, their contagious affection for the
produce. I wanted my restaurant to communicate that reverence.

In my gut, I knew that I wanted my restaurant to be in New
York City—the hardest place to succeed in the restaurant business . . . but also the only place I have ever felt free and at ease.
But I didn't just want a restaurant that would be all right or
good; I wanted a place that people would talk about. And I
didn't want it to be talked about because I was serving fancy
foams or weird textured spheres that looked like radishes but
tasted like olives, or fried parsnip ribbons or any of that froufrou culinary nonsense.

I wanted a place where I could open people's minds about
Pakistan through their taste buds—to serve the glorious, generous, hearty food of my youth, of my Nano, and interrupt Western assumptions of Pakistan being a place of bias, of oppression,
of terror. I didn't want people to think about my home like
that. When people heard the word Pakistan, it should be associated with how intoxicating those long-stewed goat hooves were
that literally melted in their mouth—a dish one cannot eat any
way other than loudly sucking, rudely, joyfully—with spices
that just barely cut through all that fat around the bone and

marrow that's slipped out. It isn't marrow that has to be forced out of a canoe-cut bone served with German mustard and a fancy knife in some gastropub! No. This is the same dish—the same marrow—that a shepherd who lives unapologetically with his herd cooks over a wood fire. It's a stew that you have to eat with fluffy, pillowy, tender, crispy, simple charred naan. I wanted to show people all this flavor and unctuousness that goat hooves can provide—without them even thinking that they are goat hooves—and somehow transport them through their taste buds to a dhaba in Karachi, sitting on a charpai squeezing lemon, with freshly cut green chilis and ginger on their plate. I'd serve the kaleji (chicken livers) that I grew up eating with crunchy-soft toothsome potains (chicken colons), fragrant with clove and cardamom, coriander, chilis, and garlic. I'd marinate meat with raw papaya to break down its toughness, barbecue it, and wrap it around a soft-boiled egg, and instead of barbecuing it to make bihari kebab, I'd coat and then fry it to make a Pakistani Scotch egg.

My guests would feel the sense of gentle care, of easygoing but exciting nourishment, that Mohammad and I felt at Nano's kitchen table. My food would speak directly to my customers. It would tell them its own story, frankly, and in doing so, they'd stop associating Pakistan with bombings and terrorism and start thinking about hot crispy chips, skewers of spiced liver, and peppers and potato and eggplant charred just right. They'd think about fluffy steaming basmati rice swirled with soft pieces of chicken. Suddenly they'd start thinking about colors and cocktails that are sour and sweet. They'd stop thinking about the bad stuff and start saying, *Hey, have you been to this place?*

But herein lies the paradox: Even as I longed to ingratiate foreigners to my home country through their palates, for myself, I find the idea of life in Pakistan anything but palatable. In

Pakistan, I was perpetually running into acquaintances from my youth—men and women who think they know me because we studied in the same classroom when we were fourteen or because they saw me on TV—in other words, people who don't know me at all. And when I was accosted on the street in Karachi by these well-meaning people, I felt a shortness, an uncomfortableness, like a dog choking on a taut leash. I felt that I was suffocating there, being asphyxiated by the societal pressure and lacking the anonymity I have everywhere else.

For all these reasons, I wanted my restaurant to be in New York City.

PART III

chapter 34

THE HEALTH
DEPARTMENT

———

Fatima

———

I RETURNED TO NEW YORK CITY TO FOLLOW THROUGH on my commitment to manage Chef Tony Mantuano's annual pop-up at the U.S. Open, waiting for *Top Chef* to air and for the accompanying gust of attention to propel me into the great unknown. I had the sense that thanks to the show, my self-realizations at Meadowood, and the seriousness with which Mohammad and I had been discussing opening a restaurant together, things were about to fall into place. I'd had an ache in my left shoulder for a while, but was certain it was from sleeping on the recliner in Nano's room at the rehabilitation clinic after her surgery. Then, on the last Friday night of the pop-up, what had been a dull and manageable ache, the kind chefs who spend sixteen hours on their feet are excellent at ignoring, became an intense burning sensation that kept me from easily moving my left shoulder or arm. I unbuttoned my chef jacket and pulled the neck hem back and down so that my bartender friend could see my bare skin. He took one look at the protruding plum-sized swell between my spine and shoulder, gasped, and said he thought I should go straight to the emergency room.

At the ER, the on-call doctors at first thought it was an abscess and tried, unsuccessfully, to aspirate it. Within twenty
minutes of seeing me, an orthopedic surgeon ordered an MRI
because I was in so much pain. I remember the doctor was ex-
ceptionally handsome, so much so that it distracted me as I wept
fearfully about what was wrong with me. When he delivered
the news that the scan came back clear apart from an anomaly in
the periphery of the scan, near my brachial plexus but nowhere
near my shoulder lump, I thought to myself, *This guy should be
on a runway.* He prescribed me oxycodone for the gnawing pain.
Not long after I'd gotten back to my apartment, the doctor
called me, and for an instant, I thought, *Okaaaay, here we go, he's
about to ask me out,* but instead he said:

"Fatima, I hate to do this over the phone, but I don't want to
waste any time. This could be something very serious. I'd like
you to call some family to help you through, because I am going
to refer you to an oncologist."

I called Mo in Sydney. It was already Saturday there, and he
was on his way to the farmers market with his girlfriend—
a world away from me in every sense.

"Mohammad, I think I'm in trouble," I began. "I don't know
what to do." I told him about the last twenty-four hours: the
pain, the emergency room, the scans, the phone call. "I might
have cancer," I said, my voice breaking.

"Hey, hey," he said. "Hey, it's okay, we're going to find out
exactly what it is, and don't worry: Just because they suspect it
doesn't mean anything, and in any case cancer is super common
now, it affects like one in three people, and there is very good
medicine out there even if you do have it."

As always, hearing his voice, his calm, his perspective, helped.

"I can't tell Mom," I admitted, beginning to fall apart at the mention of my mother hearing this news. "I won't be able to do it—"

"Fatima, take a breath," Mo said. "Breathe deep. Relax. Close your eyes for a few hours. Or if you're not sleepy, go do something nice for yourself with the rest of the day. I'll handle speaking to everyone and coordinating."

My mother flew in from California, where she was caring for Nano, my father from Washington, D.C., where he happened to be working, and Mo from Sydney—they all descended upon New York City to accompany me to my Monday appointment. It was an incredibly rare family reunion under the worst possible circumstances. One by one, they arrived to find me prostrate on a purple futon in Saadia's apartment, writhing in pain despite the medications I'd already been prescribed. How could the dull ache I'd been feeling for a couple of months have developed into this scorching pain—as though a red-hot fire poker was being twisted in my shoulder, never cooling, only going deeper and radiating more burning flesh—in a mere few days? I'm usually pretty tough, but I was sick from the pain.

On Monday, together we went in a rented van that my dad had organized to a renowned orthopedic oncologist in Long Island City. While my imaging was interpreted as cancer, the sarcoma specialist believed it wasn't, but rather something called compartment syndrome—fluid buildup caused by an injury. He was so nonchalant that he didn't insist we have a biopsy. He recommended applying ice packs and bedrest for a couple of weeks (his blasé attitude was perhaps related to his imminent departure for vacation). Call it mother's instinct, but my mom did not accept his diagnosis, not for a second. We all hoped it was an infection, something quickly treatable once we understood what we were dealing with, but whatever it was, we needed to figure out who could best help us, who was the right doctor to properly diagnose me so that I could begin treatment immediately. After insisting that we wanted it biopsied, the sarcoma specialist sent us to his colleague at the nearby Jewish hospital, who was unable to see us immediately.

It was chaos. While we wrestled with getting my insurance in order, my mother, sister, and Mo all stayed together in a one-bedroom apartment on 140th Street in East Harlem, far from the hospital. Friends all over the world referred us to friends of theirs who were doctors who we could at least speak to on the phone, and they insisted that if there was any chance it was a sarcoma, that a biopsy was critical due to the risk of cancer spreading and a "tract" being left behind from a biopsy needle, which could lead to the cancer cells seeding and the tumor becoming inoperable. The pain was grinding, blinding, and becoming unbearable.

My primary care physician refused to see me, claiming he was "too busy," and to "come back next week." We were baffled and felt trapped. The sort of pain I was in was so acute that as I tried to sleep at night, I wondered if I would wake up the next morning.

Mo took aside one of the nurses and pleaded with her to get us time with a doctor, that a young life was literally on the line. She closed her eyes, inhaled, and looked over his shoulder at me in a constant wince, holding up my elbow to find some relief. We had been there for four hours only to have been turned away.

The nurse nodded and told us to wait. She came back an hour later and snuck us in to see another doctor at the clinic who could act as my PCP. She was a woman who had beat cancer in the past, and she cared what was happening to me. She submitted an out-of-network authorization to try to get me in to a highly recommended sarcoma specialist at Memorial Sloan Kettering, one of the best cancer treatment hospitals in the world, but while waiting for it to come through, she also referred us to a sarcoma specialist at Mount Sinai. That specialist conducted a core needle biopsy to analyze tissue and diagnose conclusively, and told us that there was little risk involved and we were likely to get results quickly. The biopsy procedure triggered even more pain, and while we waited for the results, my family, frightened and exhausted already, took me to the emergency room, which treated me with pain meds and sent me home with a prescription for Dilaudid. After eight days, the biopsy results came back and were inconclusive due to "insufficient tissue," so a surgical biopsy was ordered and would be performed as soon as my insurance approved it. These early days of terror and confusion, coupled by the frustration of waiting on insurance, were a brutal welcome to the American medical system.

My friends tried to keep my spirits up. *It won't be anything serious, inshallah,* Zainie and Lala took turns telling me over dinner at Lala's one night, and I prayed they were right. Although I knew that I wasn't contagious, there was some wicked magic related to this lump on my shoulder. It had the power to suck up all the energy in a room, to kill laughter.

The pain that had begun by taking up residence in my shoulder became almost like a phantom that could move freely through my body. During these interminable days of waiting, the ghoul found his way to my head, screaming in my ears, pushing against the inside of my skull. Sometimes I thought that my family must be able to hear the wicked screeching, but it wasn't the ghoul they could hear; it was me. I was in so much pain that I couldn't stay quiet. I couldn't sleep because of the monster moving between my shoulder and my mind, and I moaned restlessly in my exhausted half-consciousness, terrifying my mother and brother. They rushed me to MSK's emergency department in the middle of the night, where I was finally admitted and a biopsy was performed with me as an inpatient. The insurance company had dragged their feet so much that it felt like they'd rather I died than have to rubber-stamp a procedure I needed. Once you are in the ER, though, approvals come in quickly. The doctors at MSK explained that my pain was so acute because it was coming both from my bones *and* my nerves, and I remained hospitalized so that they could control my pain until the results from my biopsy came in. In October, five weeks after I had made that first trip to the ER, it was confirmed that I had undifferentiated blue round cell sarcoma. My new oncologist at MSK, Dr. Lenny Wexler, a stooped Jewish grandfather-type who I'd come to find wore a yarmulke and a black suit every day, came in to talk to me.

"I'm sorry it's taken so long to get answers for you," he began. "We've finally got a handle on what this is. Fatima, you have an undifferentiated sarcoma, which means we cannot tell exactly what kind of sarcoma it is yet, but that we need to start your treatment immediately."

We were all holding each other's hands—my mother, my brother, and I, trying to be brave for each other. Each shaking inside, if not visibly.

"We want to start you on chemotherapy tomorrow," Dr. Wexler continued. "But before we start, I need to go over a few things with you."

I adjusted myself in bed, sitting up straighter, bracing for whatever was about to come out of his mouth. I looked him straight in the eye. Perhaps I was testing him. Perhaps I needed my doctor to be able to hold my gaze through whatever he was about to tell me in order to trust him, in order to give my body over to him and his care for safekeeping.

"The first thing is that chemotherapy affects your fertility. You're a young woman; probably you've thought about having children?" He paused, looking at me. I, in turn, looked at my mother. She and I locked eyes. Of course I'd assumed I'd some-day make her a grandmother. I began to nod my head yes and turned my eyes back to Dr. Wexler.

"Well, then, you may know that a woman has a finite num-ber of eggs in her ovaries. You don't produce more the way men produce more sperm throughout their life. There's a strong pos-sibility that chemotherapy will contaminate your eggs. That after you complete chemotherapy, you won't be able to have children."

Again my eyes went to my mother's. Only she could begin to fathom what this potential loss felt like for me. My gaze fell into my lap and my shoulders began to shake as I wept, begin-ning to mourn the someday-family that now would never be.

"There are options," Dr. Wexler said, while I cried quietly. "We can give you a monthly injection that will put you in a menopausal state. We can trick your body into not releasing an egg each month, so that those eggs can at least remain in your ovaries to be released on the other side of this once chemo is complete. We cannot promise that they will be viable or that you will get pregnant with them, but it's one way of trying to stave off infertility." I heard him through my tears, thinking how absurd this conversation was: a twenty-eight-year-old dis-cussing menopause with her doctor. He continued: "Or you could freeze your eggs. You could see a fertility specialist who could help you through that process, which will take several months at best, but could lead to your having eggs on ice that would be uncontaminated by the chemotherapy protocol that we'll administer once they've been harvested and frozen—"

"Let's do that," I interrupted, my gaze sweeping across the darting eyes of my family, summoning them to get aligned with me. "That seems like a good option."

"Well, it would be," Dr. Wexler countered, "except for the fact that we don't want to wait a few months to begin your treatment. We don't feel with tumors this unusual and aggressive that we have a few months to wait. We want to start your chemotherapy treatments tomorrow."

"So I have to choose between being fertile and living?" I asked in disbelief with my voice escalating from panic. Was I really asking this question? Did I really have to make this decision?

"We definitely do not recommend waiting to start your treatment," he said as a response.

"I need a few hours, or maybe a few minutes, at least, to process this," I told him. I looked at my mother. Her upper lip trembled but she kept her gaze steady. Just saying her name, the word that we utter countless times throughout life when we need help, made me falter: "Mom?"

"You can adopt a child," she said without missing a beat. My rock. "So what if you can't have a baby? Think about the good you will be able to do for someone who really needs you."

I nodded and inhaled. And then: "What else?"

"What else?" Dr. Wexler parroted.

"Yeah, what else do I need to prepare for if I start chemo tomorrow?"

I took a deep breath. I wrestled myself back into composure. I stopped crying. *This is the most excruciating thing I'll ever go through,* I told myself. *It doesn't get worse than this. If I can get through this conversation, I can get through anything.* I prepared myself for whatever he might say next.

"Lots of parts of your normal bodily functions can be affected by chemotherapy. You could lose your sense of taste—"

"My sense of taste? Doctor, I am a chef," I told him, aghast that after telling me I might not be able to have children, he was also potentially wresting my career from me. "My sense of taste is crucial to me, to my career, to my identity."

"There's a spectrum of possibilities in terms of how the chemo affects each patient. Some have no issue; some lose their sense of taste entirely, but it returns incrementally after the treatment. Some patients have a persistent metallic taste in their mouths. Some become adverse to flavors that normally are appealing."

"What will happen to my hair?" I asked, knowing full well that people treating cancer with chemo lose their hair.

I felt like I was tied to a target and being shot at. I wanted all the arrows to hit me at once.

Dr. Wexler's voice became very gentle.

"You see, chemotherapy is designed to attack rapidly dividing cells throughout your body. In this way it is indiscriminate, so those cells such as your hair, or stomach and gastrointestinal cells . . . all get damaged. So yes, you will lose your hair as you take the chemo, but it will grow back after each cycle."

He said it so softly that I could almost accept it, but then I had a horrible thought:

"What about my eyebrows?"

"They'll go too, I'm afraid."

My eyebrows. My favorite thing about my face, the thing I was a little bit proud of even during my most awkward preteen phases. My lush, thick, gracefully arched, pitch-black Pakistani eyebrows. I began to sob again, absurd as that is, about losing my eyebrows, head in hands.

Dr. Wexler let me cry for a minute.

"Fatima, I know this is a brutally difficult thing to consider, that all of this is overwhelming, but I want you to think about what is really important to you. I can tell you love your eyebrows and I wish I could promise they wouldn't fall out, but I can't. I can promise that they will grow back just as thick—it will just take time. But what I need to know from you is what's so essential to your identity that I should be aware of and consider as I create your treatment protocol, as I navigate how best to make you well again, something you cannot sacrifice."

What a question! When told I may not be able to have children, that I may lose my sense of taste, I am now being asked what's most important to me . . . what is essential. *Isn't it all essential?!* I wanted to scream. But I didn't. I took a deep breath and tried to picture myself healthy, living normally. I tried to envision myself as a regular person just living their regular life.

"I'm a chef, Doctor," I began. "I need to be able to toss pans, to chop things, to use my arms, to lift stuff . . ."

"We'll have to cross that bridge when we come to it, I'm afraid. We can't promise that you'll be the same as you used to be after this course of treatment, Fatima," Dr. Wexler said. "But I promise you we will do our best to get you healthy and strong again."

Why ask me what I'd save in a fire and then tell me that all they can do is their best? He insisted I begin my chemotherapy regimen the very next day. I agreed, as I really had no other choice.

After two rounds of chemo—about six weeks later—my diagnosis finally came. Despite it's being a form of cancer most often associated with young white males, I was diagnosed with

Ewing's sarcoma, a malignant small round blue cell tumor that manifests in the bone and soft tissue. As soon as the determination came in, they wanted to start me on a new chemo protocol: four rounds of a cocktail of five chemo drugs that were administered using a three-week cycle.

~

IT'S AS IF WITH THE DIAGNOSIS, SOME EVIL CHIMERA WAS conjured to haunt me. My vision buckled as I tried to make sense of my "new" life. I was in a state of perpetual recalibration. While I was terrified, knowing that my situation was dire and that starting treatment immediately was essential to survival, I also knew that I must remain positive, that the only way to beat it was to commit completely to positivity, to rally people around me, and to keep plowing through every obstacle that came my way.

Privately, I turned to Allah. I hated having to ask those around me for help, but asking God for help was different. Though I'd not centered my life around Him, I'd always sensed His presence, and sure enough He was there with me in my anguish, sometimes frustratingly quiet, refusing to answer my most daunting question of *Why?* but present nonetheless, making me feel less alone.

And so began the next chapter of my life. Once again, I bobbed and weaved, a weakened boxer, this time trying to evade the crushing punches that this cruel and rare form of cancer landed on my twenty-eight-year-old frame and my hopeful, ambitious, furious spirit.

My days and nights became about fighting the wretched disease, and this sort of do-or-die fighting left little time, energy, or vision for planning my future. First I had to get myself well,

I told myself, and I'd worry about the rest once I was cancer-free.

Some days, the medications themselves made me so sick, so nauseous, that my bed became a skiff at sea. If I lay absolutely still, the room would stop spinning and my stomach wouldn't retch. The mention of food made me feel violently ill, and I was losing weight faster than I could consume calories: ten pounds in six days. I was afraid that if I didn't force myself to eat I'd become unrecognizable to myself in the mirror.

Oddly, I had no appetite for the smoothies and plain pastas that sustained those in treatment around me. I made a half-hearted request for daal chawal to my mother. Yellow lentils and rice. A staple in Pakistan, and something I ate often growing up. I surprised myself; wracked with post-chemo side effects, my brain was hardwired to derive comfort from the familiar. I thought about food tentatively, testing out the images of biryani and karahi in my mind. The food of my youth kept the nausea at bay.

In a role reversal, after my umpteenth round of chemo, Zainie asked me what I was craving and I told her chicken makhani, the spicy, creamy tomato curry that tastes of warmth and comfort. She was adorably stressed about cooking for a chef. *Today, I'm just your sick best friend,* I told her, and inside I asked myself if a person who no longer cooks can be called a chef. A few days later, I longed for nihari, the spice-heavy thick beef stew derived from ancient mughals who ate it at daybreak, and she obliged again. I helped her in the end, gently fixing the seasoning, which requires an almost impossible to believe number of spices—ground fennel seeds, cardamom, cloves, coriander, cumin, turmeric, chili, powdered garlic, nutmeg, *and* masala—to give it the proper oomph. I stirred in a flour slurry to thicken it for her, and then we sat quietly together, sucking

on the fragrant beef shank bones. The silence wasn't awkward—
it never could be between us, but it felt like we were both grap-
pling with the strangeness of this new existence. Only a few
months before, Zainie had had a little health scare and had
needed to get infusions, and I'd taken the day off work to bring
her soup and sit with her for eight hours while the medicine
dripped into her. Now it was me who was weak. I needed help
with everything, even cooking.

I made plans to cook Thanksgiving in my home kitchen, despite worried protests from my family. They wanted me to rest
and avoid the dangers of cuts and burns, but they also knew I
couldn't stay away. The night before Thanksgiving, when I
should have been at home prepping in a fragrant kitchen with
music playing and a swing in my step, I was instead back at
MSK, crying frustratedly in my hospital bed. My own body had
given itself an infection and the doctors were debating my re-
lease. I held my nurse's hand as tears streamed down my face. It
could almost be comical, my crying over missing the turkey.

"I need to go home and cook," I told her. No such luck.

Thankfully, Christmas and New Year's Eve were spent laying the table with dish after dish that I'd made. Garam masala
roasted duck, cornbread pistachio stuffing, rosewater bundt
cake. Somehow the dates lined up with my chemotherapy recovery weeks, and I had the strength to spend those days slowly
dicing, slicing, and icing. Maybe someone up there was looking
out for me after all.

chapter 35

FALLEN PALMS

———

Farezeh

———

IT WAS A FRIDAY NIGHT. I WAS IN PALM SPRINGS, THERE to take care of Mummy after Fatima had to return to New York.

My phone lit up with Mohammad's name, calling me from Australia, and I smiled. It was always a tonic to hear from him.

"How are you doing, Mom?"

He sounded guarded. As if by using the wrong words he might accidentally commit a crime.

I asked him what was up. He took a deep breath.

"I need you to stay very calm. Where are you? Can you please sit down?"

"Why, Mohammad?" I slowly lowered myself onto the floor, my sinking heart following suit.

"I just got off the phone with Fatima and she's unwell. She has to get some tests done. The results of her MRI have just come back and it looks like a tumor."

There was silence, a home in California and one in Sydney unraveling as the words hung between us. Mohammad told me two things: one, that it was serious, and two, that Fatima was terrified. Fatima did not want me to panic, but she knew she would never be able to hide her own fear from me. She had needed his support to break the news to me and their father.

"Oh no, Mohammad." My voice cracked, my head in my palms. He told me he was getting the first flight out to New York and that he would meet me there.

When Mohammad was younger, he once ran into a table and hurt his forehead. Seeing him wince in pain made me start to cry—something my friends laughed at me for. But I did not want to see them hurt, not by a scrape, nor by an extra ureter. What possible reaction could there be for a tumor?

The vocabulary to describe the dread you feel when you know your child is deeply unwell has not been invented yet. Maybe because parents who have experienced it do not wish to revisit that moment ever again if they can help it. It is fear incarnate. It is an undoing.

You start to negotiate with an invisible force, telling it that perhaps it was an abscess that only needed to be cut and drained. Or maybe, you pray, it can go away on its own. Perhaps really all it needs is some antibiotics. It could be only skin-deep. But you always know when you're on the losing side of that desperate, naïve bargain.

My heart quietly whispered to me that this was not a false alarm, that the dread I felt was warranted, and despite the noise, that was all I heard. But there was no diagnosis I could obsessively research, no other condition I could blame this on. Fatima was in the best shape of her life and I had only just seen her.

I booked the early-morning flight for the following day and arrived in Saadia's apartment in New York City to find Fatima barely able to move from the bed to the bathroom, lying miserably on the futon. There was a gruesome lump peering out from between her shoulders. She had been pumped full of opioids but they seemed to have no effect. She did not complain, but her face told me everything, the pain etching itself into its contours. Fatima, the unflappable, reduced to a curled-up ball.

Imtiaz had just left New York; he had taken her to the emergency room two nights earlier. Ashtar rushed up from D.C. where, by a stroke of luck, he'd been working rather than in Lahore. Mohammad arrived the next morning, a Sunday. An unspoken anticipation of the worst happening colored every word we said to each other at this cruel family reunion. Cramped into a tiny apartment, there was nowhere to hide from the anguish that was concentrated in Fatima's body.

We all scrolled through entire contact lists, calling in favors, trawling the internet for any leads to schedule Fatima an emergency appointment to meet with the best oncologist we could find. We were in the richest country in the world with the world's best hospitals, yet we struggled to secure something as basic to treatment as a first appointment. We managed to get an appointment with a leading doctor in Long Island City whom the orthopedic surgeon had told us to see immediately.

Ashtar organized a van and the four of us found ourselves in a car together again. Nearly twenty-five years had passed since the children had seen their parents work as a team. As the layers of emotions enveloped us, we let the past be the past, because nothing was more important than what we were facing; nothing was more important than Fatima's condition.

We were at our sharpest and most polite during the ten brief minutes that the doctors found for us, for fear of getting them offside, fear of making them feel uncomfortable. We lived in fear of missing a detail, using the wrong words, overstating something, understating something. We were desperate for someone from the other side to be our ally—that is how it felt sometimes, like some sort of battle of attrition: us versus the healthcare system. One of the painful surprises of this fight was the discovery that so much of medicine is really just guesswork; for all the science in the field, it is far less precise than you would think. Sometimes we left a doctor's office more bewildered than when we went in.

This started becoming clear the moment we tried to get her needle biopsy conducted as urgently as possible: We were told it wouldn't be possible without her insurance approving it; they needed to check the claim and decide whether they think it "necessary," and with a hospital they've struck a deal with to ensure they don't have to pay too much. One absurd bureaucracy-riddled step after another. I could not believe that there were medical professionals with the means and tools to take my daughter's pain away, but they would remain out of my reach by manmade, unnecessary, and ultimately meaningless structures that turned Fatima, a human being in need, into a number on a spreadsheet.

Fatima, distraught and unable to understand the pain she was feeling, just wanted relief. We had to break up our days into thirty-minute intervals, one step after the next. We would try to make it to the night, at each step learning about what was triggering Fatima's pain, and we were trying to improvise and fix her the best we could. All the doctors did was prescribe heavier drugs. Our mission was only to help her suffer less, whatever that meant, until our next appointment, until another one hundred or two hundred steps were taken. We googled, we called, we prayed, we applied ointments, we made special teas, we brewed broths, we cooked what she felt like eating, we subscribed to all the streaming services, we encouraged her friends to come over, we looked for new apartments, we cried in the halls of the building, or silently as we tried to sleep, unsure of where to direct our own emotions. Some days, when the pain was very intense and she had taken the maximum amount of drugs she was allowed to, she would go off to sleep, and I would look over from time to time to check if her chest was moving. One evening I peered over from the bed I was sleeping in to see Mohammad with his fingers near Fatima's nose. He slept near her, checking from time to time whether she was still breathing, whether she was still alive. We never acknowledged this, for fear saying it out loud might curse us. We tried only to look at our next step, our next thirty minutes.

After much research it was clear that we wanted her to get to Memorial Sloan Kettering (MSK), New York's—and therefore the world's—leading cancer hospital. We assured Fatima that we would camp outside MSK if that was what it took to get her face time with a doctor there who could tell her what was wrong with her, and more important, soothe her agony. So far, no one's expertise seemed to do anything to help my daughter. Her pain seemed to dwell in a place unreachable to all except her. The tumor was next to a bunch of nerves—it was literally coming out of her bone. The solution? OxyContin, Dilaudid, morphine, fentanyl, pick your favorite. The effect? Momentary escape—sometimes her bright smile would make an appearance soothing our souls, but nausea and then sleep were most common.

As we bounced from one doctor to the next, the outlines of Fatima's fate began to be filled in, like a form slowly being populated. And with every answer revealed, I wanted nothing more than to erase what was said. What was wrong with her? *It looked like cancer.* How do we know? *We need to do a needle biopsy.* Did that work? *No, it only made her suffering even more unbearable—the tumor was awakened and made its presence known. So we need to do it surgically.* Okay, did that get the job done? *Well, now we know it's cancer, small blue round cell cancer, but it is "undifferentiated," i.e., an unknown type of sarcoma.* Then we finally found out it was Ewing's sarcoma, a rare and vicious cancer that normally surfaces in young white boys. What the hell was it doing in Fatima? What the hell was any type of cancer doing in FATIMA?

Why has this happened? No answers. *How has this happened?* Nothing. Chemotherapy began, as we were told by her doctors that it needed to begin immediately. The therapy had no regard for Fatima's plans. She cried to me and I told her it would all be all right. There was a lighthouse somewhere that could guide us home, even as the ship we were on seemed to be springing leaks at every turn. I suppose we all believed that there was going to be a time after this. We had to cling to that belief.

I wanted to pull my hair out, to scream at the top of my lungs and run away from all of this with the same recklessness with which the tumor had upended Fatima's life. I could feel the fear of the worst poisoning every vein in my body.

This young woman who could go toe-to-toe with anyone in the kitchen suddenly needed help to walk? Was this a joke? A dream? Every time I thought I was asleep, the pungency of the hospital disinfectant brought me back to cold hard reality. I traced the past in my mind as if I was searching for a light switch or box of matches in the pitch darkness: Where had I gone wrong as a mother? What had she been exposed to that had manifested as this growth? What could it mean that my mother *and* my daughter were unwell at the same time? We collectively decided to shield my mother from the severity of Fatima's diagnosis; with Mummy already unwell, I feared worry would make her worse. With the two women I loved most unwell at the same time, I wondered why couldn't it be me instead.

chapter 36

THE DINNER RUSH

———

Fatima

———

ETWEEN OCTOBER 2017 AND JANUARY 2018, THE intense chemo regimen that stole my hair and quashed my appetite also did what it was supposed to do: It shrank the tumor in my shoulder to an operable size. I underwent surgery that excavated 30 percent of bone and tissue from my left scapula. The surgery went well: "clear margins" around the tumor and we were told it hadn't metastasized, apparently a good sign. We were also told that since the cancer was localized, surgery to remove it plus seven more rounds of chemo should lead to a positive outcome, one in which I was cancer-free.

As a result of the surgery, I lost range of motion in my left arm—I'd never be able to high-five friends with my left hand again. I wondered how I would withstand a busy Saturday-night service, jumping behind the line if my sous chef couldn't keep up. *Maybe I'm becoming the one who can't keep up,* I thought. I tried to picture myself working the tandoor oven with one arm—a bleak thought. Establishing the perfect rhythm of slapping naan dough against the furnace-hot walls while simultaneously rotating the skewers of various marinated meats so they don't burn to a crisp is skilled and ambidextrous work, not for the one-handed.

My thoughts were perpetually tinged with worry, but I knew that the love for food and cooking was so strong inside me that even cancer couldn't cut it down. I dreamt in vivid color—of pad thai and pastina, and, in my haze of medical-marijuana-induced munchies, I chowed down, relishing every bite. (Weed was my savior, allowing me to enjoy food again and keeping the nausea at bay during my chemo weeks.)

I thought often of my early years in professional kitchens. The chaos, the whirling dervish of work. Once, at Café Centro, when I was a junior sous chef running the show and several cooks had called out sick, the person who was transporting the catering trays dropped them all onto the pedestrian walk at Forty-fifth Street and Lexington Ave. In the middle of the lunch rush, with all the cooks missing, we had to remake everything. There were plenty of days like that. But you know what? It was amazing. Managing to get through a day like that—and not only living to tell about it, but doing it again and again—it makes you understand what a human is physically capable of. We're so resilient. If I had to do it all again, I wouldn't have changed anything.

I continued to dream of my future restaurant, where the kebabs would melt against the tongue and the cocktails would be just sweet enough to calm the burn. I tried to cast the cancer out of me through sheer will, like an exorcist, despite every ache sending me into a private hell of terror that I tried to hide from my devoted, terrified mother and brother. My cancer not only derailed my life; it upended theirs and provided them with daily agonies that no drug or procedure could ameliorate.

There's no certain end date with cancer; once you have it, you worry it's going to plague you again and again forever, or rather, until the real end, the Big End. Trying to stave off its return or at least catch its return early, my doctors tested me periodically after the surgery using PET scans and MRIs. In April, scans showed some "nodes" on my lungs, but the doctors said I shouldn't worry. (Oh, I worried!) Despite telling me not to be concerned, they prescribed me precautionary additional chemo rounds to try to avoid the chance of relapse: five rounds of a new drug called irinotecan. I complied of course. I wanted to live. But I also wanted a change. I *needed* a change. New York had become nothing but hospital beds; a cycle of interminable waiting for referrals, for approvals, for answers; the icy drip of chemo and frightened family members' faces. Spring was coming, but I wanted more than a fickle New York spring, even with all its Central Park daffodils and Park Avenue tulip charm. I wanted eternal, predictable sunshine.

In April, I flew to California for the Pebble Beach Food & Wine festival. I met Eden in L.A. and we drove up the coast together to Monterey, where I got to cook with Elizabeth Falkner, Tyler Anderson, and Bruce Kalman—all *Top Chef* alumni, the latter two from my season. My friend Shilpa, who I'd been close with since CIA, came with me as my sous and tried to do the heavy lifting, to predict when my bum left arm would hold me back and to make up for it by doing things for me, but mostly I didn't let her. I'd been doing physiotherapy daily and pushing through the pain to get some strength back in my left arm. I'd somehow managed to train a different muscle to nearly make up for what had been cut out during my surgery. I've always hated asking for help.

It was glorious cooking and being one of the guys again. Feeling free. Though cancer had left its mark on me—maimed me, really—that weekend, surrounded as I was by food and friends, the scents of wood-fire grilling and pine needles, made me feel alive in a way I hadn't in months. The Pacific reflecting the sunlight, white as a flame glowing into forever; the impossible grace of the cyprus trees, balancing precariously on the ancient gray rocks, silent as mimes in the windy distance. Fans approached me and asked for my autograph. We hung out with a chef whom I've always admired and her partner, and I had the sense that my community was waiting for me, like I was standing on a doorstep outside a party, hearing the music, catching the scents of roasted meats and fragrant sauces, the banter and music on the other side of the door, if I could just get through it. It felt like a taste of what my life would be like when I got well. It filled me full of hope and determination.

Then in June, I met Joe Sasto and Joe Flamm in Aspen for the Food & Wine Classic. *Top Chef* had a big presence at the annual event, and though we weren't actually cooking together, we had so much fun. I was in remission and elated to be back with my best buddies from the show. Flamm was expecting his first child and we all felt high on life as much as dizzy from the altitude. Eden had joined me there, and Flamm hadn't seen her since Denver when she'd met us at a bar on her last night and he'd seen our spark. Flamm punched my right bicep gently, happy for me that she was still in the picture.

"I don't give a fuck, anymore, Joe," I told him over the din of the boisterous room. "I am going to do me. I'm not tiptoeing around it with my family or anyone."

"That's my girl," he said. "You do you. You show them all how it's done." Then, after a pause, Joe continued: "I never even blinked that day in the Starbucks when you said you wanted to be the next Tony Bourdain or Jamie Oliver. If anyone should be out there, on camera, cooking, eating, adventuring, it's you. Just follow your gut."

And I wanted to. When we'd filmed *Top Chef,* I'd been afraid to drink on camera, afraid to offend, afraid to set a bad example for young Pakistani girls, but after a brush with death, I felt differently: I just wanted to be myself. I just wanted to live my life and my truth.

When I told Joe Sasto a bit about the last months of treatment in New York City and my hankering for change, he encouraged me to explore the idea of living in L.A. "Your food would work so well there," he'd said of his hometown, and the more I considered it, the more I agreed. L.A. was the perfect place for something informal—but I could also start informal and then grow a project into fine dining. There was a receptivity to the Los Angeles food scene that didn't exist in the hyper-competitive, impossible-to-make-ends-meet dining scene of New York.

In typical "me" form, by the time I got back to New York City, I had a plan I was certain of: I needed a change and I wanted to move to L.A., cancer be damned. Dr. Wexler, my oncologist at MSK in New York, was not happy with the idea of me leaving mid-chemo cycle for the other side of the country, but I can be pretty convincing, and I wore him down. I did my first three rounds at MSK overlooking the East River while healing toxins dripped into my impatient veins, and then prepared to leave town for the City of Angels, praying it held mine.

In July, on my way to an imminent clean bill of health, my mom and I arrived in L.A., immediately feeling lighter and more full of hope under the California sky. We'd found a four-bedroom ranch house in San Marino with a deck, a back garden, walnut floors, big windows, and lots of light that was way out of our budget, but Mohammad wrote a letter to the owner, a Christian church around the corner, sharing my story and our love for the house, and they came down on the price for us. We'd chosen this area because it had the best school district for my little brother Bangu's last year of high school. My mother was glued to me, and though I hated to make her worry, which was inevitable, I enjoyed knowing she wasn't going anywhere. For the first time in a decade, I was back in the fold of family, but also for the first time, I was not resisting it. Mo, too, had rerouted his life to be with me. He'd convinced his boss in Sydney to transfer him to his company's California offices.

I doubled down on my health. I started to eat extremely healthily, as I'd never done before, and joked that I was just acclimating to L.A.'s healthy living culture. But far more seriously, I was looking into Gerson therapy, which would mean spending time in Mexico or Budapest in one of their two clinics and subsisting on a simple plant-based diet, taking coffee enemas and supplements to detoxify my body, to hopefully stop the cancer from regenerating. In the meantime, I ate only organic produce, I brewed my own kombucha, I made simple and nutritious meals. Any sacrifice of flavor or satisfying fatty unctuousness now was worth it to become cancer-free, to confirm that I was in remission, to buy myself more life to live.

I'd filled out my Medi-Cal California (PPO) application before we left New York so that I was sure to be covered for my last two rounds of chemo at USC Keck. I did as I was told, counting down the days until this nightmare would finally be behind me. After my first round of chemo on the West Coast (my eleventh round of chemo in ten months), I began to feel a strange pain in my hip. *The ghoul,* I thought with terror, *the ghoul is back.* The ghoul that sank its rancid fangs into my shoulder and that shrieked inside my skull in New York was back, and had decided to possess and torture me from my hip.

My mother immediately wanted me to see my L.A. oncologist, Dr. Helman, but his office told us that the essential administrative paperwork that I'd filled out when I'd gone in for my first L.A. chemo treatment had been "misplaced" by the hospital. With this paperwork literally lost in the shuffle, I'd been automatically defaulted to an HMO, L.A. Care insurance from straight Medi-Cal, which would delay my healthcare in myriad ways for months to come. When I finally did get in to see Dr. Helman, he x-rayed my hip and found a fracture. Though I couldn't fathom how I could have possibly fractured my hip, as frail and slow and careful as I'd become, part of me inwardly rejoiced: *Anything—but especially a little fracture—was better than another tumor.* Dr. Helman suggested I take Motrin for the pain and sent me home. Unfortunately, in the coming days and weeks, my pain became significantly worse. An eventual CT scan, ordered by his office while he was away on holiday, preliminarily suggested osteonecrosis or infarct, which meant that my bone tissue was not getting the blood it needed and was therefore dying and collapsing, likely a result of the intense ongoing chemo and steroid treatments that I'd been on for ten months.

Osteonecrosis is nonreversible, so I could hardly think of this prognosis as good, but, I reasoned, it was better than cancer. I could deal with the pain in my hip, I told myself, as long as it didn't take my life. I've always been stubborn. I tried to stay positive as I hobbled around our house or balanced on crutches outside it in the August L.A. heat with the sun on my face, an orange flame on the inside of my closed lids. The pain in my hip, however, was becoming so bad that I couldn't put an ounce of pressure on it. A matter of days after being diagnosed with osteonecrosis, and despite my greatest effort to ignore it, I was in too much pain to function.

On a balmy August night at two in the morning, my mother called Dr. Hu, who had replaced Dr. Helman, begging for further imaging, more tests, anything to get a better look at what was happening in my hip—anything to prove false what I feared most: that the cancer was back. On speakerphone, I could hear Dr. Hu continue to express his surprise that a fracture or osteonecrosis could cause me this much pain, but he refused to connect my condition to the cancer I'd fought for the last year and supposedly beat. Four hours later, my mom took me back to USC Keck and I was admitted for pain control: three days of morphine pumps. When Dr. Hu checked on me, my mother began her advocacy anew.

"Can't you see how much pain my daughter is in?" My mother vacillated between sounding frantic and communicating with the doctors with impressive composure. "You yourself said that it's not normal for a patient with osteonecrosis or a fracture to be in this much pain. You must order more scans. I demand you refer us to an orthopedic specialist who can perform an MRI and PET scan."

We'd all learned a new language: the language of illness. My mother and brother were also forced to become fluent in the language of advocacy.

We were informed that my insurance situation, brought about by the hospital misplacing some forms, meant that I couldn't undergo these necessary tests without a much more extensive approval process. After three days on morphine in the hospital, my pain was under control again and I was sent home, with prescription pills for pain management and a portable pump to ensure the shit went straight into my veins.

I knew things were not fine, but at home I tried to will them to be, seeking comfort in one-pan dinners that I made for my anxious family. In the kitchen, somehow, there was still conversation, just as there had been when I was young. When chicken fat is melting into buttered cast iron, and broccoli rabe is blistering in those juices, even the constantly worried can find reason to smile. One night I made up a pilaf-palau-paella cross, with chicken livers and sausage, and after Mo took the first bite and I tasted it, I felt instantly lighter. Food can do that. I couldn't fix the world, I couldn't fix my health, but I could fix a great dinner, and sometimes that has to be enough. Cancer changed me even in small ways, too: I stopped questioning myself so much, second-guessing my talent, my seasoning of a dish. What was the point? I just wanted to get on with it.

But I could only make it three days at home before the pain soared back up and once again my mother rushed me to the hospital. Over the next five days, we begged for more tests, more scans, more imaging, whatever they could do to help us understand what was happening to me, while at the same time waiting for an orthopedic surgeon to order the much-needed scans. No orthopedic surgeon ever came, but after five days I was finally approved for a PET scan.

The results came back in a day: I was riddled with it. My cancer had metastasized and I had tumors in my lungs, pelvic bone, knees, and femur.

I felt more ghoul than me.

chapter 37

86

—

Fatima

—

W E CALLED DR. WEXLER AT MSK IN NEW YORK, WHO told us to get my pain under control and get on a plane immediately so that I could be treated there.

Sitting in the airport lounge, I felt her gaze locked on the back of my head before I saw her. Her brows furrowed under dark bangs, small fists curled up around the sides of her princess dress. This maybe five-year-old girl stared at me, eyes full of curiosity and confusion. She sensed that something was not quite right. It wasn't just the baldness that gave it away or the sallow skin or baggy clothes. A cloud of death followed me. It followed me all the way to the first-class lounge at LAX. I've never flown anything but basic economy on a domestic flight, but my illness forced me to upgrade my life.

I'm in my late twenties—past the awkward stages of trying on different versions of myself. I know who I am—the things I like and don't like, the people I like and love. I'm past my college years of neglect and late-night chicken wings; I finally make time for self-care and treat my body like the peach-bottomed temple it has become. I'm in the phase when I have enough money to actually start enjoying life a little, the years of rejected ATM withdrawals due to insufficient funds a distant memory. I'm at an age still full of possibilities. New marriages. New divorces. Before the second wives and husbands and step-children that always seem to screw everyone up. Before the time when you start to lie about your age, when one wrinkle and a sag turns into four fillers and a facelift. "I'm still young!" I silently, defiantly scream. "I'm in my bloody prime!" I tell myself that I will beat this, that even if I can't work the line in a kitchen again, that I will survive and I will live well. And then the hand-knotted silk Persian rug gets ripped right out from under my unassumingly trusting, twenty-nine-year-old bare feet.

In late September, I'm given a year to live.

A year.

One year.

One.

~

THEY SAID THAT THE CANCER "IS BACK," BUT LET'S BE honest: It never really left. I'd sensed this for a while, that despite my healthy dietary regimen, my chemo protocols, my positive thinking, that the cancer was a stronger and more tenacious fighter than anything I could muster. The cancer was more stubborn than I was. I knew it as I lay prostrate on the sullied boxing mat. I'd finally met my match. And after the insult of it, the cruel, vicious punch that brings me, bloodied, to the floor, I soon begin trying to reframe it, as I am prone to do. With an iron taste and my mouth an inch above the floor, I decide that even though I know I'll lose, I'll keep fighting.

After examining my recent scans, Dr. Wexler prescribed a new chemo regimen that would hopefully stop the growth of the tumors and allow me to travel the world and eat at some of the places I've been dreaming of in the time I have left. With my pain under control thanks to Dr. Wexler and my team at MSK, I underwent my first round of this new chemo protocol. It was autumn and there I was again, back in the tower watching the silver scales of the East River, the tiny toy cars slowly making their way from Queens to Manhattan over the Fifty-ninth Street Bridge. I begged each drip of the chemo cocktail to help me as it slipped from the IV into my bloodstream. *I welcome you to my body,* I told the chemicals. *I invite you in, if you'll help me see Paris. I want to go to Rome. I'm sorry for all the times I've silently cursed you.* I was looking forward to being thirty, flirty, and thriving. Guess I have to step it up on the flirting. I have no time to lose.

Because my cancer is one that most commonly affects children, I'm treated in the pediatric oncology ward at MSK, surrounded by patients even younger than I am. It's unimaginable to see these small, frail figures fighting for their lives, and it makes me grateful for every moment I've had—in the world, experiencing life, autonomy, the messiness and bliss of it all. There's a Japanese little girl also being treated here. She's the daughter of a sushi chef and is completely obsessed with food and excited to meet me. She's only nine or ten or eleven; it's hard to tell how Ewing's sarcoma has crippled her growth. Children with cancer seem younger than they are, except in their exhausted eyes. She's terminal too. I go to visit her one day and ask her what she most wants to eat before she dies.

(Am I really having this conversation? With a ten-year-old?)

"Peter Luger's steak," she responds without missing a beat. "It's supposed to be the best in the city."

The doctors conspire to have it delivered, and one day we sit together at a hospital table that's dressed up in a starched white tablecloth and eat the room temperature steak with our families nibbling beside us, though we've got no appetite for celebration.

At one point, I share a room with another youngster: a thirteen-year-old Russian girl who is full of rage and resentment. Twice she was promised by the doctors that their regimens would make her well and twice she was deceived and forced to return to this ward, this time to die. She was gaunt and emaciated with the protruding belly of malnutrition thanks to the hunger strike she was waging against her diagnosis. When we are terminal, we take control of what we can. She took her anger out on her parents and accused them of being in cahoots with the doctors and lying to her that remission was possible.

"Why didn't you just let me die the first time?" she said through her thick accent. "Why have you made me go through this three times now?"

I wanted to soothe her, to tell her that the negativity wasn't going to do any good for her (or, frankly, for me, who was trying desperately to hang on to positivity in the bed beside her), but sometimes I understood her fury.

"Why didn't you get me help, Mom?" I snapped at my mother one day as she walked down MSK's hallway with me, corridors I traversed on crutches or with a walker to get my daily exercise. I wanted to talk about something we hadn't ever really spoken about.

"I'm *trying* to help you," my mother said, wounded. "Tell me *how* I can help you, Tatu."

"No, I mean for what Zaman did to me!" I shot back. One of the sharpest, most finely honed and rarely used spears that I carried. My mother's back straightened a little as she fumbled to adjust to what we were really talking about.

Instinctively and immediately, she said, "I'm so sorry, Tatu. I'm so very sorry." I felt the misery and anguish inside of her grow as she tried to figure out why she failed me when I most needed help, why she made the choices she did. I wanted to know what she had to say, what reasons could possibly be sufficient, and she and I both knew that there were none.

"It's too late now, Mom," I said bitterly. "I just wish you had got me help. It could have saved us so much anguish in our relationship. I know I have caused you a lot of pain," I stammered.

"No, you haven't," my mother said immediately, stopping our slow progress down the hall. "I am sorry for the pain I've caused *you*. I wish somehow I could go back and get another chance to do it right. I hope you can forgive me for how I've hurt you, how I've neglected you, for not getting you help after Zaman hurt you. I was trying to keep you from having to relive it and trying to protect our family."

And despite my weak moments of cruelty, I, too, long to spare my family any further pain. I don't want to choose the darkness of resentment over the light of forgiveness. I don't want to spend my last year in hospital beds. There's so much I want to do with my life, but like most people I've wasted so many pointless days on anger and misunderstanding, on self-doubt and stagnancy. Since my diagnosis, many people have told me that they admire me—that they respect how I've chosen to face it, to fight it, to keep pushing forward, but I often feel like a fraud. I'm just a human being who longs for more life. I, too, feel like I wasted so much time. Maybe that's just it: Since finding out I was sick, I've been trying to steal that time back, to make the most of every day.

It's funny. When we think we have all the time in the world to live, we forget to indulge in the experiences of living. When that choice is yanked away from us, that's when we scramble to feel. I was desperate to overload my senses in the coming months, making reservations at the world's best restaurants, reaching out to past lovers and friends, and smothering my family, giving them the time that I so selfishly guarded before.

In my wallet, I keep a crumpled cocktail napkin with a list of names scrawled on it. They're people I need to make amends to before I go. I have to learn how to ask for forgiveness without expecting to receive it. It's probably the most frightening thing I have ever had to do, and I've experienced some seriously terror-inducing moments.

I've spent more time in sterile hospital rooms in the past year than I have in my own apartment. This has become my new home, and the staff a part of my family. I wonder if I'll accidentally call my nurse "Mom" when she sneaks in to check my vital signs in the middle of the night. My blood pressure always stays on the low side of calm. Everyone's amazed that I'm taking it so well. But when you hit rock bottom, there really is no place to go but up.

An odd sense of relief has settled inside me, knowing that I can finally live for myself, even if it's just for a few more precious months. I reclaim myself, my body, a sense of control, by dyeing my hair. I call a local stylist to come to my hospital room to dye half my hair platinum blond and buzz the rest. He panics a little as he's setting up, whispering to my brother in his thick Italian accent, "The dye . . . it won't, uh, burn her scalp, will it?" I tell him to carry on even if it does. It's the only sense of control I feel like I have right now. I have embraced my alter-ego. She doesn't hold back.

"I love your hair!" they all say when I'm done. They think I'm brave, but really, I'm not. I'm scared. I suspect I won't last very long. There's a faint feeling deep inside my gut like a rumble of passing air, ever expanding and filling slowly until, one day, I'll pop.

Until then, every day is an opportunity for me to experience something new. I used to dream of owning my own restaurant. Now I have an ever-growing list of the ones I need to visit. From decadent uni and truffle toast at the Chef's Table at Brooklyn Fare to spice-laden Szechuan hot pot in Flushing, I'm sketching a plan to eat my way through New York and the boroughs while I can.

I think back to my favorite movie of all time, *American Beauty*. "I don't think that there's anything worse than being ordinary," Mena Suvari says as she sits with Kevin Spacey's lecherous character. I was always deathly afraid of being average in any way, and now I desperately wish to have a simple, uneventful life.

But it's too late for that. My life is not normal. I'm twenty-nine years old and am going to die in a year. Maybe my life never was normal. Maybe there is no such thing. As I finish my next round of chemo, praying it diminishes the ghoul's growth, I ask myself unanswerable questions. I scan the years like data, looking for an anomaly, wondering at what moment the first cancer cell appeared. Tumors are what happen when normal cells don't die, as all cells naturally and eventually do, but instead grow uncontrollably, becoming new, abnormal cells. Where was I when that first cell didn't die? Was I butchering a hog at Fonda del Sol? Did I do something to make that first rebel cell live longer than its prescribed healthy life span? Was it the moment I walked off the line at 8½ and gave my notice after watching investment bankers attack plates of laboriously plated, overpriced delicacies? Was I picking nasturtiums at Meadowood? Was I lying in my lover's arms?

But what then of my cancer? Did my mother lie awake at night and ask herself if *she* did something wrong—stood too near a flame? ate the wrong berries? listened to the wrong music? read the wrong verse?—to somehow make the cells that

knit together in her belly and became me outlive their prescribed cellular lives and combine to be cancerous? If she asks
herself these questions—if any parents of dying children do—
I command her and them to stop. These "wrong" cells are not
her fault. These "broken" cells are no more her fault than the
rain. Instead of blame, I ask her to take credit: for my fierce
heart that won't accept its limits.

I will live for my mother for as long as I can. I will steal her
strength, which she gives me gladly, like an organ, and fight.
When I was small, my mother often told me of my difficult
birth, how I'd swallowed amniotic fluid and had double pneumonia.

You were such a tiny little fighter, she told me. *You were so small,
but I learned you were so tough.*

My father broke down the door of the ICU in order to get
me to a better hospital with more sophisticated equipment
where I could get the care I needed.

My Nano has cancer, too. She's also been given a terminal
diagnosis. What will it do to my mother to lose us both? I don't
want to let my family down. I refuse to go out with a whimper;
if cancer is going to rob me of my life, I will not let it also rob
me of my dreams. I create a bucket list of things I want to do
before I die.

I want to return to the Basque region that helped cement my
desire to cook and this time eat at Arzak in San Sebastián, where
a father-daughter team run the restaurant and the best ingredients rule. I'll go to L'Arpège in Paris, famous for its vegetables,
where Chef Alain Passard abandoned meat when he felt what
he could get wasn't up to snuff. I picture Mo and me at Faviken
in Sweden, eating fourteen courses of creativity, like Chef
Magnus Nilsson's moose fondue.

I know I should start immediately and locally, so I add n/naka in Los Angeles to my list. I want to experience Niki Nakayama's Japanese kaiseki firsthand. I want to let the subtle choreography of her cuisine dance in front of me, to taste the wabi sabi that she worked so hard to learn and earn the right to execute—a woman not just in a man's profession but, as a kaiseki chef, in a niche solely occupied by men, until now. I've always longed to go to Osteria Francescana, specifically because of the chef-owner, Massimo Bottura. In the aftermath of the 2012 earthquake that brought Emilia-Romagna, Italy, to its knees, what Bottura did for his community—when no one was coming to Modena and all the Parmigiano-Reggiano, their most valuable local product, was at risk—he created his cacio e pepe risotto and shared the recipe all over the world, asking everyone to partake globally to save the town's economy. When most chefs might crumble and fume, Bottura came up with a plan. He expressed his country through a dish, and the support was contagious. Not one wheel of cheese was wasted! What Bottura does with his community kitchens around the world is exactly the kind of thing that sings to me. That's the kind of chef I want to be—one who thinks about more than just what's on the plate but rather about the needs of the people. Somehow, in the next year, I will get there to Modena to meet him. I will eat thick, viscous, aged balsamic and oozing mozzarella di bufala that's never been refrigerated and basil and Italian tomatoes from nearby vines and fresh pasta with good peppery olive oil and chunks and chunks of Parmesan cheese.

I hate to use my illness as a tactic, but I swallow my guilt as I slip into Noma's Instagram DMs to see if somehow the Copenhagen restaurant that's been rated the best in the world can accommodate a table for two for their already booked seafood season. I'm floored when I receive a reply from Chef Rene Redzepi himself. "Get here and we will feed you," Redzepi generously implores. Turns out that people respond when you tell them you're dying of cancer.

People say, *Someday, I want to go do this or go do that.* Well, I know I don't have enough "somedays" left. If I want to travel to Bangkok to eat at Gaa and Gaggan, two of the gastronomic standouts there, both owned by Indian chefs, if I want to see a lion in the African wild, the time is now.

Pale and on crutches, my downy head hidden under a wool cap, I went with Joe Flamm and Chef Stephanie Izzard to Masa, the famed Japanese omakase restaurant in New York City. In the taxi on the way there, they explained how the evening would work: "No matter what we are asked or offered, we say yes, okay?" Joe coached. "Yes to wine and sake pairings. Yes to truffles. Yes to a vertical uni tasting. Got it?"

"Got it," I echoed, ready to indulge, ready to feel alive through dining.

As we inhaled the ambrosian creamy funk of sea urchin— American first from Santa Barbara and Maine, followed by Japanese uni from Honshu and Hokkaido—Joe suggested we build my dream restaurant for a night.

"Sure," I said. "Let's do it. I'll find a way to incorporate uni into Pakistani cuisine. Why not?"

It was a fantasy night, after all, and after Masa's twelve-course omakase, I shook the great chef's hand.

An old kitchen crony who worked at Eleven Madison Park got us a reservation, and I went with my family to the Michelin three-star temple of fine dining in New York City. Midway through dinner, the captain led us—me hobbling on crutches— through that elegant room with my brown family members in a sea of white, up to the kitchen, where they'd re-created my Van

Pakistan Smorgasburg stall. They'd thought of everything: bottles of Pakola that made us laugh, and they even had the same tablecloth and napkin dispenser set up that I'd had in my booth. It was surreal. The chef made the most delicious, melt-in-your-mouth seekh kebabs I've ever had, with flatbread and pickled onions and green chutney they had made just for me. In a way, they'd created the restaurant of my dreams for one night: high-low, elegant and approachable, joyful and surprising. So real we could touch it, and yet, like everything else, ephemeral. For that and for much more, I am profoundly grateful.

But I'm angry too. And fearful. I question my faith in God. I learn there is no justice; I learn that lesson again and again, as the goalposts I want to sprint toward get moved further away while I fumble with my crutches. My family's love is proof that there's still beauty. Throughout all of this, my brother never leaves my side for more than an hour.

A couple of months after receiving my terminal diagnosis and submitting to the new chemo cocktail that the doctors had been confident would slow the cancer's growth, I learned a new, impossible to swallow truth.

"Unfortunately, the new protocol is not working the way we'd hoped," Dr. Wexler informed me.

"What does that mean, exactly?" I asked him, while inwardly thinking to myself that I'd been here—rock bottom—before. How could things keep getting worse?

"The most recent chemo regimen has not slowed your cancer's growth," he offered softly.

Doctors are pretty good at keeping on their poker faces, but I knew it pained Dr. Wexler to deliver this news. He never made me feel like just another patient or number on his list. Still, his discomfort was nothing compared to my own. Inwardly, I raged: *Why can't anyone or anything just stick to the plan?*

We are born and we think that by being born we are promised a life. Especially if we are born privileged, as I was. We take
for granted that it will be a long one. At twenty-eight, I was
told my life would look different, that if I wanted life, I would
have to fight for it. So fight I did. I fought for my someday restaurant, for my future. Even if I couldn't give birth to a child, I
could still have joy and laughter and adventure. I was more than
willing to work hard for any and all of it, to follow their instructions, to take the poison and the pain to gain more time. I'd
fought my way through excruciating pain and debilitating surgery to try to win myself the right to more life, only to be told
I'd get a year. A year. I'd resigned myself to their new protocols,
the new chemo cocktail meant to keep the cancer at bay, but
there I was a couple of short months into that year being told
that I wouldn't even get that.

I broke down. I cried hard.

Then, a day later, I had an idea for a show: *One Hundred
Things to Eat Before You Die!* Okay, it would only air for one
season, but it could be a great excuse to get busy. I could cram
my dreams into whatever time I had. I immediately began re-
searching who could help me realize it, putting out feelers to
bigwigs who had their agents on speed dial and could get me
meetings in a matter of days. I didn't know any other way to be.
Even in the pitch darkness, I always saw a tiny speck of light and
ran—well, hobbled, in my case—toward it. Somewhat miraculously, it seemed like the road might rise up to meet me. Pushing through my fantasy show was more attainable than curing
my cancer.

Amazed by the possibilities that seem to be opening up to
me, I decide to write a book about my last year, in life and in
food, the two forever intertwined: a book about making my
last year matter, about seeing the world. I want to leave some-

thing behind, something traceable, that could perhaps help others to ride the bull, to grab life by the horns. I write a second essay for *Bon Appétit* about living when you know you don't have much time left, and there's a monumental reaction to it that echoes in opportunities.

In November, I was invited to be on Ellen DeGeneres's show, where she presented me with a check for $50,000 to help me realize my new goal—my revised dream—of visiting my bucket list of international restaurants, of going on safari, before I die. My cancer opens up doors that would have probably remained shut to me at this point in my career. "*Top Chef* alum Fatima Ali reveals cancer is back in an emotional essay and has 1 year to live," a *Today* headline reads. *People, Us Weekly, USA Today* . . . national publications that might not cover my restaurant opening, if I had one, rush to cover my cancer prognosis. My cancer makes me famous. It's the thing that I least want to be remembered for, and yet it's given me access. What does that say about fate? About fame? I'm just a girl who wants to live. My former big plans are shot to hell. I wanted to change people's minds about Pakistan; I wanted to incite Pakistani girls to dream big, to think of the world as their oyster, to teach them how to shuck it. Instead, my only option is to wear my chains with grace.

Right after *Ellen* airs, I'm contacted by someone from Chan Soon-Shiong Institute for Medicine in Los Angeles. Its founder, Patrick Soon-Shiong, is a billionaire businessman, transplant surgeon, bioscientist, and entrepreneur who invented one of the most effective drugs to fight lung, breast, and pancreatic cancer. I'm told that I qualify for an experimental drug that's available in his El Segundo clinic in a trial overseen by a Dr. Lenny Sanders. Dr. Wexler encourages me to go and also recommends a pediatric oncologist (since my cancer is actually of a pediatric nature, remember? "Little white boy cancer," I'd quipped to Ellen) at UCLA Medical Center, a Dr. Federman. It would take two weeks for me to get approved before they could administer the experimental drug. I prayed it wouldn't take any longer, because Thanksgiving was looming and the long weekend could delay it even more.

chapter 38

KIDNEY PAIN
AND SUCH

———

Fatima

———

WE MAKE IT BACK TO L.A., AND WHILE TRYING TO coordinate the first experimental treatment at Chan Soon-Shiong, I try to enjoy living a little. *Meals out,* I tell myself. *Turn back to food. Let food resuscitate my spirit, as it always has.*

But it's like biting into a bitter, cyanide-filled almond. The taste of my own vomit is filmy on the back of my tongue like the fat from clotted cream. I sink my forehead dramatically onto my forearm, resting indelicately on the porcelain edge of the toilet, chest heaving as if I just plunged into arctic waters, and yet my brow is sweat-slicked. I stare morosely at the remnants of my excellent lunch at Kismet, a lovely Middle Eastern–inspired restaurant in Los Feliz run by two young female chefs. Sweet and musky red beets with clouds of marinated feta, snappy Persian cucumbers flecked with za'atar that Chef Sara Kramer evolved into her own proprietary blend, crusty house-made bread with a good chew, and fabulously elegant rosewater lemonade—now disfigured into green and beige globs in the basin. Two electric blue barely melted Sugar Bear Hair gummies, vitamins to help my hair grow back from chemo, float like unnatural plastic tangled in seaweed. As I brace against the cold ceramic, clawing at the side of the basin to get up, I feel a weighty pang of self-pity. In the good old days, that porcelain-induced regret was the result of downing two bottles of chilled Lambrusco—that all-too-easy-to-drink Italian sparkling wine that is particularly dangerous on an empty stomach—with friends in autumn on a rare afternoon off. This time there is no fun story; I just mixed my meds.

Don't take new antibiotics with pain pills. I make a mental note.

I rinse my mouth out and wipe my watery, sunken eyes, and I wonder: What kind of chemicals are swimming around in my system if my own body, in fear of self-poisoning, unequivocally rejects the fistful of horse pills I must swallow diligently two times a day? I tiptoe down the hall to my room, ignoring the stabbing pain in my lower back. My kidneys have been throbbing since the day before Thanksgiving, but I've gritted my teeth through the holiday, determined to be home to cook and inhale the comforting smells of sweet potatoes and stuffing. Even with my cumbersome crutches, I want to remain in the fold of togetherness in our kitchen at home and refuse to go to the emergency room because I know the catastrophic cliché it will be: third-degree oil burns from novice attempts to deep fry a twenty-four-pound turkey in a steel bucket in a backyard, sated and sedated drunk drivers who hit stop signs on their way home. *I'll wait for the doctors to get back to their clinics on Monday and make an appointment like a normal person,* I tell myself, even though I've long since forgotten what it feels like to be normal.

We return home from that appointment with a fresh orange bottle rattling with my new prescription, another to add to a collection that covers a countertop. I don't want my brother and mother to know I've thrown up again. It's not just an innocent, irresponsible vomit, filled with last night's wine and regret.

Nausea has become reason enough to spiral: *Has her cancer spread more?* is the vertiginous refrain that plays constantly in my family members' heads. I don't want to turn up that chorus, if I can help it, which I can't. We all know cancer is going to kill me, but my mother and brother spiral with every sign of it beating me, of spreading further, of speeding up the clock.

The pain is just a kidney infection. The pain is just a kidney infection. I repeat the sentence in my head pointedly, ignoring my own often fatalistic and bitchy conscience. I close my eyes. Perhaps if I can convince myself, I can convince the universe.

Breathe in and out.

The light in me buckles and bows.

It's another tumor, moron!

My inside voice isn't fooling around. But I can't help thinking like that, now I think like that all the time. And I suppose that's okay, because everything I know about my life and body has been wrestled from my grasp.

Dr. Federman runs a few tests and it turns out to really be just a kidney infection (well, a kidney infection on top of tumors in my pelvis, hips, femur, knees, and lungs). But after forty-eight hours on antibiotics, I feel no improvement and Dr. Federman sends us to the UCLA ER, where I'm admitted, medicated for the pain, and then discharged. Ostensibly, I'm buying time, waiting for approval to participate in the experimental drug trial, but my pain becomes unbearable again. Breathing feels like paring knives being forced between my ribs and twisted when I inhale, so back we go to the ER, where no oncologists are available to see me. With my lung pain—and therefore breathing—intolerable, my mother desperately begins to reach out to oncologists who have seen or treated me in the past. She leaves messages for Dr. Federman, Dr. Wexler, and a Dr. Mira Kissler at Chan Soon-Shiong, who contacts Dr.

Singh, a sarcoma specialist, and asks him to visit me at UCLA.
I'm moved from the regular fourth-floor ward to the oncology
side at the hospital, so that the team can better manage my pain.
Even though I've been referred to Dr. Federman by Dr. Wexler,
he can no longer see me due to hospital policies, so, by default,
Dr. Singh becomes my attending oncologist. If you're dizzied
by this round-robin of referrals and names, that makes two of
us. With each new white-coated specialist, I pray I've found my
savior—not someone who can literally save me (I've accepted
that I'm going to die), but someone who can help me manage
the pain enough to stay out of the hospital, to do my experimental treatment cycle, to live, just a little.

Dr. Singh immediately suggests a new chemotherapy protocol, but I've had it with chemo. We reach out to the only two
doctors whom we ever seem to be able to reach consistently,
Dr. Wexler at MSK in New York and Dr. Sanders at Chan
Soon-Shiong, and they both agree with my instincts: the chemo
Dr. Singh is suggesting would only make me more miserable.
Meanwhile, we learn that the approval for the experimental
treatment at Chan Soon-Shiong has come through, but because
of liability issues, I couldn't have the treatment at UCLA Medical Center: I must be discharged in order to receive the experimental drug at the Chan Soon-Shiong clinic in El Segundo,
which is all I want. I guess I am still holding out for a miracle:
the miracle of being pain-free, the miracle of even just a little
more time.

Enter Dr. Daniel, head of palliative care at UCLA. *Please,
Dr. Daniel, please get my pain to a point where I can go get this treatment. It's my only hope.* Dr. Daniel suggests that we try another
round of radiation, as it might help with my pain, and Dr. Wexler agrees it could. I undergo the radiation and my pain abates
from a nine out of ten to a seven, enough for me to leave the

hospital to go to the clinic. With portable pumps and an IV to administer pain meds, I make it to the Chan Soon-Shiong clinic and receive one round of the experimental treatment over two days. All I want is to get through the full cycle of this treatment. I hold on willfully to the hope that it can perform miracles, make me well enough at least to get on a plane, to fly back across the world and eat pintxos. I try not to complain about the searing pain that radiates through my body, from my broken knees through my infiltrated femur to my perforated hip, but I'm no match for it. After that first round at Chan Soon-Shiong, I'm taken back to UCLA in an ambulance, admitted through the ER. That brief patch of sky seen from El Segundo, as I'm wheeled from the clinic into the ambulance, will nearly be my last glimpse of the heavens from outside.

chapter 39

FALLING THROUGH
THE CRACKS

———

Farezeh

———

FATIMA WAS BEAUTIFUL. OBJECTIVELY. THERE WAS A magnetism to the way her gaze settled on you, a mischievous glint lighting up her huge brown eyes. Her eyebrows were the perfect crown for them. They had a mind of their own. It was often the first thing people noticed about her.

During her time in one of the hospitals, she was on a stretcher in the elevator riding up to the pediatrics ward when a woman got in on our way there. She glanced at Fatima and exclaimed, "You have the most incredible eyebrows I've ever seen!" This happened to her all the time.

And in just a few days, those eyebrows were gone. Along with her hair, her ability to walk without assistance, and the dexterity that she had spent thousands of hours honing and perfecting. Just wiped away, like all the plans she had for herself.

Youth has its gifts. Youth deceives you because you think you'll have it forever. You will always have that radiant skin, that zest for life, that invincibility, that steadfast belief that you will always have time. And it is always time that shatters those illusions, as you begin to notice your body change, and your cynicism intensifies.

But twenty-nine is too early for those gifts to fade. For Fatima, there was a thief lurking with its eyes on all of her youthful rights.

This radiant beauty, whose glow illuminated every room she was in, was suddenly a shadow, with sunken cheeks, bags under her eyes. Her nails became black, and her vomit was fluorescent—testament to the radioactive poison that was meant to make her well. Fatima, the sprinter, the junior victoress, the girl who worked eighteen-hour days, could no longer move her arm. Slowly, she lost the ability to walk, moving from her feet to a stick, to crutches, to a walker, to a wheelchair, and eventually being bed-bound. It was almost like an accelerated aging, as if her body was trying to convince those around her that it was its time to go, trying to convince her mind to give in and give up, short-circuiting her nerves, pushing up against her soft tissue, breaking out of her bones and finding the most excruciating spots to grow in. The cancer didn't care how much she wanted to live. It didn't matter that we were moving mountains to try to heal her, or even just to relieve her pain. It had its own truth, its own agenda.

Witnessing this—the cruelty and injustice—I asked a silent force, *Why?* Why did I still have hair? Why did I still have legs that worked? Why did I have all this life when hers was being taken away? I would trade all I had to give her what she needed to be okay.

All I wanted was for her pain to stop. To see my daughter, my baby, in pain like that, in constant agony, left me perpetually breathless.

No amount of drugs helped her. The combination of nerve

and bone deterioration was impossible for the doctors to manage. Dr. Daniel, a palliative care specialist, suggested that we
consider palliative sedation as an option, essentially putting her
under, making her unconscious so that she'd suffer less until life
left her body. There is something perverse about being told that
the only way to escape the pain of being alive is to be switched
off.

But Fatima was, in a sense, connected to the reality that she
wouldn't be with us for much longer. She agreed that when the
time was right, palliative sedation should occur. She signed
the documents giving her brother power of attorney, because
she knew it would be too difficult a decision to burden her
mother or father with the conflict and turmoil that must come
with such a dilemma. She wasn't at that stage then, at least not
at that point. While Fatima's body began to break down, her
mind stayed strong, alert, buzzing, and proud in its defiance.
She darted into the past to childhood memories. She dictated
anecdotes to her brother for the book she still wanted somehow
to write. She even managed to write some essays herself, laboriously typing at her keyboard, lost in her work. My busy body.
My overachiever, who was always on a mission.

It was decided that an intrathecal pump should be surgically
administered to help her get pain medicine into her spinal cord
faster. We met with the anesthesia team and they explained that
the pump could go in the skin either under her stomach or in
her back. The choice was obvious for us: As a family we all
agreed that it should be implanted in her stomach, knowing
that her tumors were aggressive in her spinal area and caused her
acute back pain already, and since she was almost entirely in bed
and on her back all day. Moving her even a few inches sent her
into a crisis that would not recede for hours.

The day of the surgical procedure arrived, and everything that could possibly go wrong did.

The palliative team had unhooked her from the pain pumps a full two hours before the surgical team was ready to take her in. Two hours. Two hours of enduring pain levels that on the pain pumps would have held steadily at an eight out of ten on the best days. Two hours when she had no pain assistance at all. The level of incompetence in the management of her procedure was flabbergasting.

We waited, pacing, praying, numb, yet every nerve in us lay exposed. White noise filled our minds and we hovered above and outside of ourselves. Time stood still. And then the nurse emerged and told us to go see her.

The theory around operations is that there is relief after one. A crescendo followed by some well-earned peace. The doctors had gone in to help solve the issue she was having, and stitched her up. She would be better, or so we were told.

But when we saw her after the procedure, Fatima was in excruciating pain, far worse, if that's even possible, than before. Frantically, I asked the nurses why she was in so much pain, when the whole purpose of the surgery was to make it better? They coldly responded that it was "because of the procedure." As if that was supposed to mean something to me. I tried to insist that Fatima be kept under the care of the surgical nurses in the post-op theater, because I felt like the ward upstairs wasn't equipped well enough to deal with her pain needs. In post-op she had a nurse dedicated to her and constantly accessible. On the ward, you ring a bell and wait your turn, and if there is a shift change coming, well, you wait even longer. She was begging for relief, tears in her eyes as she gripped her gown, willing for it to be over, for it to all end. If she could have pressed a button then to permanently check out, she probably would have. But after an hour in the recovery area, they wheeled her out to be taken back to the fourth floor.

This procedure designed to give her relief instead was a tipping point, after which Fatima's condition plummeted. Before this procedure, she could drag herself with a walker to the bathroom because she had so much dignity that she refused to take the bedpan when she felt she could muster the strength to walk, but after this procedure she couldn't even move in bed. She couldn't even turn onto her side.

When the anesthesia team came to check on her the next morning, I asked them why in God's name they had implanted the intrathecal reservoir in her back when we'd all decided and established that it should go in her stomach. The resident, Dr. Adam, told us it was the decision of the attending surgeon who made the call at that time, but no other explanation was given to us as to why that call was made. This move, done in defiance of her patient's own well-articulated and established choice, was the ultimate insult. She didn't even bother coming to speak to us, and left us utterly stupefied and in total despair.

My daughter was falling through the cracks in the medical system before my eyes. In the last fourteen months of hospitals and misdiagnoses and treatments and scans, we'd learned the doctors' language in order to communicate. We lived in their world, slept in their house in chairs and on cots. But even though we'd adapted to their rules and spoke their language, we could not protect Fatima. We could not spare her from more suffering.

We were losing her, that much was becoming clear. She willed herself to remain completely still in her bed, focusing her defiantly strong mind to lie perfectly still, to simply avoid the pain. She was left to fend for herself, and her willpower stepped in when modern medicine could not.

The pain doctors came every morning to titrate her medication through the reservoir now implanted in her back, which caused her immense pain and began to affect her psychologically. Mohammad, always at his sister's bedside, managing so many of her affairs, planning for the impossible choices that lay ahead of us, how soon or how far we couldn't be sure—it was he who asked the doctors to send a counselor, someone who understood what was happening, a therapist, someone who could help Fatima navigate this, and help all of us navigate this. Mohammad asked for, and then I insisted on, a psychologist, but no one came.

In the end, even with the implanted pump, Fatima's pain was never able to be controlled sufficiently, and in consultation with the palliative pain team, we suggested a rarely administered and controversial procedure—a lidocaine infusion, which had helped her in the past at MSK. Finally, after four more days of suffering, something that worked: Fatima's pain came down to a six out of ten before the holidays.

While Mohammad and I were battling the hospital management, Fatima was still befriending her nurses and their assistants. If she wasn't on the lookout for a date for her brother, she was thanking them for taking care of her. Through the window of relief she found from the infusion, she went back to making people smile, making her nurses laugh, despite how helpless they may have felt. Her pain had broken all of us. How did she still have so much to give?

Some of it came from her unshakable love of food. During her tough days, she'd ask for some of her no-fail comfort foods. Daal, cheeseburgers, pho, ramen, biryani, yakhni. But in the end, that source of comfort also abandoned her. She could hardly eat. Mohammad and I conspired and plotted: Could there be an elixir, a magical broth we could make that would suit her? A permutation of healing spices that could reverse her disease? That could just wash over her like a balm? Or better yet, could we somehow stumble across a secret weapon to reverse all of the tumor growth? High doses of vitamin C to jump-start her immune system and get it to attack her cancer, maybe pumping heaps of biodynamic ginger and turmeric into her food? What of these custard apple seeds that contain some scientific property, or special apricot seeds that may somehow be the key to this? Chemo and conventional therapy couldn't help us. We had lost faith in that pathway, so we clutched at whatever else we could.

I keep thinking about when we went back to Pakistan from Texas, and how I wrote an article on children of divorce. How do you love and say goodbye? And now that I am in this situation, I am constantly thinking about that. Then, the divorce was so traumatic—that was my hurdle. How do I help my children feel it's okay: We all love, and at some point in time, we learn to say goodbye. I didn't know that years later I would find myself in this situation, where I have to find that strength: to love my child . . . and how do I say goodbye to her?

chapter 40

A BOOK BY MANY

—

Fatima

—

A STRANGER ARRIVES AT MY BEDSIDE IN LOS ANGELES: a writer I hired to help me build something that will outlast me and my looming end date. Tarajia and I begin our work together, and the stories pour out as from a pierced bag of rice. The book I wanted—the life I wanted, even just for a year—is impossible. I admit that now, but maybe all is not lost. Maybe I can leave something behind that has value, something shared quietly, but even more essential than the bucket list book I aimed to write.

Tarajia sits at the end of my bed near my ankles, and her questions lead me back into myself: my childhood in Lahore, Austin, and Karachi; the market runs with Nano, with my mother when she fed the children—the children that I was supposed to figure out how to protect and feed. *It will be possible when I'm famous,* I'd told myself then, *when I'm a television star chef who can shine a spotlight on their hollow cheeks and fill their bellies with biryani and fresh naan.* What of the hungry children now? I have to give up on my dream of feeding them; it's too late. I'm not leaving this bed, so who will look after them?

"Mohammad, did you send Tarajia my essays?" I ask him. I've been recording my thoughts: memories, family lore, the fear that crept in when the rest of the house was sleeping.

"I did," Mo says.

As I lead Tarajia further through my history, we are often interrupted by the doctors. (My friends, even my family, respect my wish to focus on my final project, but the doctors know no boundaries here. I am a guest in their domain and no room is off-limits to them.)

"What have we here?" Doc interrupts us on Tarajia's first day with a condescending smile that acknowledges her: the new pale face at the foot of my bed. "Who are *you*?"

"A friend," Mohammad, Tarajia, and I respond in unison, as if we discussed or rehearsed it. Doc certainly will have something to say about a stranger, a writer, setting up here.

"Are you writing a book?" he guesses, and we all nod our heads minimally, as if we've been caught at something. "What's it going to be?" he asks me. "A book about you by a bunch of people?"

Thanks, Doc. Thanks for the faith in me, I want to say, but don't. It's undeniable, of course: I'm not going to make it and I don't have long at all, certainly not long enough to write a book.

"Very funny, Doctor. Is there something you need?" I ask him coolly instead, as if he's wandered into *my* office.

"We want to discuss pain options with you. I gather you're still only getting relief from the lidocaine. On a scale of one to ten, how would you rate your pain today?"

"Seven point five," I tell him, and we embark on a conversation about medications, doses, and side effects before he finally leaves us so that we can resume our work.

"I don't want my book to be written by several people," I tell

Tarajia after Doc and his teammates finally file out, my voice belatedly cracking.

"Neither do we," she says. But I know that as with everything else, I'll have to make concessions if I want this book to happen. Nothing simply goes my way.

"Let's keep going," Mo says, and we do.

"You're in an unusual situation," Tarajia says. "You are being forced to confront your mortality at a young age. Most people pointedly ignore their mortality, sometimes even their health, because, frankly, it's easier not to address it."

"They choose not to think about what might come; they choose not to think about the fact that nothing may come," I respond, my voice trembling, "because it's frightening; it's unimaginable, the crunching of our bones, of our physicality disappearing. They refuse to think about our eventual blackness and our nothingness, which is so frightening that it would scare the devil himself. If there is a hell, then that's what it would be: not fire and brimstone—at least those are things you can see and can feel. I think real hell is just nothingness."

"You're not going anywhere like hell," Mohammad inserts gently. "You're going somewhere infinite. It's going to be beautiful, especially when someone like you arrives."

My brother. My best friend. How can I share my fear with him—my fear that nothingness awaits me?

The fear has a rousing effect on me. The storytelling is like lucid dreaming. I am back in a field in Karachi with my brother, I am tasting sushi for the first time with our dad, and then I am spit out into the present: into the temperature-controlled confessional of my hospital room with a perpetual soundtrack of whirring machines and inhaling pumps and monitors that beep.

"Do you think that if people allowed themselves to think about this, that they would live differently?" Mo asks me.

"I cannot get into someone else's mind," I tell him, incredulously. These two and so many others seem to think I have answers. "Their synapses, their rubber bands snapping. The people who aren't thinking about that are just living: They are too busy living . . . and I am deeply jealous of them."

"Is it problematic the way we deal with death?" Mo asks.

"Mohammad, you are asking me this as if I am some kind of soothsayer, an oracle, as if I have answers, when I am shitting myself every day."

"I think you're so admired in part because of your instincts," Tarajia says. "They appear to be your compass and have led you to success and adventure. Where do your instincts lead you now? Are they giving you clues for how to traverse this? Or do you feel your instincts have abandoned you in this moment?"

Can I tell them the truth?

"I feel the world has abandoned me. I feel like everything's gone. Everyone's jumped ship. I have family, I have friends who are so dear—who I love and who love me so much, they would crack my ribs with a hug, that's how much they love me—and yet I have been abandoned. It's no one's fault."

I begin to cry. I can't help it. The defeat is too much to bear.

"Everyone reiterates, if they could change places with me, they would. And I believe them. But what good would that do? Because we are born to be abandoned. Babies are born to be brought up, taught a few things, and then left in a wicker basket to be abandoned. This is the end of my relationship with God. I am more cynical than angry. It's just a feeling. I feel let down, like life is a broken promise, a false statement."

I can barely speak. Mohammad is weeping silently too.

"When I hear you say you are abandoned I worry that you

feel alone," Mohammad says, taking my hand. "I know that no one can know what I am feeling as your brother, and I know I cannot feel what you are going through, but I don't want you to feel alone . . . that you're being left."

Our voices are so soft, communicating almost through breath.

"Actions speak louder than words," I say. "You've been there every step of the way. You don't know how much I love you. Just the way you touch me and hug me and give me my banana milkshake in the morning, how much it helps me. I feel like a cripple, I can't do anything. I can't bathe myself. I can't shit. I can't walk. But somehow because you're here, it's okay. I would be freaking the fuck out, but because of you, I am okay."

"I feel abandoned too," Mo says.

"I'm sorry."

"I know that feeling—not the way you do, but I know what you mean," Mo says.

We forget about her, the writer, the hired witness. We are lost except to each other, our kindred hands sewn together. Tears rolling down brown cheeks.

"I love you."

"I love you."

chapter 41

ORDER FIRE

——

Fatima

——

KNOCK, KNOCK, ENTER. THREE QUICK BEATS, THAT'S how the troop of doctors arrive.

"Good afternoon," Dr. Daniel says, as if he's a newscaster or the host of a children's program, as if the cameras are rolling.

"Is this very important?" I demand, not mincing my words. We are in the middle of our work on our last day with Tarajia here. I'm sharing some of my most private experiences. I want to get through it. I want to get it all done in one go, without interruption.

"It will take maybe two seconds," the doctor says. "Now, I forget," he jokes lamely, pretending not to remember why he's here. "Just kidding! How was your night?"

"I had a pretty good night."

"We're working on trying to get you an MRI, logistically," the doctor starts in. "I want to see what's going on in your neck."

"Really?" I say, skeptically.

How many MRIs have I had in the last year? I've been poked and prodded, scanned and x-rayed, poisoned and zapped, all in the name of diminishing a cancer that won't quit.

"How long is the MRI going to take?"

"Well, since you're going down, we want to get as much information as we can, but we're going to focus on your neck, because I think there's something going on in your neck causing all this pain. So a neck MRI. Once you're in the machine, thirty minutes. We're going to coordinate with Anesthesia."

"So, I'll be anesthetized?" I ask.

"You won't be sleeping."

"But I won't be *up,* either?"

"You might be like this," the doctor says.

"But this is *up,* and up is not good."

Sometimes I feel like these doctors are children. Brilliant but not capable of simple reasoning.

"Look, there are two issues with MRIs: first, pain control, how comfortable you are in the machine; second, claustrophobia and anxiety. Is that an issue for you?"

I nod, but I am catching sight of something. There, in the middle distance, then over his shoulder. If I squint, I can see a hint of it again.

"We can give you some Ativan to take the edge off. I don't want to put you in conscious sedation, but maybe we can make you sleepy," the doctor offers.

"I don't know though . . ." I begin, not meeting his gaze. Then: "I know you've put so much work into this . . ." I look the doctor in the eye. "And your face is falling as I'm saying this—"

"No, no, no," the attending avows. "You're a challenge and I like a challenge!"

"I don't think, at the end of the day, it's worth it."

There, I've said it, and these words have shifted something— the air in the room is different. And as if on cue, the white coat posse, the well-meaning chorus just behind the attending, stop writing in their notebooks or filling out their charts and they begin looking at various imaginary spots on the walls, fidgeting slightly. They don't look at me.

There's a brief silence laced with tension, as if I've gone off-script and the attending has to try to get me back to my mark.

"Your pain is so *unusual,*" Doc begins. "And if we could find something we could treat, like with radiation—"

Oh for god's sake, I want to say. "I don't want radiation, Doc. What's the point?"

"It's usually like five days," he continues, as if not having heard me. "And if we can treat the pain . . ."

"No. No radiation, please. Just let me go gently," I finally muster, with the tenderness and ease of a mother telling her teething toddler not to chew on her collar. (*Who* is caring for *whom* here?)

"Radiation can be very effective for controlling your pain," the attending begins again, like a dog with a bone. *He's* supposed to be in charge. He knows he's not supposed to let me discourage him. He's supposed to try *everything.* That's modern medicine: keep looking for something to fix, never mind the side effects, never mind the diminishment, quantity over quality.

"It's okay," I promise him through quiet breathy tears. "It's okay with *me.* I want it to be okay with *my doctors.*"

"Whatever you want," Doc says, placating me, giving in, and then slightly defensively: "But I'm only trying to help your pain."

"I know that," I tell him. I know my part, now that we've rewritten the scene. "I know one hundred percent that you are trying to help me. But I don't think that I need that much help anymore. I just don't. Keep me pain-free now, keep me pain-free here, so I can do this. That's it. Don't think about the radiation and the zapping and trying to figure out what this is."

"The issue is trying to get you home, right? With your pain controlled . . ."

"And we will get home," I interrupt to assure him. "Doc? Doc, do you believe in God?"

"I'm very religious. I couldn't do oncology if I wasn't religious."

"I don't think I'm going to last that long," I tell him, tenderly but truthfully.

"We can't predict that," he begins emphatically, stepping on my line. This part he knows by heart: Doctors don't let patients say that. Stay positive.

"I know, I know, but what I saw—if you believe in God—was my calling. I saw it yesterday. So let me go to Him. Let me be with Him. Let me meet all those wonderful men and women that they talk about in the Bible, or Torah or Quran, whatever book you read. I want to meet everybody. I want to feel that love and joy that God talks about, that God promises. This life is temporary, this life is like a grain of rice compared to the universe. Doc, let me go. And have peace in your heart that you can let me go."

One of the residents picks an imaginary piece of lint off his white coat. The medical student pretends to scratch her cheek and wipes at a cove of tears next to her quivering nostril.

"You have good moments. I see you when you are relatively well, when you are with your family, your friends. It's a gift, this time still here with them. We won't keep you alive artificially, you know that. But we have to try to alleviate any suffering. And the only thing that helps you is the lidocaine, and we can't send you home on the lidocaine at the dosage that you require."

He pauses. He seems more exhausted than I am. This speech seems like it's more for his benefit—convincing himself and the doctors-in-training that shadow him—than it is for mine.

"I've been doing oncology for a very long time, and this pain you have and how the lidocaine helps you—you were on very high doses of fentanyl when I came on, I thought, Why isn't this lady on a super-high dose, a narcotic dose, even if it hastens her life span? Then that's what we do to keep you comfortable. But you were on very high doses and you were still uncomfortable. We start the lidocaine and magically you feel better."

"Sometimes it's simple, Doc," I try to assure him. "This is because of all of you . . . There are no words . . . Thank you . . ."

"You don't have to say anything," Doc says lamely. "That was a little bit more than two minutes, sorry."

The doctors file out.

"I was seeing spiders behind them, the whole time he was talking to me, there were little black spiders everywhere," I tell Mohammad and Tarajia.

My visions began the night before, and now these things— sand flowing from electrical outlets, a toddler (the nephew I'll never know), spiders, and red stilettos—are ever present. They fascinate me, their meaning decipherable like a game.

"Mohammad, we never did the will."

"We can do it now," Mo says.

"I want to be buried in a space of land in Lahore, where I was born, the plot that Dad got for all of us in the same place where Yasmin Khala's husband is buried." And then to Tarajia: "Yasmin is my auntie who you see here every day, my mother's best friend. That beautiful woman, full of light, is a widow, can you imagine? I'll get to see him! I'll see Yasmin Khala's husband soon. So I'll be buried there in our family's plot. Someday, a long time from now, surrounded again by my family. And most important, Mr. Meow needs to be buried along my thigh. I want my funeral to be the traditional Muslim ritual, without the segregation of men and women. I want men and women to bring me together to the plot."

My mother comes in and hovers in the doorway with a bag in her arms. I ask her for five more minutes for us to get to a stopping point. When my mom closes the door again, Mohammad says, "I just want to clear out the lilies before they come in with him."

"What? What do you mean? Why?"

"Because of Mr. Meow," Mohammad says, as if this explains it.

"Mr. Meow is here?" I feel like I've stepped out of the cool shade into the warm sunlight, suddenly elated. "Mr. Meow?"

I feel ecstatic, like a child unable to control my emotions and I begin to sob, overcome.

Mohammad moves the lilies, which are toxic for cats, out of the room to prepare for Mr. Meow's visit.

Then our friends enter with Mr. Meow, here to say goodbye. If they've brought him to me, then I really must be far gone. My boy. My feline friend who loves me without judgment, as all our furry four-legged angels do.

As Mr. Meow lays on my belly, confused by his surroundings but glad of our reunion, I have a vision of seeing orange string. I stroke his gray and white face and Mom and I sing to him. I'm weeping. Mr. Meow looks concerned, and after a few minutes I ask my mother to take him away. I don't want to frighten him.

"There's been a shift," Mohammad says. "You're speaking with such clarity, such conviction, you're addressing things you haven't mentioned before."

"I feel closer to God," I tell him simply. "I got to be my sparkly self, to show off, to be in the spotlight without being in the spotlight. I hate that part of myself, but I also love it. I like being bold but having an old soul. Put the 'old' in 'bold,'" I joke. And then to Tarajia: "It's forced me to look inside myself, who I am. A stranger is asking me questions to make a story of my life. No pressure. You're going to throw yourself into this like you throw yourself into everything you do."

chapter 42

PICKLED ONIONS
AND PEACH FUZZ

———

Fatima

———

I WANTED TO WRITE A BOOK ABOUT THE LAST YEAR OF my cut-short life, brimming with delicacies, adventures, effervescence—a year dedicated to drinking cider in San Sebastián, to meeting Massimo Bottura in Modena, to indulging in Gaggan's yogurt explosion in Bangkok. But I didn't get that year; instead, I got four months. As if this pathetic abbreviation of a promised year isn't bad enough, the doctors never explicitly told me I only had four months left. I'm just too ill and in too much pain to go on. It's infuriatingly obvious. It's unsaid, but it's explicit. I'm not *going to die,* I'm *already dying.* My dying is happening in the present. Dying has become my life.

I was too sick to fly first class around the world, indulging in Lambrusco and sherry and eating at Arzak and Arpège.

Seeing the end speeding toward me, I make amends with friends and lovers, exes whom I worry I may have hurt. Eden comes to visit me. We've long since decided we should just be friends. We sit and speak and sometimes hold hands if I'm not too terrified of germs that day. She tells me that I'm beautiful, even though I'm pasty gray and immobile and swollen, and I always respond by saying how horrible I must look.

"You're still beautiful and I can prove it to you," she says one day.

"Prove it to me how?" I say.

"May I kiss you?" she asks.

Before I have a chance to protest, she takes a tissue out of the box by my bedside and she folds it in half and holds it between our lips as she gently presses hers against mine. It's filled with love, and as my eyes close, as they must when one is being kissed, instead of darkness, all I see is white light, light that seems to pour in through my closed eyelids and course through the flimsy tissue, through my throat, down my gullet, into my heart. I am weeping with love when I open my eyes again: love for life itself, which I am hungry for so much more of. We are both crying and also laughing a little at the immeasurable absurdity of it all: my extreme unwellness, our friendship, a single tissue meant to protect us from the fury of life.

I'd planned to spend New Year's Eve with my Pakistani best friends in Thailand. My mom was going to go too, with her friends. But I am too sick. Instead of meeting me on a beach in Koh Samui, my people come to me in a hospital in Santa Monica, to sit with me under fluorescent lights. Saadia and Sarah; my half siblings Zahra and Amin. My Lahore extended family—Fatimah, Tabinda, Zahra, Bano, and Mikoo and Boby (who I knew would be there to support Mohammad)—are all present. I make time for each of them, the pilgrims who have come to my bedside. I try to impart any wisdom I've gleaned from this compressed life. When the elderly are dying, we nod our heads yes when they tell us to live well, to enjoy it all, but we're preoccupied by the immediacy of living, of minutia. But I am young, and my early death frightens people; it seems to make them lean in and listen, and I want them to. *You must live now,* I want to tell them. *Forgive your enemies, your faults and flaws. Ignore the naysayers and get busy doing.*

My Karachi Grammar friends—Zainie, Mariam, Tano, Anum, and Lala—come. Family members Agul Mamoo, Talib, Aaliya, and Abrar gather around me and congregate in the evenings at our house. It should be a party, but the mood is somber. Aman from CIA comes. Gabby, whose loyalty and love never faltered . . . and Ray, who performs reiki on me. My ex-boyfriend Mark, who never tried to box me in. Josh, to offer some truths, however hard, and closure. Tammy Khala, Camron, and Adam.

I summon my *Top Chef* gang. On January 7, I text Joe that if he wants to say goodbye, he'd better get on a plane. And so they appear: Joe Sasto and Joe Flamm, Adrienne, Carrie, Claudette, Bruce, Chris, Tyler, Tanya, Brother, and Laura, congregating around me in the hospital. I try to keep them laughing; I don't want them to cry. Flamm brought his wife and newborn son with him, whom I hold, breathing in the fragrance of youth, of life that flowers from his peach-fuzz head.

"Don't worry," Flamm says. "I'll be back in L.A. in six weeks to do a dinner. I'll see you then."

"I won't be here," I remind him.

They're somber then, my funny friends; their cheeks forgetting how to grow taut with smiles. Sasto lost his mother to cancer and I'm surely triggering him; he knows how this ends. And now they all do: I've told them I won't be here for long, and now they understand. Except for the baby: the baby gurgles, plump cheeks pink, eyelashes thick and sweet, a dumpling filled with innocence, seasoned with promise.

"Tell us what we can do for you," they beg me. Everyone wants instructions from me, and sure, I'll give them some, especially if it helps them cope.

"Well, you can start by figuring out how to get better food into hospitals," I tell them, half joking. "And I wish I could have found a way to help young people who need visas. I wish there was a better way to help them navigate the red tape, the bureaucracy of immigration."

I look at Mohammad as I say this (he's always here beside me, no matter who else is visiting), as I know he's the one who will make my dreams come true when I am not here anymore to dream them. We've spoken of my family starting a foundation in my name: to feed the hungry, to help aspiring chefs find their way. I know my brother and mother and friends will do what they can to keep me with them, to keep parts of me, if only my dreams, alive.

Adrienne and I are alone at one point, and I ask her why we didn't spend more time together after filming when we were both back in New York City, living in Harlem only a few blocks from each other.

"You were blowing up," she tells me. "Becoming a rock star. I didn't think you'd have time for me . . . I guess I was intimidated."

She's talking about when *Top Chef* aired and my social media follows skyrocketed.

"None of that matters, though," I tell her. "I see that now. All I want, all that matters, is to be healthy. Is to live."

And it's true. But a younger me—only a year or two younger—wanted to be a star, to host shows on television like the food idols of my youth, to be in magazines. I told myself that fame would help me amplify the good I could do, to touch more people, to change more minds about Pakistan. To change more minds *in* Pakistan about love and acceptance; to feed more hungry children there. And maybe fame would have helped with that, with all of those things, but from where I sit now, propped up, in pain, on death's doorstep, I can tell you that all I want is more time, more life, even if it's uneventful and unremarkable. Fame doesn't matter at all, as we are each of us alone as we head around the bend.

Well, not alone entirely. God doesn't care about fame, there's no question about that. He returns to me, a friend and confidant I thought I'd lost, but as I recognize Him beside me, within me, I realize He was there all along, loving me, present but not visible.

~

MY SISTER SARAH SITS BESIDE ME, BUT HER EYES DART from my gaze.

"I'm sorry," she finally says. "I'm sorry for being so unkind to you when we were little. I'm sorry for being so petty about things that don't matter, like clothes."

I grab her hand and say, "Do you want to talk about what really happened?"

"I don't remember," she says.

"If I say his name, will you remember?" I ask.

And she says, "Yes: Zaman."

She remembers. She acknowledges it, and I tell her that I forgive her, that she was only eleven and couldn't have known what to do when I confided in her first.

I'm clearing the decks. Confronting myself and others, offering closure on both sides, I hope. I'm unequivocal in my forgiveness, but I want the people I love most to acknowledge the truth. I refuse to gloss over it and leave things unsaid. It's painful in the moment, but I want them to have a path forward, on the other side of their grief, free from blame and guilt that I don't want them to carry on into a future without me. I mean it as a gift: an opportunity to take stock and consider how they want to live their lives.

And then I see a little boy, a toddler, wearing suspenders, out of the corner of my eye. It's her someday-child that I see: my nephew. I tell her about my vision and she begins to cry.

"Why are you crying, Sarah?" I ask her.

"Because my children will never get to know you."

"I wanted to meet them, be their crazy, quirky, queer aunt," I say. "They will have my spirit—they will be a handful."

I know it sounds weird, but I believe them—the visions— even now, even when they recede. I still believe them.

Then Saadia joins us and we also reconnect.

"You've always been there for everyone, no matter what," she said. "I'm so sorry that I took you for granted. You always took care of me in New York."

I summon my fathers. A long-awaited confrontation of sorts. First, my stepdad.

"Not for one second have you ever made me feel like I was anything but your real father, your true father," he says from my bedside.

"You never really made me feel like you were my stepdad for most of my life, but there's just one thing that I wish had never happened, so that that statement could be entirely true."

He's quiet, his eyebrows trembling, as if he knows what's coming but refuses to confront it.

I say, "I love you very much, but you have let me down."

There's no greater affront than telling an Afghan man that they've let you down, that they've failed at their one purpose in life, their one mission as a man.

Incredulously he asks me, "How can you tell me I've let you down? I've been with you every step of the way—"

"Dad, I'm going to say one word," I interrupt him.

For the next three minutes he says that we shouldn't talk about it, that these are things for women to talk about, not a father figure. But then I grab his wrist and squeeze it and say, "Please let me tell you what happened to me with Zaman," and as I say this name, the face he's painted on slides away like sweat. He can't hide from me anymore. I say this man's name like a charm, a secret password to get into a club. Somehow it opens up a portion of everyone's brain to the truth, which I tell him in detail.

I confront him for the abuse that happened under his nose, and my tall burly Afghan stepfather breaks down with guilt and shame and sadness at not having protected me. He says the words that I need to hear: *I'm sorry.*

"I'm sorry," he says. "I'm sorry and I love you." And I know it is the truth, because the food he's been feeding me—the Pakistani-style brothy Chinese chicken with tons of masala and soy that my real dad made for me—tastes sweet again, and food can be good or food can be bad, but food cannot lie.

I confront my real dad, too, about his abandonment, his absence, and he, too, apologizes and tells me he loves me. I feel his love in the simple chicken stew he made me. I haven't been hungry for the last two weeks, but as I eat his food, I taste his love for me in each bite. How did he know to make that? Something that could wake my appetite? Something that tasted like childhood. He's been rubbing my feet with oil at night. I feel his love as he does this. I feel his regret at not having been there for me. It's all forgiveness now. I needed to be forgiven by some and I've forgiven everyone entirely.

I thought the next steps were going to be blackness. I've

made so many mistakes in my life and I haven't connected with God enough to deserve what's happening now. I don't know if it's real. But I keep seeing my family. From my stepdad's side, from my mom's side, places I would not expect. I don't want to lose it: the sense of not being abandoned. I'm scared to become a believer so fast. I've always believed in God, but I've never really done the things that He wanted us to do. I wanted to live my own life. But now, being in this place, where everything happens so fast, I have to choose. And I choose to accept the visions and Him completely.

Now I can see things others can't.

"I've been trying to protect the little dog all day," I tell them.

"You're such a good kind person: You've been trying to protect the little dog," my mother says patiently, full of love for me. Her voice has the quality of tears, though she's not crying.

"Yes, but he's coming with his attack dog for me, and I'm going to have to fight him off." I want them to understand, but it's so hard because they cannot see it.

"I'm going to be between you and the dog, Fatima," my mother promises. "No one can hurt you."

"He's very powerful," I warn her.

My friends remain with me through the visions, the hallucinations, the night terrors. Zainie and Binda are the last to leave.

"I'm sorry," I tell them. Though the visions are real to me, I somehow also know that they are not for others. I can recount them, but they are mine alone. Sometimes I fear they'll lose their potency if I try to explain them. "Today was tough, I know, and I'm sorry."

"Don't say sorry, Fati," Zainie tells me.

"There's so much love," I tell her. "I've seen God and I know it for sure now. I always loved my life, believing in God but living like I wanted. I haven't done enough for Him. But He loves us so much, Zainie, you have no idea. There's so much love. I want you to hear me because I know you think about this a lot. It's all about being a good person. Being good on the inside."

Zainie kisses my forehead and I close my eyes, keeping them like that as she leaves the room so that I don't see her go. While they are closed, in my private darkness, I pretend I'm a child, a teenager, dozing off beside her on a sleepover at her house. The reverie is pleasant and warm. I can do this now: intentional dreaming, navigating my memories like a librarian who knows just where to find each volume. I try to slip only into the comforting ones. Mostly I can still decide.

"I'm right in the middle," I tell my sisters. "I'm right in the middle. *Pehle jannat*—heaven, then me in the middle. One foot in each place."

chapter 43

HOT COALS ON
SMALL LIPS

———

Fatima

———

I DIDN'T CHOOSE MY RELIGION. I WAS SIMPLY BORN INTO it. From a very young age, I understood, subliminally or otherwise, that without blind faith in a deity, one with attributes utterly overwhelming to an eight-year-old, my destiny was the seven layers of hell. Skin-peeling, hair-singeing, demonic-creature-filled hell. My religious education was split between school and my grandmother, who told my brother and me stories of the prophets when we were very young. My favorite one was about Musa. As an infant, he was tucked in a woven basket and sent floating down the river Nile into the waiting arms of one of the handmaidens of the Pharaoh's wife—the very same Pharaoh who had ordered a decree throughout Egypt that all the baby boys be slaughtered because of a premonition from his soothsayer, who had seen a vision of a man able to perform miracles and rally the Egyptians in a way the Pharaoh never could. With this beautiful infant Musa in her arms, the Pharaoh's wife beseeched her husband to allow her to adopt the baby, since they couldn't have any children of their own. After seeking his fortune-teller's advice, the Pharaoh devised a test for the infant: If the boy were to crawl toward the piles of shiny riches and jewels they had collected on one side of the room and ignored the furnace-hot coals on the other side of the room, he would be buried alive like so many of the baby boys in the kingdom.

A gurgling Musa was brought to sit in the middle of the hall, where all of Pharaoh's court had convened to watch eagerly. The baby, oblivious that the next few minutes were crucial in determining his fate, began to crawl slowly toward the chest of gold. The onlookers murmured and whispered, convinced of the child's demise. Halfway through his wriggling, however, he stopped in his tracks and changed trajectory. The baby now sat in front of the sparking embers of coal, and before the Pharaoh's wife could gather him up, he had grasped a burning coal and tried to put it in his mouth. The trusted soothsayer proclaimed that no son who could overlook the riches of Egypt for a bite of excruciatingly painful embers could be a threat who would be able to defeat Pharaoh and his army, so Musa was raised in the palace like one of their own, thanks to Allah's interventions, and continued his exceptional path toward prophethood.

I was fascinated by stories like these about Islam. Being a storyteller myself, I was drawn to the human sides of all the messengers. Their struggles and strife and victories and conquests, their families and relationships—that was what I expected when I began studying religion at school. However, at school there was instead a heavy emphasis on rote learning passages of the Quran and not much else. The dismissal of analyzing it as theory to use as guidance rather than dogmatic ideology confused me, and I found myself questioning my faith constantly. Needless to say, I grew up confused and frightened by God. On one hand His wrath is incomparable, smiting entire civilizations for

their insubordinations, and on the other hand, love and magna-
nimity are His core. He is capable of love like a mother's love for
her child, amplified ten thousand times.

Did I believe it? I wasn't sure . . . and what is true belief anyway?

My mother didn't emphasize a show of our faith as a presen-
tation of our virtue for others. Yes, she prayed—but not five
times a day as is prescribed—and she encouraged us to pray as
well, but she never forced us to. The same philosophy carried
over to the other commandments: fasting for the whole month
of Ramadan was not obligatory like it was for many of my
friends. I think my mother had the wisdom to know her teenage children would only stubbornly shun ideologies they
couldn't fathom. I always thought it was bizarre that my classmates would compare the number of fasts they had kept and
compete to see who received the most eidi (the pocket money
all the adults hand out to children during the celebratory finale
and probably the best thing about Ramadan, apart from the lavish feast for Eid). It was always critical that you went to the right
relatives' houses to celebrate the new moon of the lunar calendar because of the menu they would curate. I distinctly remember the decadent spread at my father's khala's house and that
gut-panging feeling of greedy eagerness as we arrived, enduring the next hour of heavily perfumed aunties giving us wet
kisses on the cheek as they cooed over how big we'd gotten.
Once that khala passed away and took the many phenomenal
family recipes with her, Eid never felt quite the same.

As I aged and religious study was no longer a part of our syl-
labus, I found myself moving further away from God. Conve-
niently, since I had never bothered to read much of the English
translation of the Quran to make my own judgments, the infor-

mation I had about my own belief system was from interpretations by others. After moving to the United States for college in 2008, I was exposed to vastly different cultures and people and all the judgment that comes along with that. In Pakistan, I was simply in a homogenous Islamic Republic, where notions like alcohol prohibition and martial law were commonplace, but in a secular society, concepts like lynching previous government rulers was too foreign and barbaric a notion to grasp.

Any time there was news of a terrorist bombing, I would squeeze my eyes shut and chant feverishly in my head: *Please don't let it be a brown person . . . please don't let him be Muslim.*

With each passing incident, my own self-worth began to chip away. I carried nagging guilt around with me as if I was somehow connected to those heinous monsters committing crimes against the innocent. I know I didn't know very much then, but I was certain that hate and murder were *not* what my religion was about.

If my God had chosen some of these prophets as exemplary role models to represent Him—generous beyond their means, patient and noble, benevolent even, in the grips of cruel torture . . . these were the prophets I knew, and if they were made in His image, surely that was His true reflection. I was adamant about that theory, adamant that the Quran was a guide and not a dogmatic decree with mandatory rote regurgitation. I wanted to be able to take all the *inspiring* theories about my religion and discard the ones I could not grapple with like a stack of cards during a game. I wanted it—no, I *needed* it—to match up to my contemporary living. And now as I've read that "no soul does Allah place under a greater pressure than it can bear" (Baqarah 2:286), I long to believe it. It's been fourteen months of getting my ass handed to me by cancer. Game after game, the cards are stacked and the house keeps winning and here I am underneath the table with not a chip left, knowing I should have stuck to go fish.

Now, knowing the end is near, I feel bathed in His presence. I feel complete conviction that I can bear what is coming and that I am not alone. When fear makes my chest shake and my vision blurs with tears, I ask my mother or brother to read me certain passages from the Quran, and my panic subsides. My fear of the nothingness abates and I feel certainty that what awaits me through the punctuated black paper of the night sky is not nothingness after all, that it's nothingness's opposite.

chapter 44

A FLOCK OF
WILD PEACOCKS

———

Farezeh

———

WE TOOK HER HOME FROM THE HOSPITAL, WITH
assurances that when it was time, she'd be relieved of her suffering so she could go peacefully. As we prepared to leave, she
made me promise to give gifts to every single person, every
resident, every doctor, every nurse's aide, who had helped her
over her months in this ward.

"Thank you," Fatima said to every nurse, ambulance driver,
and assistant that we passed. "Thank you so much for taking
care of me."

Some of her best friends flew in from all over the world to be
by her side, took leave from their jobs across oceans to say goodbye to her forever. They saw themselves in one another's grief,
and were all united by their love for Fatima. They helped her
make thank-you cards for everyone in her hospital ward. The
head chef was still in control, ordering her sous chefs around,
directing their moves to make sure she got what she needed to
get done. They took turns sitting with her and did their best to
help in whatever way they could, but they, like all of us, were
powerless to prevent the inevitable. They held themselves to-

gether with bright and positive energy, their presence filled the rooms they were in with lightness and warmth, laughter, but behind all of it they, too, were breaking. When they were alone, or away from Fatima, they let themselves cry. The moment when three of them realized that they would never see their friend again as they said goodbye to her and left the hospital for the airport will stay with me. The shock of the inevitable.

They will ultimately all remain close to me. I will continue to see my daughter in them, and they will see their best friend in me—a physical tether to hold on to, to see with their eyes, to touch, feel, and hear.

When we arrived at the house and they pulled her from the ambulance on the folding gurney, she lightly touched the hand of the paramedic who was unloading her and asked him to wait a moment. She closed her eyes and inhaled deeply.

"The air here. I love the air," she said as if she was standing on a Provençal hillside planted with lavender or a freshly mown hay field in England or a Tuscan vineyard, all places that she'd never been. The fresh air of San Marino under the sky was enough for her.

Our swollen home awaited her, full of people and grief. Fatima's friends from all over the world had come to see her, silently waiting for their moment with her. There were mattresses all over the lounge, suitcases everywhere. I glanced around at the fullness and emptiness of that house. It could have been Fatima's wedding. On what other occasion would the best friends of a twenty-nine-year-old girl flock to the same city on the other side of the world? And yet, somehow, life had led us all there— a beautiful house bracing for unbearable sadness.

Fatima worried about everyone's comfort and was afraid that her various friends from different chapters of her life would clash. "Mom, what if they don't get along? I don't want people to have a bad time."

I shook my head at her. I wish she worried more about herself. I know she would be happy to know that all the friends she feared wouldn't get along are all incredibly close now. They tell me all the time that Fatima brought them together. Perhaps Fatima knew that they'd all need each other after she was gone. She was leaving instructions and cushioning the inevitable falls that were to come.

She would have tried to leave instructions for me too, but for us, her family, she did not have answers. Moms are supposed to be the ones with answers. But I only had questions: *How will I face each day knowing she's not with us? How will we live our lives knowing she won't share any more moments together? What even is the point of living without her?*

~

MY DAUGHTER IS DYING. THE SLOW, DRAWN-OUT AGONizing process of watching her die has left me in ruins, and yet, rudderless as I am, I feel my journey has just begun. I have my whole life ahead of me. I wake up and go to sleep with this every day: the fact that she won't be here with me. I can still touch her now, but never being able to hold her hand, to feel her, to hug her . . . I don't know how to make sense of it.

Why hadn't I gotten her the help she needed to heal from her molestation? I've begun to ask myself the nagging questions that will stay with me always, in her absence. I'd wanted to turn the page: I hadn't wanted her to relive the trauma by retelling it. I'd meant well, but I'd been selfish. It was I who was afraid of the retelling, of the power those words might have on my new, fragile marriage. I was afraid that shining a light on her wounds would also reveal my shortcomings as a mother, as a wife. The impossible standards of a society that rules with shame and secrecy rather than acknowledgment, acceptance, and tenderness.

She told me one morning, "Mom, I am going to write something—I think it can become a movie! It will be about the sister-in-law I will never know. She can read it one day and know me." Because she's so close to Mohammad, she feels that by dying, she'll miss out—so many things she was excited about. But it's we who will miss out after she goes: her company, the love she radiated, her presence.

In theory, Yasmin is in charge of food and the kitchen, but with Chef Fatima in the house, of course she must share that space. Fatima asks for a boiled egg, and when Yasmin brings her one, Fatima's humor kicks in.

"Yasmin Khala, I'm going to teach you how to boil an egg."

And of course, Yasmin patiently listens and prepares it just as Fatima tells her to. And of course, Fatima's technique was right: It was a perfect egg.

~

I KNOW THAT I MUST SEEK OUT SUPPORT, A COMMUNITY to help me through this, that others have lost their children too, that technically I am not alone in this. But I feel utterly alone. There's a vacuum inside me; I already feel hollow. Something's missing. I feel lost. Even though I wake up and go through the same motions every day, I watch her, I help her, I talk to the doctors—eat, sleep, whatever . . .

When they were young, I used to say to them, *It's all right, it'll be okay.* And I don't know why, but I keep repeating this sentence. And I look at Fatima and I keep saying it in my head:

It's all right, it'll be okay, even though it's not all right, and it's not okay. Why do I say this then? Is it to comfort myself?

As she feels herself getting closer to death, Fatima wants to know what awaits her. She asks me for the green Quran that's become an extension of my body throughout her illness. She reads it robustly. Sometimes she smiles, as if she found an answer. Other times she furrows her brow. Then quietly says, "How beautiful" and stares at that page for hours. In and out. There and yet not there.

I seek her out constantly. I want to pull out my veins and knot them into hers so I can keep her, just a little longer. I sing off-key to her:

> *You are my sunshine,*
> *My only sunshine,*
> *You make me happy*
> *When times are blue.*

"Mom, it's *when skies are gray,*" she giggles.

I know the right lyrics, but I knew it would make her laugh, momentary comic relief at my expense—a mistake I make again and again for my only sunshine.

It will be days now, not weeks, until she's fully on the other side.

~

THIS MORNING, I WOKE UP TO A TEXT FROM YASMIN. IT'S a photograph: *There is a peacock on our roof. A peacock.*

I looked out the window and there was a peacock in the backyard. I thought I was dreaming, but when I rubbed my eyes and looked again, it was still there. I got out of bed and washed my face and looked out the window again and there was another. One by one, peacock after peacock landed in our yard until there were eleven of them parading around our yard and our roof like royals at a lawn party. Fatima's cat was beside himself.

Peacocks are Fatima's spirit animal. She loves their unapologetic majesty, their beauty and grandeur. And they had come—as her angels, guides promised by the Quran—to welcome her to the next world.

At dusk, they left, one by one, as inexplicably as they'd arrived. I don't need outward signs to know that something unusual is happening, that my daughter's passage is extraordinary, but they are there to remind me. Then a halo around the full moon, directly over our house. I can't make sense of these last days of her life and I won't try to. I accept their painful chaos and their strange, purposeful mystery. The gory intensity of her death is a distorted mirror to her tenacious, complicated birth. I thank God that I could hold her in both.

I wanted to walk with her on her journey until the end of my days. But during our time together—which even if she had lived to be a hundred would have been too brief if I had continued living on after her—we both arrive at the same point: Fatima regrets not having enough time in this world. I regret not having enough time with her. We wasted so much of it living apart, misunderstanding each other and worrying about so many useless things when we needed to do the opposite—to trust each other.

"Mom, you and I are for a reason . . . I don't want you to be sad," she tells me in her last days with us.

And I beg her to stay.

"I don't want you to go, I don't want you to leave."

"I will always be there, Mom. I am part of you; you and I are one. God's calling me. I have to go."

~

THE NIGHT BEFORE GOD TOOK HER, I SPOKE TO HIM directly. With my claws still deep in my daughter's life, I begged him, *If You're going to take her, take her peacefully. No more pain.*

Fatima keeps asking for Nadeem, Yasmin's husband, who died a few years before.

"I'll call him. If I could just ask him a few questions . . ." she says. Nadeem, who protected me in my sudden divorce. Nadeem, whose affection for me and my children never wavered. "I'll see him soon," Fatima says, as if he's picking her up on the other end of a long flight.

Three hours later, I stand beside her bed. Fatima looks up at me and makes eye contact. She is there, it's really her.

She manages to whisper, "Mom, I can't breathe."

How could she live, if she couldn't breathe? Those instants when she's still with us, too brief, yet elastic somehow. In those instants, my mind irrationally searched for a method to help her breathe, to keep her breathing, a tool, a procedure, but my heart kept me still, catatonic and helpless as I was—a state I've never grown accustomed to in the fourteen months of powerlessness. I would be still for her. I hold her hand.

Yasmin and Erum call out my name. They never leave me. Their grief, their pain at watching their little "niece" suffer, takes a back seat to mine. It's what true friends do: They dig their nails into each other's palms. They bite their fists and ignore their tears to try to help me survive this. Their hands hold my shoulders, keep me upright in the moment a mother cannot fathom in the abstract and dreads from the moment she's warned it's coming.

~

MOHAMMAD CALLED THE HOSPICE WORKERS. HE TOLD them to increase the medicine to help her through. He held her hand, gently stroking it.

"It's okay, Fati. We love you so much—don't worry about us, we're going to be okay. You don't need to hold on for us anymore. Let go, and be free. It's okay, just let go."

And Fatima listened to her brother, as she has always done.

chapter 45

MY DREAM, ABBREVIATED

———

Fatima

———

INSTEAD OF MY BUCKET LIST BOOK, THIS IS THE STORY of my abbreviated life, short but nonetheless possessing secret love, joy and pain, adventure and hard work, luck and its opposite. I'm a daughter, a sister, a friend, a Muslim, a Pakistani. I am a chef. I'm queer, I suppose, if we must find a word to define my attraction to people's spirits rather than the bodies that contain them. I'm a person who is dying. Even now, I don't know how to unravel which of these identifiers is greater or less significant than the others, but the one I want least to be associated with is that I am dying. This book is my way of still fighting, of surviving beyond my expiration date; of hopefully helping other small brown girls who feel strange—who kiss their best friends and find they like it, but in doing so hate themselves due to their desires—to forgive themselves and to be themselves. Perhaps if parents could look at their children and ask, "Are they kind? Are they giving? Are they honest?" and finding that they are, feel there's reason enough to love them, no matter what else they are, then there would be less suffering. This book is the only way I can think of to replace the restaurant I dreamt of opening: a vehicle that could close the gap between colors and faiths, contradict assumptions, teach people tolerance and curiosity about my beloved Pakistan through their taste buds. This is my way of saying goodbye, of letting go, of hanging on. This is my way of being free—of judgment, of pain, of cancer— and leading with love even as I take my leave.

ACKNOWLEDGMENTS

By

MOHAMMAD ALI

———

THIS IS A CHAPTER FATIMA NEVER GOT TO WRITE, BUT is our attempt to acknowledge and pay tribute to many of the people who made her life and our lives richer.

The grownups who lovingly fostered a child's love of cooking, never letting Fati feel like she was too young for the kitchen. Nano, Fati's first teacher, a wise and steady hand that guided her through this life and followed her into the next. Mrs. Ricks, who gave Fati her first recipe book in kindergarten, setting her on the path to discover what cooking meant to her. Kadir, who relished being Fati's first sous chef and indulged her varied and whacky menu requests. Itrath, whose limitless love envelops our family, who handed Fatima her first apron and helped prepare that fateful feast with Fatima.

To Ashtar, who gave Fati her first olive, her first taste of sushi, who knew he had met his match when it came to the bravery with which one should explore food. Who enabled Fati to travel across the world to study culinary arts and proudly watched her overtake his own considerable cooking skill.

Fati could graft herself new friendships wherever she went

in the world, and that's what kept her rooted and gave her the anchor she needed as she stepped out into the unknown. To her oldest co-conspirators, Fatimah and Binda, who held her heart and hand with so much care and love, throughout her life.

To her girls Anum, Ariana, Danesh, Eman, Lala, Mariam, Manhal, Pogo, Tano, Yasir, Zainie, and so many others at Karachi Grammar School, who understood before so many others how special she was.

To her pack now in Lahore, including Bano, Shezzy, SS, and Zahra, who celebrate their friend at every chance they get. To her New York crew, including Gabi, Raymond, Mark, and Mel, who made a city as bewildering as New York her home. To Bobi, Meeku, and Usman—our childhood brothers who also lost their little sister that day, for being with us through those dark days.

Fati found loving homes in her friends' parents, who continue to be the mountains that help hold the sky above us. To Erum and Afi, for opening their homes and caring for Fati like she was their own and being by her side until they couldn't. To Yasmin and Nadeem, for being an immeasurable source of support, safety, and warmth for our family and for being there at every step as our lives unfolded. To Afshi, Aamna, Naila, Talat, and everyone who makes up our formidable squad in Lahore— for their unconditional love and support through all these years. To our newfound California family Ayesha, Kishwar, Misbah, Ruqiya, and their wonderful husbands, who took us in with open arms when we found ourselves rudderless and without much of a compass after Fatima. For opening up your homes and kitchens, for including us in your adventures, and for just being by our side as we attempted to come to grips with our new reality.

Fati cooked in many kitchens—all of them made her a better

chef, some through their generosity, some through fire. To the Culinary Institute of America and her teachers there, to the extraordinary talent she found in her fellow chefs Amaan, Aya, Eric, Mark, Mike, Miro, Robert, Sandra, Shilpa, and Amaan, who inspired her and kept tabs no matter where they found themselves in the world. To the crew that went to Spain, and the Basque chefs and craftspeople she met there, who reaffirmed her deep desire to devote her life to cooking honest food. To the dishwashers, front of house staff, the servers, the line cooks, the people hustling day in and day out to feed the city, the big-hearted, hard-working backbone of the restaurant industry.

Then there are the people who saw Fati's lofty goals for her life and instead of scoffing, did what they could to push her closer to them without blinking. To Chef Maneet Chauhan, who helped Fati understand she had a place in the industry, and that she could both embrace her culinary identity and be successful, and that Pakistani food can be done in an inventive, playful, and delicious way. Who helped her get her first job out of college and encouraged her to step into the spotlight at the Food Network.

To the folks at *Chopped,* who opened Fati's eyes to just how much talent she possessed at such a young age. To the team at Chef's Roll, who gave Fati the opportunity to travel and work at Meadowood in the Napa Valley, and Chef Kostow, who comfortably knew that Fati would achieve the success she did and was part of her journey of rediscovering her perspective on what being a chef and doing what you love for a living meant.

The road to becoming a chef is paved with one obstacle after the other. For a brown Muslim Pakistani woman, they seem to multiply at every turn. To the people who cleared the way for Fati to live out her dream of working New York kitchens. To the two Franks and many chefs at the Patina Group who shared hot, busy kitchens with Fati and saw her rapid rise within the ranks, and who backed her early in her career. To Omer and Yasmin, for believing in Fati enough to want to invest in her and connecting her with her brilliant lawyer Seth, without whom she would never have gotten her visa to stay in the United States and work independently.

Then there are those who have built platforms for Fati to shine through. To the entire team over at *Top Chef*—to Padma, for being an early inspiration and later a dear friend to a little girl who had starry-eyed dreams of one day being on the screen like she was. Adrienne, Brother, Bruce, Carrie, Claudette, Chris, Eden, Joe Flamm, Joe Sasto, Laura, Melissa, Rogelio, Tanya, Tu, Tyler—and the folks behind the scenes making everything work. It makes us very happy knowing so many of you got a chance to see and interact with Fati as she came into her own. That you got to see with your very own eyes the sparkle in hers, and take in big gulps of Fati while you could.

To Abdullah, Vanessa, Farideh, and Arooj from Munchies and Vice, celebrating her unique voice in the culinary landscape, enabling her to share her creativity with the world, and for opening your arms and doors for us when we hosted her memorial in Brooklyn. To everyone who showed up that day from all the different parts of her life to be together and share some of her favorite food, including Madhuri, who penned a beautiful essay that captured so much of what Fatima had always longed for and fought to achieve.

To Smorgasburg and all the patrons that came to eat at Van Pakistan and supported Fati as she began firming up what Chef Fati was going to be all about.

While we wish it wasn't Fatima's cancer that brought these people into our lives, we are grateful to know them and proud that they will always be a part of our family. They all tried their best to make Fati's pain better and do their part in healing and helping her, which is all one can really ask for. To her first orthopedic doctor in New York, who was a guiding light for her as she navigated the first few terrifying days of discovering a suspected tumor. To Dr. Max Vaynrub, a young, talented, and dedicated surgeon and Fatima's first doctor at MSK, who patiently helped us understand what was happening to her and took it upon himself to ensure she had access to the best care possible by connecting us with Dr. Lenny Wexler, who will forever have a special place in our hearts, as he does with so many children and their families. To him, and his tireless team of nurses and doctors, specialists, and the entire Memorial Sloan Kettering staff. Nurses that became Fati's friends and confidants, Carly, Jaimie, Jessie, Kelly, Kristin, Maggie, Mel, Nicole, Tori, and so many big and beautiful hearts that help carry those broken families dealing with impossible circumstances every day. To Dr. Patrick Soon-Shiong and his team, including Dr. Lenny Sanders and Dr. Mira Kissler, who offered us real hope when we had no options left, who worked for and with us to help heal Fatima when the traditional pathways failed us. For advocating for her, and being there for us in what felt like an all-consuming abyss.

When Fati's illness took her away from the kitchen, some people turned the light on Fati's other gift: her beautiful mind. To Amanda Shapiro and *Bon Appétit* magazine, for giving Fatima a platform to share her voice and story with so many others. For encouraging her to write and amplifying her voice. To the James Beard Foundation—for recognizing the power of her story, and the skill in her writing.

To Gordon Ramsay, for reaching out and offering whatever

he and his team could to help Fatima and our family make the most of our time left together. Elvia, for pushing us and creating opportunities for us to make a dream reality.

To Ellen DeGeneres, for sharing her hefty platform with Fati so that she could share her story with the world, and help inspire so many others through her own gift of storytelling. To Ellen Rocamora and the team at *Ellen,* who did everything they could to make us feel special, even off-camera, and supported us throughout her last months in California. Rebecca, who helped us deal with the media world in the aftermath of Fati's passing.

To CBS, for allowing Fatima to reflect so beautifully on what she would share with her younger self, allowing her to share some of her recipes, and amplifying her voice to help her reach millions.

To our dear friends Mohsin and Zahra, for helping us believe that we could help Fati seize back the control of her story that her illness had wrestled away from her by empowering her to make her show and write her book. For introducing us to his agent at WME and our dear friend who has worked for years with us to help us get this book out there, Jay Mandel. To Josh, who early on helped us gain swift momentum in creating a show Fati always wanted but was ultimately too unwell to do.

A lot of people struggle with knowing what a family losing one of their own needs. Some know exactly what to do. To Ming Tsai, who understands more than most what a battle with cancer brings, and who embraced Fati and had her on his show to share her with his world. For supporting the Samfund along with so many of Fati's *Top Chef* friends. To Sam, for starting the Samfund and dedicating an award for resilience and survival in Chef Fati's memory, and helping thousands of young cancer survivors across the country.

To Pam, Linzi, Rebecca, Dimitri, and the team at Eleven Madison Park—for giving us an unforgettable meal, and treating us with such respect, dignity, and honor. For putting up Fatima's Van Pakistan stall inside of their three-star kitchen, for making us the best seekh kebabs we've ever had, and for the everlasting memory and full hearts you left us with that night.

To Jason, for getting us impossible-to-get tickets to *Hamilton* before we left New York one last time, and the gentleman who sat next to us and invited us backstage after the show to meet the cast and be onstage.

To Chef Masa, for standing in front of Fatima, Flamm, and Stephanie and hand-making each dish of the omakase for her to enjoy.

To Chef Michael, who reached out to invite Fatima and her family and had them eat some of the best pasta you can have, with mountains of fresh truffles.

To so many other chefs who opened their kitchens and their hearts to Fatima, and made exceptions and broke rules to feed us their creations and give us moments of joy and escape, and helped Fati feel normal, and more than okay, even if for just a few moments. Sara at Kismet for making our way back home after dreaded checkups one afternoon much more delightful; Xi'an Famous Foods for their spicy lamb noodles; Guisados, for coming to our door one day with trays and trays of the greatest hits, which our family ate for at least two days; Sasto and Bella for that focaccia and staying by our sides in L.A.; Bruce for the pasta and chicken parm; and the marvelous small-plates restaurant whose food Fati wanted on New Year's Eve, who made an exception to deliver us their entire menu.

To Peter, who involved Fati in his film "Her Name Is Chef," as she began to grapple with what was happening to her, allowing her to stay engaged and productive, and made a beautiful film about chefs that showcased Fati's story and touched so many.

To Massimo, a culinary hero for Fatima, and his lovely wife, Lara—for embracing Fatima's mother, Farezeh, as she embarked on the journey to Modena her daughter so desperately was hoping to go on, to meet this great chef, taste his food, and indulge in a dream of hers she thought she would get to achieve at some point in her life. For connecting us with Jill, and for helping us work on something Fatima would be so thrilled to see come together.

To Nigella, Martin Yan, and her many food heroes from BBC Food and the Food Network. *Yan Can Cook* turned cooking into a fantastical adventure in our living rooms, transporting Fatima into a world that she would make her life's work. To Johnathan Gold, for seeking out and celebrating the delicious richness that cultural diversity and diaspora bring to a place, and for elevating humble and dedicated cooks and chefs across America. Fatima was destroyed when she heard of his passing, knowing she wouldn't get the chance to share her food with him, a man she had a lot of respect and admiration for. To Liz, Kerry, and Evan, our silent and distant cheerleaders, without whom California would have been a lot harder.

To the San Marino St. Edmund's Episcopal Church and its members, who leased us our home in San Marino and held services for Fatima at various times. The generous, supportive, and warm spiritual community who called us in and checked on us as we packed up our lives after Fatima's passing.

To all of Fati's followers and fans who welcomed her into their lives, people she touched and inspired, who constantly sent positivity and encouragement her way through their Instagram messages. She drew an immense amount of strength from the kind words people had to say to her—so many battlers have to fight this fight alone, but we had the world on our side, and we are deeply grateful and fortunate to have had this. To the many wonderful, kind, and generous people who reached out in whatever way they knew how to comfort us, and console us, and share in our grief and loss. Fatima would receive packets in the mail containing letters and gifts from people all over who just wanted to reach out and touch her in whatever way they could, to let her know she was on their minds and in their hearts. So many have shared with us how and what Fati means to them, and what they have learned about themselves and this life through her.

To Tarajia, our friend and collaborator, who dropped into our lives at such a precarious time and did not shy away from what must have been a daunting and bizarre scenario, with so much unknown. Her steadfast dedication to this project, her commitment to help us finish what Fati started, her patient ear as we trawled through our lives and dug up all sorts of painful memories to write an honest book are deeply appreciated. Without her with us, this book would not have been possible.

To Pamela, our editor, for jumping into the deep end and taking on such an emotionally charged project and navigating the development of this book with us. For your patience and careful and sensitive hand-holding, and giving us the time we needed to try to finish what Fati started. For believing in her story and for embracing her family wholeheartedly. To Ballantine for giving Fatima the platform to share herself with the world, and for supporting us to fulfill a dream she always had.

To Rimmel, someone Fatima never got a chance to meet even though she wanted so dearly to one day. For helping us sift through so much pain, patiently and steadily, so that we could fulfill our promise to her. For not flinching.

To Qari Muhammad Azam, for being a beacon of spiritual guidance in the pitch black of such despair. Helping us understand the power of storytelling, the lessons that can be learned from stories like Fatima's, and how we need not fear the judgment of people.

To Farezeh, Fatima's mother, her friend, her caretaker, her everything. "I am yours, and you are mine—you and me are one, Mom—I will always be with you," Fatima looked at her and said toward the end. The deepness of the love they shared cannot be described, and the magnitude of the loss of your own flesh, blood, body, and soul cannot be expressed. For raising one of the most exceptional human beings, for being fearless when you needed to be, for fighting for Fatima at every turn, for pushing her to be the best, for believing in her and making sure she didn't fall prey to the things that you did. For pushing through immense tsunamis of grief, being completely overwhelmed and overcome having to think about what has happened, what you had to witness, recalling all of those moments, time and time again so that this book could take its shape, confronting all those things and putting them out into the world by following your daughter's lead. For your courage, for your love, and for being by Fatima's side every waking minute of her battle, through every step, trying as hard as you could to absorb her suffering, to somehow suck it out of the air and hold on to it so she could be spared. You are human, and you made choices wanting the best for your children; it's okay that you could not be everything for everyone—nobody can. Replace regret and remorse with what your daughter asked from everyone around her: love, compassion, and forgiveness, including for oneself.

And finally, to our family—Fati's illness and death brought up many things that lay dormant, glossed over, or neglected over the years. These sorts of things tend to shine light in areas we don't always want to look, but now we dare not look away and forget the many lessons her passing has to offer us. In our attempt to share her story as she wanted, we have tried to do as she asked of all of us: to be honest, no matter how much the truth hurts.

Fati was the best of us, and that much became very clear as we watched her stripped bare, with nothing left but what is at her core—the very essence of her being. How we will choose to live our lives going forward is our own individual path to take— she is here for us just as she was when she was alive, and we owe it to her to live life differently, think differently, love differently, forgive differently.

To Fati's cousins, who've all had their chance to play a part in her life, Zain and Zainab, Ilsa, Ike, and Adam, Haider, and Mahvish. To Tammy, for taking us in when we found ourselves lost, and to Saby for keeping the ship steady after Agha Jani went too soon. To Mohammad Ali for bringing pure unadulterated delight with spontaneous joy rides to grab ice cream, tickle torture, and his infectious humor—your cheeky smile will always fill our hearts and brighten up any room you are in. For teaching us how to eat two-minute noodles properly, and everything we know about cars. Mamu and Fati have a lot more in common than they had the chance to discover. Fatima's Dadi and Dada, who doted on her and treated her like the royalty she was, and her Api Kicho, who calls out her name every day and shares stories of her childhood to anyone willing to listen, her Nana whom she never met but who had such a big impact on her life, and her Nano, who left this world only five nights after Fatima did, calling out for a child who only she could see needed her.

To Imtiaz, Farezeh, Mohammad, Saadia, Sarah, Saadi, and Ali-Imtiaz, and to Ashtar, Afshan, Amin, and Zahra—the empty seat at our table is tough to look at. But we're lucky our hearts are so full, and that they continue to make room for more and more love that we share for her. Don't hesitate to ask her what you ought to do when you face a decision in your life— she has a way of setting us on the path we should be on.

To the thousands of parents and children out there battling cruel diseases in pediatric wards in cancer hospitals, scrambling to find clinical trials, struggling to access proper medical care because of apathetic insurance companies, families fighting together, people fighting alone: We see you now, and we know you know. This world is full of heartache, and if we only knew just how close to the surface it is for all of us, how it lurks around every corner ready to steal away so much, we might begin to cut to the bone to what actually matters.

TO KEEP HER LEGACY ALIVE, Fatima's family and friends launched the Chef Fatima Foundation in 2020 to "spread joy and make change through food." To learn more about the foundation and how you can get involved, please visit www .cheffatimafoundation.org.

Born in Pakistan, FATIMA ALI was a chef in New York City. She received her education from the Culinary Institute of America and, at the age of twenty-three, competed in and won an episode of *Chopped* on the Food Network. Ali was a contestant on the fifteenth season of Bravo's *Top Chef,* where she was voted "Fan Favorite." She wrote several essays for *Bon Appétit,* the last of which was posthumously awarded a James Beard Award in January 2019.

TARAJIA MORRELL is a native New Yorker who grew up at the table. In 2011, Morrell created the food and travel blog The Lovage. Her reporting and essays have since appeared in *WSJ. Magazine, T Magazine, Food & Wine, Departures,* and *Cherry Bombe,* among others. Morrell is also the author of *Soul of New York: A Guide to 30 Exceptional Experiences.* She lives in Manhattan with her daughter.

@tarajiamorrell

About the Type

This book was set in Bembo, a typeface based on an old-style Roman face that was used for Cardinal Pietro Bembo's tract *De Aetna* in 1495. Bembo was cut by Francesco Griffo (1450–1518) in the early sixteenth century for Italian Renaissance printer and publisher Aldus Manutius (1449–1515). The Lanston Monotype Company of Philadelphia brought the well-proportioned letterforms of Bembo to the United States in the 1930s.